MEDITATIONS FOR ALL THE DAYS OF THE YEAR

VOLUME 5. FROM THE SEVENTEENTH SUNDAY AFTER PENTECOST TO THE FIRST SUNDAY IN ADVENT

REV. M HAMON, S.S.

SENSUS FIDELIUM PRESS

Gastonia, North Carolina

Nihil Obstat.

D. J. McMahon, **D. D.,**

Censor Librorum.

Imprimatur

MICHAEL AUGUSTINE,

Archbishop of New York

New York, July 14, 1894.

Print ISBN: 978-1-966961-13-0

SensusFideliumPress.com

PRAYERS

Morning Prayers

In the name of the Father, and of the Son, and of the Holy Ghost. Amen.

Place Yourself in the Presence of God and adore His holy Name.

Most holy and adorable Trinity, one God in three Persons, **I** believe that Thou art here present: I adore Thee with the deepest humility, and render to Thee, with my whole heart, the homage which is due to Thy sovereign majesty.

An Act of Faith.

O my God, I firmly believe that Thou art one God in three divine Persons, Father, Son, and Holy Ghost; I believe that Thy divine Son became man, and died for our sins, and that He will come to judge the living and the dead. I believe these and all the truths which the holy Catholic Church teaches, because Thou hast revealed them, who canst neither deceive nor be deceived.

An Act of Hope.

O my God, relying on Thy infinite goodness and promises, I hope to obtain pardon of my sins, the help of Thy grace, and life everlasting, through the merits of Jesus Christ, my Lord and Redeemer.

An Act of Love.

O my God, I love Thee above all things, with my whole heart and soul, because Thou art all-good and worthy of all love. I love my neighbor as myself for the love of Thee. I forgive all who have injured me, and ask pardon of all whom I have injured.

Thank God for All Favors and Offer Yourself to Him.

O my God, I most humbly thank Thee for all the favors Thou hast bestowed upon me up to the present moment. I give Thee thanks from the bottom of my heart that Thou hast created me after Thine own image and likeness, that Thou hast redeemed me by the precious blood of Thy dear Son, and that Thou hast preserved me and brought me safe to the beginning of another day. I offer to Thee, O Lord, my whole being, and in particular all my thoughts, words, actions, and sufferings of this day. I consecrate them all to the glory of Thy name, beseeching Thee that through the infinite merits of Jesus Christ my Savior they may all find acceptance in Thy sight. May Thy divine love animate them and may they all tend to Thy greater glory.

Resolve Avoid Sin and to Practice Virtue.

Adorable Jesus, my Savior and Master, model of all perfection, I resolve and will endeavor this day to imitate Thy example, to be, like Thee, mild, humble, chaste, zealous, charitable, and resigned. I will redouble my efforts so that I may not fall this day into any of those sins which I have here* tofore committed *(here name any besetting sin),* and which **I** sincerely desire to forsake.

Ask God for the Necessary Graces.

O my God, Thou knowest my poverty and weakness, and that I am unable to do anything good without Thee; deny me not, O God, the help of Thy grace; proportion it to my necessities; give me strength to avoid anything evil which Thou forbiddest, and to practice the good which Thou hast commanded; and enable me to bear patiently all the trials which it may please Thee to send me.

The Lord's prayer.

Pater noster, qui es in coelis, sanctificetur nomen tuum: adveniat regnum tuum fiat voluntas tua, sicut in coelo, et in tetra. Panem nostrum quotidianum da nobis hodie: et dimitte nobis debita nostra, sicut et nos dimittimus debitoribus nostris Et ne nos inducas in tentationem: sed libera nos a malo. Amen.

Our Father, who art in heaven, hallowed be Thy name: Thy kingdom come: Thy will be done on earth, as it is in heaven. Give us this day our daily bread: and forgive us our trespasses, as we forgive those who trespass against us. And lead us not into temptation: but deliver us from evil. Amen.

Hail Mary.

Ave, Maria, gratia plena Dominus tecum: benedicta tu in mulieribus, et benedictus fructus ventris tui, Jesus. Santa Maria, Mater Dei, ora pro nobis peccatoribus, nunc et in hora mortis nostrae. Amen.

Hail, Mary full of grace; the Lord is with you; blessed art thou among women, and blessed is the fruit of Thy womb, Jesus. Holy Mary, Mother of God, pray for us sinners, now and at the hour of our death. Amen.

The Apostles' Creed.

Credo in Deum, Patrem omnipotentem, Creatorem caeli et terrae; et in Jesum Christum, Filium ejus unicum, Dominum nostrum; qui conceptus est de Spiritu Sancto, natus ex Maria Virgine, passus sub Pontio Pilato, crucifixes, mortuus et sepultus. Descendit ad infernos; tertia die resurrexit a mortuis; ascendit ad caelos, sedet ad dexteram Dei Patris omnipotentis; inde venturus est judicare vivos et mortuos. Credo in Spiritum Sanctum, sanctam Ecclesiam Catholicam, sanctorum communionem, remissionem peccatorum, carnis resurrectionem, vitam aeternam. Amen.

I believe in God, the Father Almighty, Creator of heaven and earth; and in Jesus Christ, His only Son, our Lord : who was conceived by the Holy Ghost, born of the Virgin Mary, suffered under Pontius Pilate, was crucified, died, and was buried. He descended into hell; the third day He rose again from the dead; He ascended into heaven, and sitteth at the right hand of God, the Father Almighty; from thence He shall come to judge the living and the dead. I believe in the Holy

Ghost, the holy Catholic Church, the communion of saints, the forgiveness of sins, the resurrection of the body, and the life everlasting. Amen.

Ask the Prayers of the Blessed Virgin, your Guardian Angel,
and your Patron Saint,

Holy Virgin Mother of God, my Mother and Patroness, I place myself under thy protection, I throw myself with confidence into the arms of thy compassion.
Be to me, O Mother of mercy, my refuge in distress, my consolation under suffering, my advocate with thy adorable Son, now and at the hour of my death.

Angel of God, my guardian dear.
To whom His love commits me here, Ever this day be at my side, To light and guard, to rule and guide. Amen.

O great Saint whose name I bear, protect me, pray for me, that like thee I may serve God faithfully on earth, and glorify Him eternally with thee in heaven.
Amen.

Evening Prayers.

In the name of the Father, and of the Son, and of the Holy Ghost. Amen.

Come, O Holy Ghost, fill the hearts of Thy faithful, and kindle in them the fire of Thy love.

Place Yourself in the Presence of God and Humbly Adore Him.

O my God, I present myself before Thee at the end of another day, to offer Thee anew the homage of my heart. I humbly adore Thee, my Creator, my Redeemer, and my Judge! I believe in Thee, because Thou art Truth itself; I hope in Thee, because Thou art faithful to Thy premises; I love Thee with my whole heart, because Thou art infinitely worthy of being loved; and for Thy sake I love my neighbor as myself.

Return Thanks to God for All His Mercies.

Enable me, O my God, to return Thee thanks as I ought ter all Thine inestimable blessings and favors. Thou hast thought of me and loved me from all eternity; Thou hast formed me out of nothing; Thou hast delivered up Thy beloved Son to the ignominious death of the cross for my redemption; Thou hast made me a member of Thy holy Church; Thou hast preserved me from falling into the abyss of eternal misery, when my sins had provoked Thee to punish me; Thou hast graciously continued to spare me, even though I have not ceased to offend Thee. What return, O my God, can I make for Thy innumerable blessings, and particularly for the favors of this day? O all ye saints and angels, unite with me in praising the God of mercies, who is so bountiful to so unworthy a creature.

Our Father. Hail Mary. I believe.

Ask of God Light to Discover the Sins Committed this Day.

O my God, sovereign judge of men, who desirest not tha death of a sinner, but that he should be converted and saved, enlighten my mind, that I may know the sins which I have this day committed in thought, word, or deed, and give me the grace of true contrition.

Pere Examine your Conscience; then Say:

O my God, I heartily repent and am grieved that I have offended Thee, because Thou art infinitely good and sin is infinitely displeasing to Thee. I humbly ask of Thee mercy and pardon, through the infinite merits of Jesus Christ. I resolve, by the assistance of Thy grace, to do penance for my sins, and I will endeavor never more to offend Thee.

The Confiteor.

Confiteor Deo omnipotent, beatae Marine semper Virgini, beato Michaeli Archangelo, beato Joanni Baptistae, sanctis apostolis Petro et Paulo, omnibus sanctis, et tibi Pater, quia peccavi nimis cogitatione, verbo, et opere, mea culpa, mea culpa, mea maxima culpa., Ideo precor beatam Mariam semper Virginem, beatum Michaelem Archangelum, beatum Joannem Baptistam, sanctos apostolos Petrum et Paulum, omnes sanctos, et te, Pater, orare pro me ad Dominum Deum nostrum.

Misereatur nostri Omnipotens Deus, et dimissis peccatis nobis, perducat nos ad vitam eternam. Amen.

Indulgentiam, absolutionem, et remissionem peccatorum nostrorum, tribuat nobis omnipotens et misericors Dominus. Amen

I confess to Almighty God. to blessed Marv, ever Virgin, to blessed Michael the Archangel, to blessed John the Baptist, to the holy apostles Peter and Paul, and to all the saints, and to you, Father, that I have sinned exceedingly in thought, word, and deed, through my fault, through my fault, through my most grievous fault. Therefore I beseech blessed Mary ever Virgin, blessed Michael the Archangel, blessed John the Baptist, the holy apostles Peter and Paul, all the saints, and you, Father, to pray to the Lord our God for me.

May Almighty God have mercy upon us, and forgive us our sins, and bring us unto life everlasting. Amen.

May the Almighty and merciful Lord grant us pardon, absolution, and remission of our sins. Amen.

Pray for the Church of Christ.

O God, hear my prayers on behalf of our Holy. Father Pope ___, our Bishops, our clergy, and for all that are in authority over us. Bless, I beseech Thee, the whole Catholic Church, and convert all heretics and unbelievers.

Pray for the Living and for the Faithful Departed.

Pour down Thy blessings, O Lord, upon all my friends, relations, and acquaintances, and upon my enemies, if I have any. Help the poor and sick, and those who are in their last agony. O God of mercy and goodness, have compassion on the souls of the faithful in purgatory; put an end to their sufferings, and grant to them eternal light, rest, and happiness. Amen.

Commend Yourself to God, to the Blessed Virgin, and the Saints.

Bless, O Lord, the repose I am about to take, that, my bodily strength, being renewed, I may be the better enabled to serve Thee.

O blessed Virgin Mary, Mother of mercy, pray for me that I may be preserved this night from all evil, whether of body or soul. Blessed St. Joseph, and all ye saints and angels ol Paradise, especially my guardian angel and my chosen patron, watch over me. I commend myself to your protection now and always.

Amen

—·—

"Joseph wrapped Him in fine linen, and laid Him in a sepulchre that was hewed in stone."—St. Luke xxiii. 53.

CONTENTS

Seventeenth Sunday After Pentecost.

The Gospel according to St. Matthew, xxii. 35-46.

"At that time the Pharisees came to Jesus: and one of them, a doctor of the law, asked Him, tempting Him: Master, which is the great commandment in the law? Jesus said to him: Thou shalt love the Lord thy God with thy whole heart, and with thy whole soul, and with thy whole mind. This is the greatest and the first commandment. And the second is like to this: Thou shalt love thy neighbor as thyself. On these two commandments dependeth the whole law and the prophets. And the Pharisees being gathered together, Jesus asked them, saying: What think you of Christ? Whose son is He? They say to Him: David's. He saith to them: How, then, doth David in spirit call Him Lord, saying: The Lord said to my Lord: Sit on My right hand, until I make Thy enemies Thy footstool? If David, then, call Him Lord, how is He his son? And no man was able to answer Him a word: neither durst any man from that day forth ask Him any more questions."

Summary of the Morrow's Meditation.

We will meditate tomorrow upon the commandment of the love of God, recalled to us by the gospel, and we shall see: 1st, the reasons for loving God; 2nd, the manner of maintaining and increasing love towards God. We shall thence deduce the resolution: 1st, to perform all our actions, little ones as well as great, through love to God, and from a great desire to please Him; 3rd, often to utter, by day and by night, ejaculatory prayers or loving aspirations. Our spiritual nosegay shall be the words of St. Ignatius: *"Lord, give me Thy love, and it suffices me."*

Meditation for the Morning.

Let us adore Our Lord Jesus Christ giving His enemies, when they came to tempt Him, the commandment of the love of God, which He calls the first and the greatest of all the commandments. Let us thank Him for this lesson and beg Him to make it sink deeply into our heart.

The Love of God.

FIRST POINT.

Reasons for Loving God.

Why should we love God? Because, first, He is God; that is to say, the supreme Being, the necessary and eternal Being, the Being who is infinitely perfect, infinite goodness and beauty, wisdom and holiness in their essence; our Father, our all, to whom belongs so essentially all the love of which our heart is capable, that God Himself could not dispense us from loving Him. Wherefore should we love God? It is because love is the means of becoming perfect. When we really love God we have no other will than His; we only love what He loves, and only hate what He hates; we do all that He commands, nothing that He forbids; and thus we accomplish the whole law. Wherefore love God? It is because we find all good things in this one sole good. We find therein the most perfect satisfaction of our soul and our mind, and there remains nothing to desire. *"Give me Thy love, my God,"* said St. Ignatius, *"and that suffices me."* We may do without all other knowledge; we cannot do without the knowledge of divine love. Possessed of the knowledge of all the sciences, we may yet be unhappy with the love of God we are always happy; and the most ignorant of men, who knows how to love God, is worth more than the wise one who does not love Him. Wherefore love God? Because not to love Him is a triple crime: a sin of criminal want of appreciation, because God and His perfections merit all the love of our hearts infinitely more than all creatures put together; a crime of injustice, because man, not being able to live without love, and, therefore, loving creatures more than he loves the Creator, thereby prefers what is finite to what is infinite, nothingness to everything, some few drops of beauty and goodness to be found in creatures to the ocean of all goodness and of all beauty which is in God, which is supremely unjust; lastly, a crime of ingratitude, since we have received all from God, and nothing from creatures except the few good things which God has enabled them to bestow upon us; since, also, we expect from God eternal happiness, and nothing from creatures except as regards this present life. God does us nothing but what is good; creatures often do us nothing but evil. O God, how just it is to love Thee with all the love of our hearts!

SECOND POINT.

How to Preserve and Increase in our Hearts Love for God

1st. We must avoid, as much as possible, even slight faults. Faults, however slight they may be, cool the heart of God and our own heart, weaken love, diminish grace. 2nd. We must watch over our heart continually in order to hinder it from attaching itself to creatures. The love of God and the love of creatures are incompatible things; it is for us to choose between these two loves. Now could we be blind enough to permit love toward creatures to take the upper hand over love to the Creator? The love of God so fills the heart as to leave nothing lacking, no other desire than that of always loving Him more and more; whilst, on the contrary, the love of creatures leaves the heart constantly empty and thirsting for something further. The love of God is full of sweetness, whilst the love of creatures is always mingled with bitterness. The thought, I love God and am loved by Him, consoles us in all the troubles of life; the love of creatures gives but little consolation, and is often the origin of the greatest troubles. 3rd. We must give up our heart to love, with a great and continual desire to be entirely filled and enkindled with it, and to make as many acts of it as possible. This is what St. Francis de Sales advises. "How," he was asked one day, "can we increase in divine love?" "By loving," he replied. In the same way as we learn to read by reading, to write by writing, so also we learn to love God by loving Him; that is to say, by multiplying aspirations of love night and day. Each act of love is like wood put on the fire; it heats, kindles, and augments the flames of holy love. 4th. We must often take an account of the state of our soul, examine to what degree holy love is dominant in us, whether it is really the motive of our acts and sentiments; and after this examination conceive a great desire to love God more, ask of Him grace to do so, and make the resolution that we will. Yes, my God, I desire to annihilate in me whatever is human and according to nature; I desire that Thy love alone should direct and lead me, without taking into consideration any natural repugnances; I desire amidst all that changes around me to remain invariably fixed in Thy holy love, and in dependence upon its holy inspirations.

Resolutions and spiritual nosegay as above.

— · —

SEVENTEENTH MONDAY AFTER PENTECOST

Summary of the Morrow's Meditation.

We will meditate tomorrow upon the first remedy to be applied to the digressions of the imagination. It consists in repressing curiosity, which desires to see everything, to know everything, and to hear everything. We will then make the resolution: 1st, to be more modest in the use we make of our eyes, and more reserved in regard to questions about things there is no need for us to know; 2nd, if others give us news which we have not asked for, to receive it with moderation, almost with indifference, and with none of the avidity which puts the mind into a state of disorder. Our spiritual nosegay shall be the advice of the Holy Ghost: Watch over yourselves and take heed of what you hear (Ecclus. xiii. 16).

Meditation for the Morning.

Let us adore our divine Saviour in the divine use which He made of His imagination. He never occupied it with vain and superfluous ideas, but much rather with useful and holy ones, keeping it always subject to the will of His Father, and making it serve only for His adorable designs. Let us render our homage to this divine Saviour, and ask for grace to imitate Him.

FIRST POINT.

The Influence of Curiosity upon the Disorders of theImagination.

Curiosity represents all exterior objects in the imagination as in a mirror, wherein are reflected all our sensations, and wherein they are preserved for a long time, even after they have passed away; for, when ceasing to see objects we do not cease to imagine them. Once perceived, they remain within us in the, imagination, which, a too faithful guardian, represents them to us without waiting for us to ask for them, often, even, just when we do not wish it Some time since, a curious object or a beautiful spectacle offered itself to our sight. Unmortified as we were, we looked at this object with an avidity which approached very nearly to passion ; and, as a punishment for this imprudence, the imagination reproduces it to us at prayer, at meditation, at our different exercises of piety, and that in pictures so full of life and truth that we seem to see it once more, and imagine we are speaking with people even months and years afterwards; for it has the dreadful talent of ceaselessly prolonging the existence even of things which exist no longer, and to make the most distant facts present. And this is the reason why we have so much difficulty in praying, in living in recollection, in preserving interior peace, in acquiring true and solid piety. Let us examine ourselves upon so important a subject.

SECOND POINT.

The Necessity and Manner of Correcting Curiosity.

To give a free course to curiosity, to endeavor to see, know, and hear everything, and, after that, to complain of the ramblings of the imagination, of distractions in prayer, of importunate images which pursue us and keep us in a state of incessant dissipation, is to imitate the child who, placing an object before a mirror, would be offended at seeing it represented in it. To read a letter with too much human eagerness, to let our eyes wander with entire freedom along streets, greedily and inquisitively to ask about all that is being said or done, to read newspapers with passion, and books which contain things more or less interesting, and, after that, to expect that our interior will have an aptitude for prayer, and that the imagination will leave us at peace, is to desire to obtain calm out of a tempest, light out of darkness, order and peace out of turmoil; it is to desire the impossible. Therefore, we read of a St. Charles, that, when worldly things were spoken of in his presence, he kept himself on his guard, that he might not be taken up by them. All the saints have acted in the same manner. Occupied with their souls and the duties of their position, they felt little curiosity to hear all that was going on, and it was thus that they preserved themselves from the greater portion of the ramblings of the imagination. Following their example, we ought to watch over our eyes, and deprive them of seeing what if is not necessary for them to see; we ought to watch over our words, and not ask for news or indulge in questions about things we have no need to know; we ought to watch over our thoughts, and not allow them freedom to wander and be occupied with a thousand useless objects or a thousand reveries; otherwise the imagination seizes upon them as realities, presents them to the soul with their forms and circumstances, and places them on the scene, accompanied by things and persons. We see them, we hear them, we enjoy their society, we exhaust ourselves with desires, seeking for means to reach the phantom which we pursue; and nothing more is wanting to dissipate our interior and trouble our exercises of piety. The spirit of the world is to desire to know everything, to snatch at all kinds of news, and to fill ourselves with a thousand vain things. The spirit of God, on the contrary, leads us to ignore voluntarily all which is of no use in regard to our spiritual advancement and the duties of our state. Happy ignorance which renders the knowledge of divine things easy to the soul, which disengages it from all that might disturb its peace, and renders it so entirely mistress, of itself that it disposes of itself at the good pleasure of its virtue! Let us here examine ourselves. How many times have we been uneasy on account of our having learned what there was no necessity for us to know, and preoccupied about things which we could perfectly well do without?

Resolutions and spiritual nosegay as above.

SEVENTEENTH TUESDAY AFTER PENTECOST

Summary of the Morrow's Meditation.

We will meditate tomorrow upon two new remedies suitable for employing against the ramblings of the imagination, which consist in correcting: 1st, frivolity of the mind; 2nd, attachments of the heart. We will then make the resolution: 1st, to send away all useless thoughts and replace them by sweet pictures of Jesus Christ and His mysteries; 2nd, to detach ourselves from all to which we cling the most, in order to prevent pre-occupations which distract the imagination. Our spiritual nosegay shall be the remark made by the Evangelist upon the Blessed Virgin, that she fed her mind and her heart upon all she heard which was edifying: *"But Mary kept all these words, pondering them in her heart"* (Luke ii. 19).

Meditation for the Morning.

Let us adore Our Lord in the supreme dominion He maintained over His mind, His heart, and His imagination. Let us admire the perfect manner in which all was regulated, and, prostrate at His feet, let us beg Him to help us to keep our imagination in subjection, seeing that it is an enemy greedy of independence and possessed of the strength of many years of empire; an enemy which, being chased away, always returns; which, being cast down to the ground, rises again; which, being conquered, renews the attack. Let us ask of Him to infuse into our heart a love which, although it may ceaselessly give way to distractions, ceaselessly returns; which, ceaselessly led away from God, ceaselessly comes back to Him; and in this way to destroy in us the frivolity of mind and the attachments of the heart whence so many disorderly imaginations proceed.

FIRST POINT.

We must Correct Frivolity of Mind, the Habitual Cause of the Ramblings of the Imagination.

When we have had the unhappiness of contracting a habit of frivolity of mind which amuses itself with vain thoughts, which holds in aversion grave and serious reflections, the wandering and uneasy imagination, having nothing to fix it, runs from one object to another, and turns with every wind, like a fugitive slave who is not at work in his master's house. Hardly have we begun a prayer than our imagination steals us from ourselves and runs to all the ends of the earth. It is otherwise with serious and recollected souls. The serious thoughts with which they habitually occupy themselves offer to the imagination nothing but holy images, which fix its frivolity and inconstancy. David beholds God taking him by the hand to guide him (Ps. lxxii. 24); Jerome, in the desert, sees solemn pictures of the last judgment, the dead issuing from the dust at the sound of the trumpet, and the Sovereign Judge descending from the clouds. The saints picture to themselves heaven with its throne, the crown and the glory which await them; the joys of the holy family, which is composed of God our Father, of Mary our mother, of the saints our brethren. At other times they transport themselves by means of their imagination to the crib, to Nazareth, to Calvary, or else they represent to themselves Jesus conversing with men, performing the actions they themselves have to do, and they take Him as their pattern. Is this the use we make of our imagination? Do we not belong to those frivolous minds who will not occupy this wandering faculty with anything useful that may interest and captivate it?

SECOND POINT.

We must Correct the Attachments of the Heart which are a less Fruitful Cause of the Disorders of the Imagination.

The imagination is a slave of the heart; it follows it wherever it goes and is at its orders to paint the objects which interest it, which excite its complaisance or its aversion. Do we feel too purely natural a friendship for someone, the imagination brings him before us, we converse with him and take pleasure in his company. Do we, on the other hand, feel an aversion for him, imagination cites the person before our tribunal, we dispute with him, we prove to him that he is in the wrong, and we overwhelm him with reproaches. We are passionately attached to some affair or other; the imagination preoccupies itself with it, and we think less of what we do than of what we desire to do. We allow our heart to be too strongly attached to the success of an enterprise; the imagination seizes upon the good that we desire or the evil that we fear, troubles us with joy or casts us down with fear. Lastly, we are dominated by pride or vanity; immediately the imagination asks us what is said of us, and makes us go down into the conscience of another person in order that we may read therein whether we are esteemed or misunderstood; at other times it represents to us the eulogiums and the applause which we believe to be due to us, and makes us assist at interviews in which our merit is brought to light. If anyone has the misfortune to wound our self-love in the slightest degree, it forms an odious portrait of him, which we contemplate with annoyance and displeasure. There is no longer possible for us any tranquil reflection or any work. If, on the contrary, friendship and esteem have been shown us, the imagination fills us with pictures of our own merit, makes us contemplate by day and night pictures of our own excellence, transports us into the future, amuses us with chimerical projects, and desires that we should be spoken of. Let us conclude from these remarks, to which so many others might be added, how important it is to detach ourselves from all which is not God or according to God if we desire to repress the ramblings of the imagination.

Resolutions and spiritual nosegay as above.

SEVENTEENTH WEDNESDAY AFTER PENTECOST

Summary of the Morrow's Meditation.

We will meditate tomorrow upon a fourth remedy applicable to the wanderings of the imagination, which consists in a diversion, 1st, prompt; 2nd, humble; 3rd, peaceable. We will then make the resolution: 1st, never to be disquieted, whatever may be the wanderings of our imagination, and always to maintain patience and courage; 2nd, constantly to combat them by means of a prompt, humble, and peaceful diversion. Our spiritual nosegay shall be the words of Job: *"The dissipation of my thoughts has been the torment of my heart"* (Job xvii. 11).

Meditation for the Morning.

Let us adore Our Lord, tempted in the desert, turning away the temptation by passages from the Holy Scriptures, by prayer, and by union with God, His Father. Let us thank Him for His example and ask of Him grace to imitate it.

FIRST POINT.

We must Combat the Imagination by Means of a Prompt Diversion.

To attempt to arrest the imagination by pure violence would be to attempt the impossible. A diversion is the only resource; we turn our backs to the enemy by occupying ourselves with more ardor with what we are doing, and lovingly cast ourselves into the arms of God by effusions of the heart, like the child who, when an attempt is made to take it from the breast of its mother, clings all the more to it in proportion to the efforts made to take it away. The essential point is not to delay; for, being already so evil in itself, what is there the imagination would not do if we allowed it to be mistress for even a few moments only? It would carry us away, seduced as we should be by its pleasing pictures; it would make us lose time, often even something more precious still, by mixing ideas which are permissible with ideas which are dangerous, and then with bad ones. This is what we gain by trafficking with the frivolities of the imagination instead of putting them away from us at the very first moment. Let us here examine ourselves. Do we habitually watch over the gate of our interior, so that we may not allow any vain fancies to enter therein? Do we not, on the contrary, knowingly entertain ourselves with certain imaginations? Do we not recall them, even when they escape us, and do we not form new and more vivid ones? Do we not allow ourselves to indulge in the illusion that, at certain idle moments, we may give license to our imagination?

SECOND POINT.

We must Combat the Imagination by a Humble Diversion.

The imagination being of all the faculties the most degraded, and one of our greatest miseries, we ought to humble ourselves profoundly before God and, prostrate at His feet, say to Him, inspired by a lively sentiment of our misery: "Alas, Lord, I am but as a leaf carried away by a breath of wind, a *'wind that goeth and returneth not'* (Ps. lxxvii. 39); I have lost the respect due to Thy presence and I deserve nothing but to be rejected by Thee. My place is beneath the feet of all creatures. Let millions of angels glorify Thee by their recollection, let holy souls enjoy the delights of piety. As for me, unworthy to satisfy Thy love, it is too much honor for me to be here beneath Thy feet, to satisfy Thy justice by combats, privations, and aridities. Nakedness, misery, powerlessness, these things are my portion; abased in my nothingness I accept it, and submit to it." Such is the humble diversion to be opposed to the importunities of the imagination. The soul which is faithful to it attracts the eyes and the complaisance of God. He consoles it, He enlightens it, He unites it to Himself, in such a degree that a pious author has said that distractions, when we know how to humble ourselves before them, are a path which leads us to contemplation.

THIRD POINT.

We must Combat the Imagination by a Peaceful Diversion.

Peace of heart is the most precious of all possessions, and to take it from us would be a triumph for the devil, even supposing that in making us give way to a rambling imagination he was to leave our heart innocent. And wherefore give this enjoyment to the enemy of our salvation? To be distracted is not to be culpable, as long as we do not seek opportunities or give our consent. Job was not the less holy when the dissipation of his thoughts was the torment of his heart (Job xvii. 11), or David, when the illusions of his imagination importuned him (Ps. xxxvii. 8), or all the saints, when their imagination carried them where they did not desire to be. We must not therefore lose peace, or be annoyed, or be cast down even if the imagination were to make us suffer until death. St. Teresa suffered from it even after forty years of prayer.

Resolutions and spiritual nosegay as above.

SEVENTEENTH THURSDAY AFTER PENTECOST

Summary of the Morrow's inebriation.

As all our senses are like so many doors by which sin attempts to enter into our soul, we will meditate tomorrow upon the mortification of two of our principal senses, sight and hearing. We will then make the resolution: 1st, not to lose time in looking at useless things and watching from a door or a window those who come and go, or in visiting vain worldly curiosities; 2nd, to keep ourselves from gossiping and the retailing of news, which always dissipates us, even if it does not compromise us. Our spiritual nosegay shall be the words of the Holy Ghost: "The *eye is not filled with seeing, neither is the ear filled with hearing*" (Eccles, i. 8).

Meditation for the Morning.

Let us adore Our Lord Jesus Christ in the admirable use which He made of the senses of sight and hearing. What modesty in His eyes; what a turning away from all vain conversation and from all which serves only to flatter the ear! Let us render to Him all our homage of adoration, admiration, and praise.

FIRST POINT.

The Mortification of the Eyes

The Holy Spirit tells us by the mouth of the Sage that nothing upon earth is capable of doing us more harm than too great liberty in the use of our eyes. St. Jerome, commenting upon those words of Job, *"Have the gates of death been opened to thee?"* (Job xxxviii. 17) says, in the same sense, that our eyes are the gates of death, because it is by them that the death of sin enters into the soul; they are, according to the words of Jeremias, the windows by which death penetrates into us (Jer. ix. 21). Thereby, in fact, enter evil thoughts and imaginations which are dangerous, lascivious representations which often kindle and entertain in our heart the fire of the passions. Thereby the soul contracts a habit of dissipation which renders us incapable of prayer and spiritual things, which makes us lose time, deranges the whole of our interior, ravages the virtues we have acquired, and destroys all energy for good. If you do not watch over the gates of your senses, says the Imitation, you will lose in one moment all that you may have amassed during a long period and with a great deal of trouble. If you do not accustom your senses, says St Dorothea, not to wander amidst the vain frivolities of this world, the license that you grant them will distract you from the care to be given to your salvation. St. John Baptist, says St. Jerome, shut up in his desert, believed that his eyes, which were destined to behold Jesus Christ, ought to disdain the lower things of this world (St. Jerome, *Ep.,* iv.). With this example before us, we should feel that our eyes, destined for eternity to contemplate the splendors of the saints together with the glorious humanity of Jesus Christ, the brilliancy of which illuminates the whole of the holy city, ought not to wander in streets and in public places, gazing upon things we have no need to see, and upon so many persons with whose comings and goings we have nothing to do. They ought to serve us for what is useful in regard to the glory of God, for the service of our neighbor or our own interests; and, apart from these exceptions, to be kept in restraint, modest and reserved everywhere, but more especially at church and at prayer; otherwise we shall either not pray, or we shall be thinking of what we see rather than of what we are saying. Restraint in regard to our eyes is the safeguard of innocence, of recollection, of the spirit of prayer, of all the virtues; and there has not been a saint who has not habitually kept a restraint over his eyes. Are we of that number?

SECOND POINT.

Mortification of the Hearing.

Mortification of the hearing demands that we should not lend our ears to murmurings, to calumnies, to ridicule, to improper words, to speeches having a double meaning, to conversations which conscience reproves. It even requires that we should not lose time in listening to frivolous talk, which is devoid of usefulness and of dignity; still less to listen to our own praises, when flatterers permit themselves to indulge in such things, and that we should, as soon as possible, turn the conversation in another direction. It does not approve of running after news or frequenting those who make a practice of giving it; of entertaining ourselves with romances, comedies, and a thousand things which distil an impure venom into the heart. It condemns still more severely profane songs, music which tends to enervate and to lead to licentiousness, and it only tolerates with regret concerts which have only pleasure and amusement for their object. Lastly, it recalls to mind the counsel of the Holy Ghost: Take heed of what you hear (Ecclus. xiii. 16), that is to say: Do not lend your ears to vain and useless words which are of no use in regard to salvation. Let us examine what we have to reproach ourselves with in regard to these rules and let us have courage to deprive ourselves here below of these satisfactions of the sense of hearing, that we may the better listen in heaven to the concerts of angels and saints.

Resolutions and spiritual nosegay as above.

SEVENTEENTH FRIDAY AFTER PENTECOST

Summary of the Morrow's Meditation.

We will continue tomorrow to meditate upon the mortification of the senses, and in particular, 1st, upon the mortification of the sense of taste; 2nd, upon the mortification of the sense of touch. We will then deduce the resolution: 1st, in our meals not to seek the satisfaction of our sensuality, and to see in our food only the good pleasure of God, who feeds us at His pleasure, without our having the right either to be pleased if the food be to our taste or to be discontented if it be not; 2nd, heartily to accept all that our body may meet with in the way of suffering, never seeking to flatter it or procure for it pleasure. Our spiritual nosegay shall be the words of the Apostle: *"I chastise my body, and bring it into subjection; lest perhaps I myself should become a castaway "* (I. Cor. ix. 27).

Meditation for the Morning.

Let us adore Our Lord giving us a beautiful example of the mortification of the sense of taste and of touch. In order not to satisfy His palate, He often deprives Himself of food and of drink. When He eats or drinks He never does it because of the pleasure He finds in it; and during His Passion He takes nothing but gall and vinegar. He is more admirable still in regard to the sense of touch, seeing that in His Passion He does not leave, from the sole of His foot to the crown of His head, a single portion of His body free from suffering (Isaias i. 6). Let us thank Him for these great examples, which so greatly condemn our sensitiveness.

FIRST POINT.

Mortification of the Taste.

The mortification of the sense of taste forbids us to seek after good cheer, exquisite aliments, delicate meats, which the saints call the food of incontinence and voluptuousness. In the use of common food, it wishes that we should take, without thinking of it, such food as is given to us; if it suits our tastes, let us bless God who treats us so well; if it is not palatable to us, let us still bless God, who gives us an opportunity for mortifying ourselves; and if the choice be free to us, let us leave the best morsels to others. It forbids us to pay attention to the greater or less savor of aliments, to think of them after our meals, and still less to speak of them. It is not worthy of a Christian soul to let its thoughts descend to things which are so much below it. The mortification of the sense of taste forbids us to eat anything between our meals, not even fruit, or someone or other of the delicacies in which people of the world indulge, and which are nothing more than satisfactions accorded to sensuality. It is pleased when it can partake of things which have a bad taste, to swallow them slowly, in order the better to feel the bitterness of them, and thereby honor the bitterness Our Saviour tasted on the cross Are these the rules of our conduct?

SECOND POINT.

Mortification of the Sense of Touch.

The sense of touch, being spread over the whole body, is, on that very account, all the more dangerous, says St. John Climacus; its attacks are more frequent, its assaults more multiplied, and the war to be sustained more continual. It is this which led the saints to torment their flesh by exterior mortifications, and St. Paul in particular to chastise his flesh and reduce it to servitude, from the fear that he should be a castaway. In conformity with these great examples, we ought not either to touch ourselves or touch others without necessity; or allow ourselves to indulge in that effeminate delicacy which will not allow of anything coarse or hard coming near the flesh; which is always on the lookout for what is most comfortable, most sensual, softest to the flesh, and is on the search for all the means invented by the love of comfort for satisfying the sense of touch. We ought to bear, if not with joy, at least with patience and without complaint, cold, heat, all the discomforts of the season, and take only such care of ourselves as our health requires, without giving way to eagerness, and do all in moderation. We ought, in the same spirit, to accept sickness, infirmities, all that can make the body suffer, seeing in it all an opportunity of giving God solid marks of our love, of deadening our passions, and expiating our past faults. Lastly, not content with the sufferings sent us by Providence, we ought to impose voluntary ones on ourselves, according to the maxim of the Apostle, that all Christians must crucify their flesh (Gal. v. 24), in order to honor the Passion of Our Saviour, and to accomplish in our flesh, like St. Paul, what was wanting in His sufferings (Col. i. 24). Do we observe these rules?

Resolutions and spiritual nosegay as above.

Seventeenth Saturday after Pentecost

Summary of the Morrow's Meditation.

We will meditate tomorrow: 1st, on the happiness with which God recompenses mortified souls here below; 2nd, on the unhappiness to which He abandons unmortified souls. We will derive from these reflections the resolution: 1st, to be generous in the service of God, and cheerfully to make all the sacrifices which present themselves to us; 2nd, for the love of God frequently to impose voluntary sacrifices on ourselves, even if they should consist of nothing but a desire, a look, or something agreeable to the senses. Our spiritual nosegay shall be the words of the Apostle: *"I exceedingly abound with joy in all our tribulations"* (II. Cor. vii. 4).

Meditation for the Morning.

Let us adore the infinite goodness of Jesus Christ, who at the same time that He imposes upon us the law of mortification takes from it all that is painful to nature by declaring to us that therein consists our true happiness. My law is a *yoke*, He says, but I render it *sweet* to those who will wear it; it is a *burden*, but I make it *light* to those who will bear it (Matt. xi. 30). Let us thank Him for willing thus to temper by the unction of His grace the hardness of the cross, and to share the burden with us that He may lighten it.

FIRST POINT.

With what Happiness God Recompenses Here Below Mortified Souls.

When God beholds in His service generous souls who are not afraid of making sacrifices to Him, He does not allow Himself to be vanquished in generosity; He delights to shed upon them His consolations and His delights; He renders to them in proportion to what they give Him, and there is, as it were, a holy emulation of love between Him and them. Such great hearts as these and such true Christians are delighted to find opportunities for suffering and doing violence to themselves. Far from allowing any such opportunities to escape them, however opposed they may be to their temperament, they seize them joyfully, as being one of the greatest happinesses of life, and they never say: "It is not an obligation incumbent on me; I shall meet with enough opportunities for mortifying myself; it shall be for another time." If anyone mortifies them, they are not troubled; they do not feel the least resentment, and they act always with the same cordiality towards them. It never occurs to them to complain of difficulties accompanying virtue, nor to cry down exercises of piety under the pretense that they are painful. Always ready to renounce every pleasure, even such as are permitted, which they might enjoy in this life, they keep themselves continually at a distance from the voluptuousness of the world, the satisfaction of the flesh, from all kinds of luxuries and superfluities. Lastly, knowing that the body is a slave which, when it is well fed, revolts against its master, they weaken it, they keep it in subjection; they never dwell on the pleasure to be found in the use of creatures, and endeavor to conform themselves in everything to Jesus crucified. But, on the other hand, God compensates them magnificently for these privations. Let us believe what the great Apostle says when he cries out: *"Blessed be the God and Father of Our Lord Jesus Christ, the Father of mercies, and the God of all comfort, who comforteth us in all our tribulations ... I exceedingly abound with joy in all our tribulations. God comforteth the humble"* (II. Cor. i. 3, 4; vii. 4, 6). Let us believe St. Francis Xavier; great sufferings were shown to him in the career on which he was about to enter; he asks for still more. At that very moment he is recompensed by an ocean of joy and happiness which he cannot contain, and which obliges him to cry out, "Enough, *O Lord,* enough!" And we also, let us have the courage to renounce self-will in order to infuse order into the employment of our time, to sacrifice even only a desire, a look, a pleasure of the senses, a word, and we shall feel what joy and happiness there is in doing something for God, and grace entering into our soul will make us repeat the words of St. Aloysius, that a little sacrifice made for God procures a thousand times more happiness for the soul than the thing sacrificed would have done.

SECOND POINT.

To what Unhappiness God Abandons Unmortified Souls.

How unhappy such souls are! For them there is no unction and grace in the service of God; it is nothing but disgust and tepidity; piety is insipid, devotion has no attractions. We see others advance and we remain behind, because we will not detach ourselves as they do. Prayer is nothing but a weariness, because neither the heart, which is a slave to its attachments, nor the mind, which is habitually dissipated, is in a proper state for the reception of celestial communications; and where the generous soul complains that the hours are too short, the unmortified soul finds them always too long. What is, however, the most pitiable is, that often a trifle, a nothing, stops it; it is only a thread, but as long as the thread is not broken, the soul which it keeps back will never fly into the bosom of God, where repose and happiness are found; it will do nothing but turn round and round in the same labyrinth, nothing but painfully torment itself around that which holds it back. Is not this our history?

Resolutions and spiritual nosegay as above.

EIGHTEENTH SUNDAY AFTER PENTECOST

The Gospel according to St. Matthew, ix. 1-8.

"At that time Jesus entered into a boat, and passed over the water, and came into His own city. And behold they brought to Him one sick of the palsy lying in a bed. And Jesus, seeing their faith, said to the man sick of the palsy: Be of good heart, son, thy sins are forgiven thee. And behold some of the scribes said within themselves: He blasphemeth. And Jesus, seeing their thoughts, said: Why do you think evil in your hearts? Whether is easier, to say, Thy sins are forgiven thee: or to say, Arise and walk? But that you may know that the Son of man hath power on earth to forgive sins (then saith He to the man sick of the palsy), Arise, take up thy bed, and go into thy house. And he arose and went into his house. And the multitude seeing it, feared, and glorified God, that gave such power to men."

Summary of the Morrow's Meditation.

We will meditate tomorrow upon the gospel of the day, and we shall learn from it; 1st, to have recourse to God in all troubles of life; 2nd, to occupy ourselves more with the eternal destiny of our souls than with any temporal evils. We will thence deduce the resolution: 1st, to make Our Lord the confidant of our trials, and to cast them all into His bosom; 2nd, to place our eternal interests before everything that belongs to this present life. Our spiritual nosegay shall be the words of the gospel: *"Lord, to whom shall we go? Thou hast the words of eternal life"* (John vi. 69).

Meditation for the Morning.

Let us adore Our Lord Jesus Christ graciously receiving the man sick of the palsy and those who present him to Him. When we go to Him with confidence, we are sure of always being graciously received. How good He is, how worthy of all our homage! He alone is the true friend of souls! Let us prostrate ourselves at His feet and pour into His heart all our feelings of gratitude.

FIRST POINT.

We must have Recourse to God in all the Troubles of Life.

This is the lesson given us in our gospel. As soon as Our Saviour had arrived in His city, that is to say, at Capharnaum, where He habitually resided, a man sick of the palsy was brought to Him. The house within and all around was encumbered by a crowd of people, and, in order to present the sick man to Him, no other means were available except to uncover the roof and to let down through the opening the bed on which the poor palsied man was laid. The example of such great faith therein set us teaches us to have recourse to God in all the troubles of life. It is, indeed, He alone who decrees the trials which afflict us, He alone consoles us, He alone recompenses us. He decrees them; for nothing happens in this world except by the express will or permission of Providence, and not even a hair of our head falls to the ground except by its intervention; and this Providence is always full of loving kindness. If it wounds, it gives the remedy which softens the wound; if its hand strikes, it also heals (Job v. 18). Wherefore, then, instead of having recourse to men, who can do nothing, why not have recourse to God, who can do all? Besides, He consoles us in all trials. Men, as Job says (Job xvi. 2), are only troublesome consolers; we tell them our troubles and the majority of them either do not compassionate us or do not know how to speak the words of faith which alone can console us. Let us tell our troubles to God in a fervent prayer at the foot of a crucifix or in a visit to the Blessed Sacrament, and we shall return from it feeling better, strengthened and consoled. Lastly, God alone recompenses us for trials borne in a Christian manner. If we speak of our trials to creatures we often lose the merit of them; our self-love seeks to make itself pitied and admired; if we speak of them to ourselves, our nature murmurs, lays the blame on God and on man, and we derive nothing from it but a greater degree of sadness, of discontent with ourselves, and of sin. If, on the contrary, we cast our troubles into the heart of God, we sanctify them by resignation, by prayer, by the hope of eternal possessions, and the assurance that our hope will not be confounded. Let us here recognize, in the presence of God, how much harm we do ourselves by all these stories of our sufferings and our troubles which we recount to creatures.

SECOND POINT.

The Eternal Destiny of our Soul ought to Occupy us more than all Temporal Evils.

This is the lesson the Saviour gives us in the gospel of the day. The Jews present to Him the man sick of the palsy and beg of Him to cure the poor suffering body. Our Lord replies to them by curing his soul, which is still more sick. He enlightens it, He touches it, He penetrates it with sincere contrition and a true love of God, and He says to the sick man, "My son, have confidence, your sins are remitted you." The cure of the body will come, but it will be only in the second place. The essential must precede that which is accessory, heaven must come before earth; the interests of eternity before those of time; the soul before the body. Is it thus that we appreciate all things? The holy Cure of Ars once lighted his lamp by mistake with a bank-bill. His servant uttered a cry and was greatly distressed. "How little faith you have," the holy priest said to her. "If you had seen me commit a venial sin, you would have said nothing, but for a little money thus lost you cry out loudly." How many Christians are there in the world who attach less interest to their salvation than to their money; who have less fear of a sin than they have of the loss of their fortune, of their honor, and their reputation? Let us examine ourselves as to whether we are not of the number.

Resolutions and spiritual nosegay as above.

EIGHTEENTH MONDAY AFTER PENTECOST

Summary of the Morrow's Meditation.

We will terminate tomorrow our meditations upon mortification, by considering: 1st, the happiness which the mortified soul enjoys in its relations towards its neighbor; 2nd, the happiness it finds in itself. We will thence deduce the resolution: 1st, not to allow a single day to pass without performing some act of mortification, either of the will, or of the disposition, or of self-love, and we will set down two such acts for the day; 2nd, to obey the Holy Ghost in all the acts He may suggest such as sacrificing a caprice, a desire, a pleasure. Our spiritual nosegay shall be the words of the Imitation: *"Leave all, and you will find all; relinquish your attachments, and you will have peace"* (III. Imit. xxxii. 1).

Meditation for the Morning.

Let us admire Our Lord, who is full of esteem and of love for mortification. It would have been easy for Him to have been born in opulence, to live in pleasure, to die without suffering; and yet He willed, through choice, to be born in a stable, to live in continual labors, and to die upon a cross. Oh, how admirable this choice is! How it reveals to us the excellence of mortification, that incomparable virtue which procures happiness for us in our relations with our neighbor and enables us to find it also in ourselves. Let us thank Our Lord for it.

FIRST POINT.

The Mortified Soul finds Happiness in its Relations with its Neighbor.

Mortification is the secret of being on good terms with everyone. There is never any dissension, because the mortified man accommodates his will and his character to the will and the character of others. There is never any altercation, because, never believing his own judgment to be the sole rule of what is true, he never thinks of entering into any disputes, and his conversation is always sweet, tranquil, calm, and charming. There are never any rivalries or contentions, because he prefers to yield his rights rather than uphold them at the expense of charity. Therefore, everyone is devoted to him; and as he is attentive to procure happiness for others, they, on their part, are attentive in ministering to his. It is quite otherwise with the unmortified man, who is always striving to make his own will, his own ideas, his interests, and his way of looking at things prevail. Everywhere he meets with nothing but disputes and quarrels, dislike or hatred, affronts or deceptions of self-love, engendered by the conflict of interests, of wills, of tastes, and of characters where mortification does not reign. And thus it happens that the man whose whole desire is not to suffer, suffers on all sides; he repels the hearts of his fellows by his haughtiness and his pretensions, by his determination not to render any service in the least degree annoying to himself, by his self-love, which is always on the search for what is most agreeable to himself, without having any fear of putting others to inconvenience; lastly, by his words, which are often bitter and hard, his somber and disagreeable manners, his impetuosity, and his violent temper. Let us examine our conscience with regard to all these points.

SECOND POINT.

The Mortified Soul finds Happiness within Itself.

The mortified man is always happy in himself. All may change around him; whether he be in the midst of enjoyments or of privations, in one place or another, he is content with everything, content everywhere, because he does not cling to anything; he desires nothing but the good pleasure of God, whom he sees, whom he adores, whom he loves in everything. Created objects cannot trouble him, because God is all in all to him, and because he says to himself: "God only suffices; he who has God has everything." This is why the saints were the happiest of men here below. Raised above all events, their days flowed on in an independence and tranquility which nothing could disturb; within them reigned a constant calm, a repose, a continually uniform serenity; the wind of a thousand desires never came near to agitate them; still less did emotions and passions overwhelm them; never the very slightest murmur of discontent passed over the surface of their souls. "I desire very few things," said one of them, "and the little that I desire I desire in a very small degree." In these few words, oh, what an admirable secret for being happy is contained! What movements, what agitations, what troubles and annoyances we may spare ourselves, what happy liberty, what delicious peace we may acquire! (III. Imit. xxxi. i.)

Resolutions and spiritual nosegay as above.

Eighteenth Tuesday
After Pentecost

Summary of the Morrow's Meditation

Our preceding meditations have had for their object the emptying of our heart from all attachment to creatures; it is time now to fill it with divine charity. This is why we will consider tomorrow what charity is, and we shall see that it: 1st, in loving God for Himself; 2nd, in loving Him above all things; 3rd, in loving Him with all our power. We will then make the resolution: 1st, as much as possible to multiply aspirations of love towards God, in order to ask of Him grace to love Him always more and more; 2nd, to perform all our actions from love. Our spiritual nosegay shall be the words of St. Augustine: *"O fire which burneth always, inflame me, that I may love thee with my whole heart" (Conf,* lib. x.; *Solil.* 29.)

Meditation for the Morning.

Let us adore God giving us the sweet precept of love: *"Thou shall love the Lord thy God"* (Deut. vi. 5; Mark xii. 30). Although the love with which He loves Himself suffices for His happiness, He desires also to be loved by His creatures. Although all the angels and all the saints burn with the most ardent love towards Him, it is not enough for His heart; He wishes that earth should have a share in the happiness of heaven, and that we should love Him also. Not only does He permit this commerce of love between ourselves and Him, but He commands it, and He threatens us with His anger if we do not love Him. Let us, with St.

Augustine, admire this excess of charity. For what am I to Thee, O my God, that Thou shouldst desire to enter into such intimate heart-to-heart relations with me, and that Thou art angry with me if I refuse to do so? *(Conf.,* lib. ii.)

FIRST POINT.

We ought to Love God for Himself

God doubtless deserves that we should love Him infinitely, because of all that He has done for us since we are on earth, as well as for all the good things He destines us throughout eternity. But to love Him for this reason is not to accomplish the precept of charity; it is to satisfy the law of gratitude. True charity makes abstraction of all self-interest, and, raising itself up to God, considered in Himself, it loves His infinite perfection, worthy of itself alone to ravish all hearts; the supreme goodness, the incomparable beauty which can never be sufficiently loved, even though we had no recompense to expect from it. At the sole sight of these infinite amiabilities, the soul bursts forth into transports and cries out with the saints, *"God alone, God alone is everything to me."* And there is nothing in heaven or upon earth that I desire if it be not Thee, O my God, Thou who art all good (Ex. xxxiii. 19); Thou who art beauty ever ancient and ever new; Thou after whom I sigh (Ps. xli. 3), and the sight of whom will maintain ma throughout eternity in a continual ecstasy of joy, of happiness, and of love (Ps. xvi. 15). In this happy state, we have at heart but one desire, the desire of pleasing God. We love Him, not only because He infinitely merits it, but because He wills it, because such is His good pleasure, and because His good pleasure is everything for the soul which loves. Let us examine whether we have thus loved God. Have we not loved Him only for the sake of what He has done for us, of the glory which He promises us, of the paradise which we expect? Do we often make acts of pure love towards God, and have we deeply implanted in our hearts the sentiment of the love of God purely for Himself? *"The reason for loving God,"* says St. Bernard, *"is because He is God."*

SECOND POINT.

We ought to Love God above alt Things.

To love God above all things is to be ready to sacrifice everything and to lose everything rather than offend Him or displease Him; it is to maintain our whole being and our whole existence at the disposition of His good pleasure; it is to prefer the glory of being His, of serving Him and pleasing Him, to all the riches, to all the grandeurs, to all the pleasures of this world, and to be ready to separate from our parents or our friends; to break with those to whom we cling the most; to immolate our own satisfaction, our health, out life even, if it be necessary, rather than be wanting in what God asks of us. What can be more just than this frame of mind? *"He who loves his father and mother more than Me, is not worthy of Me,"* Jesus Christ has said. God in His place before everything, God before riches, God before pleasure and well-being, God before the *"what will they say,"* God before the whole of the universe. How little is this truth understood! When the men of whom the gospel speaks are invited to the wedding, I have bought a farm, says one: I am obliged to go and see it (Luke xiv. 18). What is that compared with the enjoyment of God, of which this marriage is a symbol? It is a nothing, and this nothing costs a thousand cares and a thousand anxieties. It does not signify; for the sake of this nothing God is lost. I have bought five pair of oxen, says another: I must go and try them (Luke xiv. 19). The man, then, does not even know them, and yet he attaches himself to them. Oh, how we should be on our guard against attaching ourselves to the world, did we but know what are its miseries, its sorrows, and its infidelities! I cannot accept the invitation, others say (Luke xiv. 20), and thus, some on one account, and some on another, lose heaven and lose God because they do not love Him above everything else. As for me, Lord, I will love Thee above all things. Take from me everything except Thy love; I shall be content, and I will cheerfully lose all things for love of Thee. In leaving me Thy love, Thou leavest me all I desire. Thy love is everything to me, and without it everything is nothing to me. Even immortality is not dear to me except that through it I shall always enjoy Thy love. I would rather cease to be from this moment, than be one moment without Thy love. Let us sound our hearts. Are these really our dispositions?

THIRD POINT.

We ought to Love God with all our Power.

That is to say: 1st, *with all our heart,* in such a way that we love God only, nothing but in God and for God; 2nd, *with all our mind,* taking pleasure in thinking of Him and on the means whereby to please Him; 3rd, *with our whole soul,* subjecting to Him all our passions, and using our senses, whether interior or exterior, only according to His good pleasure; 4th, *with our whole strength,* sparing ourselves nothing when there is a question of accomplishing His will, and employing our whole strength in serving Him. Is it thus that we love God? *In our heart,* what attachment to our own ease, to sensuality, to self-love, what affections and intentions which have no relation to God! *In our mind,* what forgetfulness of God, what habitual dissipation! Most frequently we speak and act as though God did not exist, solely occupied, as we are, in pleasing the creature, or finding pleasure in ourselves. *In our soul,* we allow free course to curiosity, to our imagination, to our passions, in regard to everything which does not actually bear the character of mortal sin. *In the use of our senses and of our faculties,* we expect to serve God without annoyance and without subjecting them to Him. As soon as the cross presents itself, we draw back. As long as duty is in accordance with pleasure, we are faithful to it; as soon as He asks a sacrifice of us, a violence to be done to ourselves, an effort over ourselves, we neglect it. Evidently, this is not to love God with all our strength. Let us examine ourselves, therefore, and see if we can flatter ourselves that we love God with our whole power.

Resolutions and spiritual nosegay as above.

Eighteenth Wednesday After Pentecost

Summary of the Morrow's inebriation.

We will meditate tomorrow upon the love of complaisance, otherwise termed joy in God. We will consider: 1st, in what this joy consists; 2nd, the great advantages which it procures for the soul. We will thence deduce the resolution: 1st, often to meditate upon the infinite perfections of God, His immensity, His goodness, His omnipotence, and to place our whole happiness in losing ourselves in these sacred abysses, admiring His greatness and His elevation above all beings; 2nd, always to be content with God and with the guidance of His providence, whatever of good or evil may happen to us. Our spiritual nosegay shall be the words of St. Augustine: "*God is content with whoever is content with Him*" *(In Ps.* xxxii.).

Meditation for the Morning.

Let us adore Our Lord contemplating with supreme joy the immense and incomprehensible perfections of God His Father; His heart plunges with delight into these sacred abysses; in them He finds all His complaisance and all His joy. Let us rejoice at the joys He tastes and the glory He thereby procures for His Father.

FIRST POINT.

In what Consists the Love of Complaisance, or Joy in God.

When we are filled with ardent love for someone, it is great joy to think of his beautiful qualities; we speak of them to others, we dwell upon them in our thoughts, and all which raises him, and which aggrandizes him, gives us pleasure; we are happy in his happiness. Now, if amongst ourselves the beautiful qualities of the person beloved cause joy to him who loves, what joy ought it not to be for a person who loves God to see that He is so beautiful, so perfect, so holy, so great, and, at the same time, so full of kindness! "How beautiful Thou art, my beloved!" exclaimed St. Francis de Sales; "may my God be blessed forever for being so good! Whether I live or die, I am but too happy to know that my God is rich in all kinds of possessions, and that His goodness is infinite!" It was this joy which the Blessed Virgin felt when she sang in her canticle: *"My soul doth magnify the Lord, and my spirit hath rejoiced in God my Saviour"* (Luke i. 46, 47). It was this that the Prophet-King had sung before her, when he exclaimed: *"My heart and my flesh have rejoiced in the living God"* (Ps. lxxxiii. 3). In this holy ecstasy of love, the soul, delighting in the ineffable beauty of its God, rejoices that He possesses in His essence the plenitude of all good; that He finds in Himself His own beatitude; it rejoices that so many saints love Him in heaven and upon earth; that the Church everywhere resounds with His praise; that His Son honors Him as He merits to be honored; and this joy is as an anticipated paradise to it Do we often exercise ourselves in this love of complaisance towards God, which is so dear to holy souls?

SECOND POINT.

The Great Advantages Procured by the Love of Complaisance or Joy in God.

1st. Nothing is more suitable for detaching the soul from the earth and filling it with holy desires for heaven. Enchanted with the beauties of God, it feels that here below there is nothing real, nothing worthy of it Everything outside God seems to it nothing but vanity, and it exclaims with the saints, God of Himself is sufficient; all that is not God is nothing to me! Freed from all attachments, it flies to heaven by means of holy desires, to see, face to face, the God whom it loves; to praise Him unceasingly, to love Him in an eternal ecstasy. 2nd. The soul which is thus enamored of the beauties of God finds supreme felicity in abandoning itself lovingly to all the decrees of the infinitely good Father, decrees of which it desires the accomplishment a thousand times more than it does its own personal satisfaction. It wills all that God wills, desires all that He desires, loves all that He loves, hates all that He hates, and wills, desires, hates, and loves nothing else. In adversity as in prosperity, in abandonment as in consolations, in sickness as in health, in privation as in enjoyment, it cherishes the divine good pleasure; and content with God, whatever He may do, it always says, with an abandonment full of sweetness, It is well, my God, because it is Thy good pleasure (Matt. xi. 26). 3rd. Being thus detached from the earth and united to the divine good pleasure, it rapidly advances in virtues, above all, in holy love, because it feels that God merits all its love, and, in proportion as it loves Him more, it feels Him to be always more amiable ; and, advancing thus, it feels nothing to be painful, because there exists nothing painful to him who loves, or if there does, he loves the pain itself.

Resolutions and spiritual nosegay as above.

— · —

EIGHTEENTH THURSDAY AFTER PENTECOST

Summary of the Morrow's Meditation.

After having meditated upon the love of complaisance, or of holy joy which the contemplation of the divine perfections excites in the soul, we will meditate tomorrow upon the sentiment of loving kindness, which is a second effect of the love of God in the heart; and we shall consider, 1st, in what this love consists; 2nd, what ought to be the practice of it. We will then make the resolution: 1st, in all circumstances to sustain the cause of the glory of God and His religion, of His Church and of His worship; 2nd, every time that we shall see or hear God offended to make Him reparation or honorable amends by means of acts of love. Our spiritual nosegay shall be the words of the prophet Elias: *"With zeal have I been zealous for the Lord God of hosts: for the children of Israel have forsaken Thy covenant"* (III. Kings xix. 9).

Meditation for the Morning.

Let us adore Our Lord in the incomparable sentiment of loving kindness of which He made proof towards His Father. He descends upon earth in order to destroy His enemies, to make Him known by the whole world, to establish His kingdom there, to procure for Him all kinds of honors. Let us admire this loving kindness, and let us thank Our Lord for the beautiful example which He gives us.

FIRST POINT.

In what Consists the Sentiment of Loving Kindness towards God.

This sentiment consists in a great desire that God should be known, loved, and served; His holy name blessed by all hearts, exalted by all mouths, and His will be accomplished by all men (Matt. vi. 9). The soul which loves with the sentiment of loving kindness would willingly sacrifice for the cause of God and His glory its possessions, its reputation, its repose, its health, its life; and, in order to obtain one heart more in the world to love the Lord, there would be nothing it would not be ready to do. Therefore it is never without extreme suffering that it beholds God offended in the world; and when it hears His holy name blasphemed, when it sees His commandments despised, His worship neglected, His holy day violated, His Church insulted and delivered up to spoil, it is as though its heart were transpierced by a sword. It sighs over it, it entreats God to pardon it, it does penance for it, it offers reparation and honorable amends for it, it offers itself and all its actions as an expiatory victim, consenting willingly to suffer everything, even death itself, that God may no longer be offended and that sinners may be converted. Lastly, in its powerlessness to love God as much as it desires to do, it invites all beings, even the inanimate creation, to join themselves with it to celebrate His praises: O all ye whom the Lord has created, bless Him, praise Him, and glorify Him forever. Say with me, How great God is, let us exalt His name together (Dan. iii. 5; Ps. xxxiii.), and if it could it would enkindle the whole universe with a great fire of love towards the God whom it loves. Oh, that I could, said St. Teresa, hold the hearts of all men in my hands to consume them all in a furnace of love! Let us examine if these be our dispositions; if we have not beheld with indifference religion dishonored, the Church despised; if we have the interests of God at heart; if on many occasions we have not preferred our private interests to those of His honor and glory.

SECOND POINT.

What are the Practices with which the Sentiment of Loving Kindness towards God
ought to Inspire us.

When the love of God has really entered into the heart, it begins to seek after
all possible means for honoring Him, and in its own sphere does all that is
possible. From afar it follows with lively interest the Catholic missions which
labor to gain new children to the faith; and it seconds them on the one hand by
its prayers, and on the other by the efforts it makes to develop the good works
of the Propagation of the Faith and of the Holy Infancy. In its own country,
seeing the wicked attack Holy Church, her august head and her ministers, it
compassionates these calamities, and, together with prayer, it opposes them by
language, which is firm without being bitter, when the opportunity presents
itself. At the sight of the energy displayed by the genius of evil, of the associations
and institutions he creates, the sacrifices and the trouble he imposes upon
himself in order to pervert the peoples, it feels itself to be urged by a great desire,
or, rather, by a holy passion, to do at least as much for the glory of God, and
not allow the devil to enjoy the pleasure of being able to boast that he is better
served by his adepts than Jesus Christ is by His disciples. In consequence, it is
always actively engaged in doing all the good it can, and sacrifices cost it nothing.
At the sight of sinners, who, with eyes closed, are hastening to their eternal
ruin, it prays, it endeavors to bring back these wandering souls, now by good
counsel and a word in season, now by some holy ingenuity, always by a good
example; and, knowing the influence of external worship upon the mind of
the people, it obtains, in as far as is possible, the decoration of churches, the
ornamentation of altars, the neatness of the sacred vessels, propriety in singing
and in ceremonies, perfect piety in the administration of the sacraments and
of holy things; finally, burning with thirst for the glory of God, it says every
day, with all its soul: *"Glory to the Father, to the Son, and to the Holy Ghost!"* It
communicates and performs various good works for the conversion of sinners,
the exaltation of Holy Church, and the triumph of religion. Is it thus that we
practice the sentiment of loving kindness towards God?

Resolutions and spiritual nosegay as above.

EIGHTEENTH FRIDAY AFTER PENTECOST

Summary of the Morrow's Meditation.

We will meditate tomorrow upon a third effect of the love of God, which is conformity to the divine will; and we shall see: 1st, in what this conformity consists; 2nd, how it is a logical consequence of the love of God. We will then make the resolution: 1st, to be always content with God, with the condition in which He has placed us, the talents He has bestowed upon us, the position He has assigned us; 2nd, never to desire anything, to ask nothing, to refuse nothing, but in all things to will simply the good pleasure of God. Our spiritual nosegay shall be the third clause of the Lord's Prayer: "*Father, Thy will be done on earth as it is in heaven.*"

Meditation for the Morning.

Let us adore our Lord Jesus Christ subjecting Himself, from His first entrance into the world, to the good pleasure of His Father, and thenceforth placing this good pleasure in the midst of His heart, there to be the sole rule of His conduct. Let us admire His constant conformity to the most holy, most amiable, and most adorable will of God, and let us beg Him to enable us to understand and practice it.

FIRST POINT.

In what Consists Perfect Conformity to the Will of God.

There is to be understood by it an intimate union of our will to the will of God, which makes us desire nothing else but the divine good pleasure, which wills all that it wills and as it wills, which is ready to go peacefully and cheerfully wherever it calls us, and to do all that it asks of us. In this happy state, all things are done with entire sincerity of soul, without being troubled, without being eager to finish anything, without being kept back by dislike or weariness, without being preoccupied with the prospects either of success, which we desire only in so far as God wills it, or of failure, to which we submit beforehand, if God wills it. We are not more attached to one thing than to another, but are indifferent to all, having no choice or preference in regard to anything whatever, feeling no other love but that of the divine will, because we love, not the things themselves which God wills, but the divine good pleasure which wills them; and this divine will is as a most amiable attraction, which makes us happy to go wherever it wills. A holy indifference, which is neither apathy nor carelessness, but, on the contrary, the heroism of the will, accepting all that God wills, not only in the natural order, like health or sickness, beauty or ugliness, strength or weakness, life or death ; not only in things belonging to the civil order, such as riches, honors, and dignities; but also in things belonging to the spiritual order, such as aridities or consolations, tastes or drynesses, in all the events of life, all the occupations of every day, in such a way that we are as content to apply ourselves to one thing as to another, and that it makes us happy to repeat the words of St. Francis de Sales: "*Desire nothing, ask nothing, refuse nothing.*" At what point have we arrived in regard to this practice?

SECOND POINT.

Conformity to the Divine Will is a Logical Consequence of the Love of God in the Heart.

It is impossible to conceive of a heart which loves God and which yet does not find its whole happiness in pleasing Him. Even amongst men, with whom love is imperfect, there is no sweeter enjoyment than that of conforming ourselves to the good pleasure of the person who is beloved. Therefore, to please God is the sole ambition of the heart wherein holy love reigns; it is its sole ambition in this world, the one aim of all its actions as well as of all its projects. We live then only to say with the Apostle: "*Lord, what wilt Thou have me to do*" (Acts ix. 6), or with the Psalmist: *"What have I in heaven and, besides Thee, what do I desire upon earth"* (Ps. lxxiii. 25.) To wish anything else would be to subtract from the love of God a part of one's self, and this partition would make the soul which loves shudder; it would be to substitute the will of the creature for the will of the Creator, and this substitution is revolting to God; it would be to forget that God knows better than we do what is good for us, that nothing is wiser or better than His divine good pleasure, and this forgetfulness is an intolerable injury inflicted upon love. This is why the soul which loves preserves such a perfect serenity of heart in the midst of the great inequality of events. All may be thrown upside down, not only around, but within it; whether it be sad or joyful, in sweetness or bitterness, in peace or in trouble, in light or in darkness, in pleasantness or weariness, whether the sun burns it or the dew refreshes it, it is always the same; and, with its eyes fixed upon the good pleasure of God, it sings the canticle of eternal acquiescence: *"Father, Thy will be done on earth as it is in heaven."* It takes delight in solitude when God places it there; it takes delight in conversation when God so wills it. It does not cling more to one way of serving God than to another; and if it prays, it is not impatient to have its prayer answered; it awaits in peace God's time. Are these our dispositions?

Resolutions and spiritual nosegay as above.

EIGHTEENTH SATURDAY AFTER PENTECOST

Summary of the Morrow's Meditation.

We will continue tomorrow our meditations upon conformity to the will of God, and we shall see: 1st, that this conformity is the sum-total of all the virtues; 2nd, that it is the highest degree of perfection. We will then make the resolution: 1st, never to complain at the mishaps or disappointments which may happen to us, and to receive them as coming from the fatherly hand of God; 2nd, to bless God in adversity as well as in prosperity. Our spiritual nosegay shall be: *"The Lord gave, and the Lord hath taken away, blessed be the name of the Lord"* (Job i. 21).

Meditation for the morning.

Let us adore Jesus Christ declaring to us that He came down from heaven to earth, not to do His own will, but in all things to follow the good pleasure of His Father; that therein was His food, His life; that it was His all (John iv. 34; vi. 38). Let us admire, let us bless such holy dispositions, and let us ask of Him a share in them.

FIRST POINT.

Conformity to the Will of God the Sum Total of all Virtues.

This perfect conformity, leading the soul through all the events of life, makes it practice sometimes humility, at other times obedience; in such a situation, patience; in another, poverty; always and everywhere it establishes mortification in us: here of the will and the desires, there of the inclinations and of natural tastes; because, through this conformity, the whole man is sacrificed to the divine good pleasure, which alone remains alive in his soul; then, upon the ruins of immolated nature, is raised the love of God in its highest perfection; for if, as the pagan philosopher Sallust says, true friendship consists in having but one same will and one same non-will as our friend, it is evident that the more perfect we are in conforming our will to the will of God, the more we shall love Him; and it is an equally consoling fact that, together with the love of God, the love of our neighbor will be perfected in our soul, since the will of God is that we should love one another tenderly and greatly; that we should mutually bear with one another; that in our brethren we should honor the image of our heavenly Father, the living members of Jesus Christ, and the temples of the Holy Ghost. Let us here examine ourselves. Have we properly understood the excellence of this conformity to the will of God? Have we seen that its practice is identical with the practice of all the virtues, and that it is in itself a magnificent summary of them?

SECOND POINT.

Conformity to the Will of God is the Highest Perfection.

We can do nothing greater for God, nothing more perfect, nothing more exquisite, than to sacrifice ourselves to Him by conforming our will to His. In other virtues we sacrifice a portion of ourselves; for example, in temperance, the pleasures of the mouth; in modesty, restraint in the use of our eyes; in patience, sensitiveness; in humility, the pride of the heart; but in conformity to the will of God we sacrifice the whole of ourselves to Him; we put ourselves, body and soul, into His hands, that He may do with us all He wills, without any exception or reserve whatsoever. It is the perfect holocaust from which we do not steal anything. We give Him the whole of our affections, all our desires, the whole of our being, in accordance with the request He makes to us in those sweet words: *"My son, give Me thy heart"* (Prov. xxiii. 26), and we thereby raise ourselves to the summit of perfection. For God being supreme perfection, we shall be all the more perfect in proportion as we resemble Him the more, and our resemblance to Him will be more or less complete in proportion to our will being more or less conformed to His. This is why the Holy Spirit says: *"Wait on God with patience, Join thyself to God, and endure, that thy life may be increased in the latter end"* (Ecclus. ii. 3). This is also the reason why St Bernard remarks that the words of St Paul, Lord, what wouldst Thou have me to do? few as they are, include so many things that he says everything. This is, doubtless, also, why St Francis de Sales teaches that it is impossible to God not to place in His paradise whoever dies in perfect conformity to the divine good pleasure.

Resolutions and spiritual nosegay as above.

Nineteenth Sunday after Pentecost

The Gospel according to St. Matthew, xxii. 1-14.

"And Jesus spoke this parable: The kingdom of heaven is likened to a king who made a marriage for his son. And he sent his servants to call them that were invited to the marriage; and they would not come. Again, he sent other servants, saying: Tell them that were invited: Behold, I have prepared my dinner; my beeves and fatlings are killed, and all things are ready; come ye to the marriage. But they neglected, and went their ways, one to his farm, and another to his merchandise. And the rest laid hands on his servants, and, having treated them contumeliously, put them to death. But when the king had heard of it he was angry, and sending his armies he destroyed those murderers and burnt their city. Then he saith to his servants: The marriage indeed is ready; but they that were invited were not worthy. Go ye therefore into the highways, and as many as you shall find call to the marriage. And his servants going forth into the ways, gathered together all that they found, both bad and good: and the marriage was filled with guests. And the king went in to see the guests: and he saw there a man who had not on a wedding garment. And he saith to him: Friend, how earnest thou in hither not having on a wedding garment? But he was silent Then the king said to the waiters: Bind his hands and feet, and cast him into the exterior darkness; there shall be weeping and gnashing of teeth. For many are called, but few are chosen."

Summary of the Morrow's Meditation.

We will meditate tomorrow upon the last sentence in the gospel of the day, where, under the figure of the chastisement inflicted upon the man invited to the wedding who had not on the wedding garment, are represented to us the torments of hell reserved for the sinner who has soiled the robe of his innocence, and who has not bleached it by penitence, and we shall see that the thought of hell is: 1st, a remedy against sin; 2nd, an efficacious help for forming the soul to virtue. We will then make the resolution: 1st never to remain for twenty-four hours in a state in which, if we died, we should be damned; 2nd, to encourage ourselves in the midst of difficulties imposed by virtue by this thought: What is this compared with hell, where, if I am not a saint, I shall always burn? Our spiritual nosegay shall be the words of St. Augustine: *"Let us go down to hell during our life, that we may not go down there after our death."*

Meditation for the Morning.

Let us adore Jesus Christ reminding us of the pains of hell, to the end that we may be impelled to avoid them. These are a terrible darkness, a weeping and gnashing of teeth caused by torments; these are bound hands and feet, that is, a will compelled to desire obstinately the evil which it hates, and to hate furiously the good, the excellence of which it recognizes. Let us think seriously and often of this unhappy state. We shall find in this thought a remedy against sin and an efficacious help to form the soul to virtue.

FIRST POINT.

The Thought of Hell a Remedy against Sin.

This remedy has the triple effect of making us expiate our past sins, correct our actual sins, and prevent those to which the future may expose us. 1st. We must expiate our past sins. Filled with the thought that we have deserved hell, and that God has pardoned us only on the condition that we offer Him a compensation by penance, there is no penance which seems too hard, and the soul need rather to be restrained than excited, as in the case of the hermits of Egypt who, because of a single fault, condemned themselves during their whole life to austerities at which our effeminacy would tremble. 2nd. The thought of hell corrects actual faults. Seriously meditating upon this thought makes it impossible to remain a single day in a state of sin, even when it is doubtful. It is folly to risk our eternity and not to take the sure means for escaping a misfortune which is, at the same time, terrible and eternal. 3rd. This thought prevents sins to which the future might expose us. When we say, like St. Teresa, *always, never; always* suffer, *never* an end to our sufferings, *never* a moment of freedom from them, it is impossible to expose ourselves voluntarily to the danger of sin; not to watch over ourselves, our actions, our words, our thoughts; not to fly from everything that would expose our salvation to danger, even occasions and appearances of sin, dissipation, idleness, dangerous society, books, or conversations into which too great freedom enters ; it is impossible, lastly, not to pray with our whole heart, and not to take every precaution to avoid sin.

SECOND POINT.

The Thought of Hell an Efficacious Remedy for Forming the Soul to Virtue.

This thought, in point of fact, lays the foundation of virtue through the humility which it inspires; it raises the edifice of it by the acts which it gives us courage to practice; it puts the crown on it by the love which it kindles in the heart, 1st. This thought renders us humble. We have already seen, on the Friday of the second week after Pentecost, that if we had committed but one single sin, and that even had this sin been forgiven, we should never be anything more than a person who has escaped hell, who has deserved to be, throughout eternity, insulted and despised by devils; and we are ignorant whether we do not still deserve this treatment, for no one knows whether he is worthy of love or of hatred, nor do we know whether, supposing that we are worthy today of heaven, we shall not, on some future day, render ourselves worthy of hell; in order to do so, nothing more is wanted than a moment of weakness, a thought of pride, of which the rebel angels are a proof; nothing more than a calumny, an impurity, according to St. Paul; nothing more than a desire, a look, according to Jesus Christ; now, are not all these considerations supremely suitable to keep a soul abased in humility? 2nd. The foundation of virtue being thus laid, the thought on which we are meditating raises the edifice of virtue by acts which it gives us courage to practice. Doubtless it costs us something to renounce ourselves, to break with frivolity, dissipation, self-love; to subject ourselves to a rule of life and no longer to lose our time; but when we think of hell, what is all that, we say, compared with hell, wherein, if I am not a saint, I shall always burn? And then we hesitate no longer. It costs us something to mortify and humiliate ourselves, to suffer grief, contradiction, contempt, and insults; but when we think of hell, what is all that, we say to ourselves, compared with hell, wherein, if I am not a saint, I shall always burn? And thence we conclude: Ah, if it were necessary to wean myself from all kinds of pleasures, to practice upon my body the severities of the most austere penance, if I had to pass days and nights in prayer, bury myself alive, cut off my hand, tear out my eyes, sacrifice possessions and liberty, health and life, I ought not to hesitate a moment, for what is all that compared with hell, wherein, if I am not a saint, I shall always burn? Thus, full of courage, the soul reasons which thinks of hell; thus St. Augustine reasoned, when he begged of God to make him suffer fire and iron here below, provided that He would spare him in eternity. It was thus that an ancient hermit understood is when he said to a young religious who was wearied of his cavern, "Ah, my son, you can never have meditated much on what hell is, from which you are preserved therein." It was thus that all the martyrs understood it, all the anchorites, all the illustrious penitents, in a word, all the saints, for it was through it that they attained the courage whereby they became saints. It is thus that the thought of hell raises the edifice of virtue. 3rd. It is the consummation of virtue through the love which it kindles in the heart. For there is no medium; either we must burn here below with the flames of holy love, or we must burn eternally in the flames of divine justice. Now, in the presence of such an alternative there is no room for hesitation. Nothing is so cruel as hell; nothing is so sweet as love. Besides, how could we help loving God, who places us so high in His esteem and love that He desires, at all costs, to be loved by us, since He has only made hell in order to force us to love Him? How could we help loving God, whose anger, even though it be provoked by our crimes, creates an order of things which is in our greatest temporal and eternal interests? Now this is what He has done in creating hell; for, if there were no hell, what would the consequences have been to us? Natural, divine, and human laws would be without sanction, passions without any bridle, vice without any barrier; there would be no virtue, no guarantee of order for society here below, no elect for heaven, and paradise would be a kingdom devoid of inhabitants. Be Thou therefore blessed and loved, O my God, not only for having prepared for us the happiness of heaven, but also for having created hell to frighten our passions. Thou hast thereby made it a kind of necessity for us to save ourselves, and Thy anger has served the designs of Thy love. How, lastly, not love a God who has worked so many miracles and has had recourse to so many means to preserve us from hell?

The Incarnation, the Redemption, the maintenance of Thy Holy Church, the priesthood and all the sacraments, all interior and exterior graces, all the solicitations of the Holy Spirit in the bottom of our hearts, all the instructions given us, and all the good examples set us, are as so many ingenious devices of God, who desires to save us all. Oh, how greatly does such goodness merit the whole of our love! And what shall we say of the divine patience which did not allow us to fall into the depths of hell, when we deserved to do so? It kept us, as it were, suspended by a hair over the abyss; it had only to open its hand, let us go, and we should have been lost (Ps. xciii. 17; lxxxv. 13). O God, who hast waited for me to do penance, may all creatures bless and love Thee! (Dan. iii. 57, 58.) Alas! how many others, after a single sin, have fallen into the abyss, whilst I, who am much more guilty than they, still breathe. I have at my disposition all Thy graces whereby to save myself. O divine goodness! O ineffable predilection! Touched by so much love, O my God, I will henceforth make my whole life a permanent testimony of my gratitude. I ought to be sacrificed to Thy anger, I will sacrifice myself to Thy love; I ought to blaspheme Thee, I will everywhere proclaim Thy praise and Thy goodness; I ought to curse Thee, I will bless Thee always; I ought to suffer forever, I will love Thee always!

Resolutions and spiritual nosegay as above.

NINETEENTH MONDAY AFTER PENTECOST

Summary of the Morrow's Meditation.

We will tomorrow resume our meditations upon conformity to the will of God, and we shall see: 1st, that this perfect conformity is the secret of happiness even here upon earth; 2nd, that outside it there is only unhappiness. We will then make the resolution: 1st, to attach ourselves solely to the good pleasure of God, to cherish it in all events, whether they be joyful or sorrowful, and never to allow ourselves to be troubled by anything whatever; 2nd, to place our whole joy in being led in all things by the divine will, like a child by the hand of its mother. Our spiritual nosegay shall be the words of the Psalmist: *"Thou hast held me by my right hand, O Lord, and by Thy will Thou hast conducted me"* (Ps. lxxii. 24).

Meditation for the Morning.

Let us adore the interior of Our Lord, always perfectly submissive and united to the good pleasure of His Father. Never did He seek His own satisfaction (Rom. xv. 3); in all things and at all moments He had nothing in view but the good pleasure of His Father (John vii. 29). How admirable are these dispositions, how worthy of all our praises, and, above all, of our imitation.

FIRST POINT.

Perfect Conformity to the Will of God is the Secret of Happiness even Here Below.

When we receive all things as being sent by Providence, and when we live in a state of entire abandonment to all that this adorable Providence wills, we never meet with any vexations. As we have no other will and no other desire but the will of God, and see this most amiable will in all that happens to us, we have always all that we will and all that we desire. Imitating the example set us by the holy king David, we joyously give our hand to the good pleasure of God, who leads us from one action to another, from a second to a third, and thus our whole life passes sweetly, joyously, holily. No accident has power to disturb or trouble us, because we know that all comes from God, and that His will, which is a thousand times amiable, presides over all. This thought changes sufferings and troubles into joy, bitterness into sweetness; and things that plunge other souls into desolation console the soul which is united to the good pleasure of God. Hence there is in it a tranquility and a peace which nothing can ruffle, a constant serenity, a calmness in acting and speaking which proves how truly the Apostle and the sage had spoken when they said, the Apostle in affirming that "To *them that love God all things work together unto good"* (Rom. viii. 28), and the sage in declaring that *"Whatsoever shall befall the just man, it shall not make him sad"* (Prov. xii. 21). He may be tried by God, as was the holy man Job, but, like him, he will say to God: Thou triest me in a manner which ravishes me (Job x. 16); and neither his interior peace will be troubled nor his exterior allow a word or a gesture of sadness, of anger, or of impatience to escape it, and it may be said of him, as of Tobias, *"He repined not because the evil had befallen him "* (Tob. ii. 13).

SECOND POINT.

There is no Happiness for those who do not Identify their Will with the Will of God.

Every man, says St. Augustine, desires happiness, but all do not seek it where it is to be found. We seek it elsewhere than in the good pleasure of God, and from that time we condemn ourselves to an unhappy life. We find nothing but deceptions in the things, the persons, or the places to which we attach ourselves, because everything changes here below. Even if all were not to change, we ourselves change, and what gave us pleasure yesterday displeases us today. Israel liked the manna at the beginning and thought it had a marvelous taste,

but a little while afterwards it was disgusted with it. It was glad to be delivered
from the tyranny of Pharao, but a little while afterwards it wearied of the liberty
of the desert, and wanted to return to Egypt Now, with these variations of taste,
how could it be possible not to be unhappy? He who seeks contentment in
himself, says St. Augustine, shall be afflicted; he alone is always happy who puts
his joy in God alone, because God is always the same. Filled with this truth, a
holy religious, a witness to the extremes of joy and sorrow, and to the variations
of temper in which men allow themselves to indulge, according to the variety
of the things to which they attach themselves, exclaimed: As for me, nothing
can take away my joy, because nothing can take from me Jesus Christ, who is
all my happiness; and St. Augustine addressed God in these beautiful words:
*"Thou hast made us for Thee, Lord, and our hearts cannot enjoy repose save in
Thee alone."*

Resolutions and spiritual nosegay as above.

NINETEENTH TUESDAY AFTER PENTECOST

We will meditate during the whole of this week upon a fourth effect of divine love, which is fidelity in walking in the presence of God; and for tomorrow we will consider: 1st, what the exercise of the presence of God is; 2nd, how dear this exercise ought to be to every Christian heart. We will then make the resolution: 1st, seriously to undertake a life of recollection and of union with God; 2nd, to maintain in ourselves perfect purity of heart and of conscience, without which union with God is impossible. Our spiritual nosegay shall be the sixth beatitude: *"Blessed are the clean of heart, for they shall see God"* (Matt. v. 8).

Meditation for the Morning.

Let us adore the Holy Spirit inviting us to be attentive to the presence of God, and to exercise an effort over ourselves that we may constantly remain in His august presence (Ps. civ. 4). Let us thank Him for so useful a lesson, and let us ask of Him grace to profit by it.

FIRST POINT.

In what the Exercise of the Presence of God Consists.

1st. It is to have a lively and habitual faith in this truth, that God fills heaven and earth (Jer. xxiii. 24); that He sees at night as well as by day; that He discerns not only our acts, but even our most secret thoughts (II. Paral. xvi. 9; Heb. iv. 13); that He envelops us with His essence, penetrates us as water penetrates a sponge in the midst of the sea, so that it is in Him that we have life, motion, and being, and that He is more intimate with us than we are with ourselves (Acts xvii. 28). 2nd. This lively faith ought to be accompanied by a profound feeling of religious veneration for the grandeur and infinite perfections of God; an acquiescence full of love to His adorable will, to His desires, to all His designs, whatever they may be, to all His graces, which only ask, in order to save us, a heart faithful in corresponding to them; and from thence there arises between God and the soul a holy intercourse full of confidence and of love, a holy jealousy to be agreeable to Him in all things, by doing every moment what is pleasing to Him, and in the manner which pleases Him most. 3rd. This lively faith and this religious veneration of the presence of God ought to be accompanied by perfect detachment from all the pleasures of the senses, from all exterior things, even those which are in the order of God with regard to us, in such a manner that, whilst lending ourselves to them from duty, we do not deliver up ourselves to them to the extent of being absorbed by them; otherwise the presence of God would produce nothing more in us than a secondary sentiment; created things, news, and earthly trifles would alone have the privilege of exciting our interest and our avidity, to the detriment of God, whom even the best things have not the right to banish from our mind and our heart St. Mary Magdalene at the sepulcher did not pause to look at the beauty of the angels which appeared to her; she saw them without allowing herself to be distracted from the thought of Jesus; she continued to seek Him, and had no peace until she had found Him. Let her be our model.

SECOND POINT.

How Dear the Exercise of the Presence of God ought to be to the Heart of a Christian.

When we have the eyes of our heart sufficiently enlightened to see everywhere, and principally in ourselves, the three Divine Persons, with all their glory, their infinite amiability, their ineffable attributes, it is the delight of the soul to keep company with them, to contemplate them, to bless them, to praise them, to love them; and to live in the forgetfulness of the many marvelous things which we possess in ourselves would be a monstrosity. If, in the world, we do not leave to himself a beloved friend who has come to make us a visit; if we are delighted to converse with him and to remain in his society, how could the soul which loves God, and which sees Him everywhere with it and in it, not delight also to keep company with Him! If things which are extraordinarily beautiful occupy the mind to the point of its being difficult for us to tear away ourselves from them, with how much greater reason ought the infinite perfections of God, present in the midst of us, to be the delight of our mind and of our heart; and the more we give ourselves up to it, the more the delight increases, the more love is inflamed, for the reason given by the author of the Imitation, that we cannot remain near a great fire without bringing away with us some of its heat; or, rather, for the reason that we cannot live in the midst of flames without being burned, be plunged in love without loving, and because God is a consuming fire and love itself (Heb. xii. 29; I. John iv. 16): we can only escape the fire by forgetting it. Happy he who, understanding these holy truths, is not contented with an act of the presence of God made in the morning and speedily stifled by the dissipation of the day, but who applies himself to love God only, constantly, in the use of creatures, in his actions and his sufferings, in life and at death, and who often utters, from the bottom of his heart, this cry of a holy soul: "*In the love of God is three Persons; all for the love of the Holy Trinity living in me.*"

Resolutions and spiritual nosegay as above.

Nineteenth Wednesday after Pentecost

Summary of the Morrow's Meditation.

We will tomorrow consider the exercise of the presence of God, not only as a practice dear to every Christian heart, but as a religious duty; and in order to understand this duty well, we shall see: 1st, that we ought to keep ourselves habitually in the presence of God; 2nd, that we ought to maintain supreme respect, as well exterior as interior, in His presence. We will then make the resolution: 1st, in all places and at all times to respect the presence of God, not to allow ourselves to do anything in His sight which we should not dare to do in presence of a great personage; 2nd, often to utter acts of adoration to God present We will retain as our spiritual nosegay the words of Jacob: *"Indeed the Lord is in this place, and I knew it not"* (Gen. xxviii. 16).

Meditation for the Morning.

Let us adore Jesus Christ teaching us by His example the respect due to the presence of God. From the first moment of His incarnation His holy soul did not lose sight of it for one single moment; it kept itself continually abased in the most profound respect in presence of His lofty majesty and merited thereby to attract towards Himself the complaisance of the Father, according to the revelation He made of it to the earth (Matt. iii. 17). Such perfect homage rendered to the presence of God is indeed worthy of our praise and our adoration.

FIRST POINT.

Religion Obliges us to Maintain ourselves Habitually in the Presence of God.

What should we think of anyone who, being admitted into the company of a great monarch, did not pay any attention to his presence?—did not think of it even, went and came, acted and spoke exactly as though the monarch were not there? To act in this manner would be doubtless a most offensive proceeding. How much more reprehensible, then, would be the Christian who did not pay any attention to the presence of the great God, compared with whom all the monarchs of the earth are but as a grain of dust; who permitted himself to act as though God did not see us, to speak as though He did not hear us, to think as though He did not assist at our most secret thoughts; who did not make any account of Him in his projects, his deliberations, and his acts; who, lastly, spoke to Him only at rare intervals, often without even thinking of what he was saying, and who behaved in every way with the utter absence of restraint of a person who had forgotten in whose presence he was? *I am in the presence of God!* These sole words ought to make a deep impression upon us, and keep us abased in the most profound religious respect; for what is it to say, *I am in the presence of God?* It is to say, I am in presence of His divine perfections, which enchant all heaven; in presence of His greatness, which commands all my respect; in presence of His omnipotence, which demands my profound submission; in presence of His ineffable beauties, calculated to ravish all hearts; in presence of His goodness, which so well deserves all my love; in presence of His mercy, which calls for all my confidence; in presence of His justice, which I ought to fear; His holiness, which I ought to adore; and His providence, into the hands of which I ought everywhere to abandon myself. And living day and night in the midst of so many marvels which keep the angels in perpetual admiration, how ill would it become me never to think of it, to forget continually that I am in the hands of the best of fathers, a Father infinitely rich in mercy, always ready to pardon my sins as soon as I confess them to Him, to assist me as soon as I have recourse to Him; always attentive to me, to the extent of counting the number of the hairs of my head (Luke xii. 7), and of watching at my bedside during my sleep! Does not my conscience bid me pay attention to so kind a presence, so that I may not incur the reproach St. John addressed to the Jews: "There *hath stood One in the midst of you whom you knew not*" (John i. 26)? O Lord, open my eyes that I may see Thee! (Ps. xii. 4; Luke xviii. 41.)

SECOND POINT.

Religion Obliges us to Unite Supreme Respect, Exterior as well as Interior, with the Remembrance of the Presence of God.

Interior respect due to the presence of God consists in a profound abasement of all the powers of the soul in presence of His lofty majesty; in a sweet attention to perform in a proper manner all that we do, even the most common actions, such as eating and drinking, conversation and repose, because of the holiness of the eyes which are fixed upon us; lastly, in the sacrifice of the whole of our being, made with gladness, and reiterated at every action by these sweet words, or others like to them: *"All for Thee, O my God!"* Exterior respect consists in an ever-modest deportment (Philipp, iv. 5), like that maintained by St. Francis de Sales, which was marked by as much restraint and reserve when he was alone as when he was in society; in a manner of speaking and acting which is always sweet and charitable, always worthy, in which is revealed a soul convinced that God listens to and is looking at it; lastly, in a Christian moderation, which performs and says all things in a suitable manner, without any haste as well as without any negligence, even in its recreations, which it knows how to indulge in gaily when it is the season for them, like a child of God under the eyes of its Father.

Resolutions and spiritual nosegay as above.

Nineteenth Thursday after Pentecost

Summary of the Morrow's Meditation.

We will consider tomorrow: 1st, the exercise of the presence of God as a duty owing to gratitude; 2nd, the forgetfulness of God as being horrible ingratitude. We will then make the resolution: 1st, to make use of the sight of all created things to raise ourselves to God and to converse with Him; 2nd, to associate with all our actions the spirit of gratitude which they are calculated to inspire. We will retain as our spiritual nosegay these words of St. John Climacus: *"Every creature is a ladder to raise us to God."*

Meditation for the Morning.

Let us adore Jesus Christ always engaged in thanksgivings in presence of His Father, whether in the Eucharist or in heaven. Let us unite ourselves to the perpetual hymn of His gratitude and let us endeavor to enter into the same sentiments: *"Let us render thanks to the Lord our God."*

FIRST POINT.

The Exercise of the Presence of God is a Duty owing to Gratitude.

There is not a moment in life in which we do not receive some particular benefit from God; consequently, there is not a moment in which we ought not to thank Him and bless Him. We rise in the morning: Thanks, my God, we ought to say to Him, thanks for having kept me during last night, in which so many others have died, and for granting me another day in which to serve Thee and save myself! We put on our clothes: Thanks, my God, many poor have hardly any clothing or only a few rags! We say our morning prayer and make our meditation: Thanks, my God, many others have neither the leisure, nor the thought, nor the good-will! We move our feet to walk, our hands to act, our tongue to speak; we open our eyes to see, our ears to hear: Thanks, my God, so many others are deprived of the senses which I enjoy! We eat and drink: Thanks, my God, it is a present given me by Thy love; so many others have nothing to eat and drink today! We draw in our breath and then exhale it: Thanks, my God, this inhalation is a blessing of Thy providence; if Thou wert for a single moment to cease dispensing air to me in suitable measure and conditions, I should die at that very moment; it was a thought which made St. Gregory Nazianzen say that the remembrance of God ought to be as habitual to us as is breathing. In the evening we take our rest: Thanks, my God, for having preserved me during this day, in which Thou hast taken away life from so many others, and for giving me this night to take the rest so necessary to me. A good thought enters into our mind, a good feeling into our heart, good examples offer themselves to us, we listen to good sermons, we read good books: Thanks, my God, I owe to Thee this good thought, this good feeling, this good example, this sermon, this book; all this is a grace I did not deserve, it is a present made me by Thy love. If, turning away our eyes from our own person, we cast them upon all that surrounds us, everything cries out to us to think of Thee, O my God, and to love Thee. All creatures are images of Thee, and as it were mirrors which reflect Thy perfections; heaven is the palace of Thy glory; earth the footstool under Thy feet; men the ministers of Thy providence; all events are the effects, now of Thy justice, now of Thy goodness, always of Thy wisdom. Everything here below is full of Thy love and calls for our gratitude. Above our heads, Thy sun lights us during the day, the moon and the stars by night; around us, harvests, fruits, flowers, the grass of the field, procure for us what is necessary, useful, agreeable; the animals which walk upon the earth, which fly in the air or swim in the waters, all tell us that Thou hast made them, some to feed and clothe us, others to serve us or amuse us; even the good offices our fellows render to us are a blessing of Thy love; it is Thou who dost inspire them and who dost infuse into their hearts the benevolence they show us; lastly, the whole creation contains nothing but what serves for our good. How then live, surrounded by the munificence of the divine love, and yet forget Him who is the author of it? Shall we be obliged to say with much more reason than St. Bonaventure, *"I am surrounded by love on all sides, and I do not know what it is to love?"*

SECOND POINT.

To Live in Forgetfulness of God is Horrible Ingratitude.

Is it not, indeed, horrible ingratitude continually to be receiving blessings and never to give thanks to our benefactor, and to think of him no more than if he did not exist? It is the sad story of the man who lives in forgetfulness of God. Through love for him, God, who is everywhere present, gives or preserves life in all that lives, movement in all that moves, being in all that is; and yet man cannot raise his eyes in gratitude towards his benefactor! Absorbed in things belonging to this world, he thinks but rarely of Him who never forgets him. O forgetfulness of God, what strange ingratitude thou dost display, well deserving to be wept over with repentant tears! Alas! what reproaches have I not to address to myself on this subject! what habitual dissipation! How rarely I think of God to love Him and thank Him for His continual goodness, His mercy, shown at every moment! I must, at all costs, correct myself.

Resolutions and spiritual nosegay as above.

Nineteenth Friday after Pentecost

Summary of the Morrow's Meditation.

We will consider tomorrow the exercise of the presence of God from the point of view of our own interest, and we shall see that it is: 1st, an excellent preservative against sin; 2nd, a powerful means of sanctification. We will then make the resolution: 1st, to recall to ourselves as often as possible, day and night, the holy presence of God; 2nd, to avoid wandering eyes, ramblings of the imagination, curiosity about news, ardor in our desires, things which all form an obstacle to the exercise of the presence of God. Our spiritual nosegay shall be the words of God to Abraham: *"Walk before Me and be perfect"* (Gen. xvii. 1).

Meditation for the Morning.

Let us adore God giving to each of us, in the person of Abraham, a counsel so important with regard to the proper regulation of our life, and so necessary for combating the kind of fascination which sensible things exercise upon us. *"Walk before Me and be perfect."* Let us thank Him for having revealed to us this secret of spiritual life, and let us ask of Him grace thoroughly to profit by it.

FIRST POINT.

The Exercise of the Presence of God is an Excellent Preservative against Sin.

The cause of all our evils is dissipation, which renders us inattentive and consequently unfaithful to grace, which keeps us leading a wholly natural life, wholly sensual, wholly pagan: a shameful life, in which the soul, allowing itself perfect freedom in thinking and desiring, saying and doing whatever pleases it, forgets God during whole days just as though He did not exist. The reiterated and persevering thought of the presence of God would, on the contrary, make us live a supernatural life; it would rule all the movements of our heart; it would moderate all our passions; it would repress the movements of our temper; it would purify our intentions; finally, says St. Jerome, it would banish all sin, because we sin only because we lose sight of God, and we should perhaps never sin if He were always present to our thoughts (Ps. x. 5). Where, indeed, could the servant be found who would be wanting in his duties beneath the eyes of his master, or the malefactor who would permit himself to commit a crime before the eyes of his judge? The elders of Babylon, when they were about to commit a crime against Susanna, cast down their eyes that they might not see the sky which recalled them to the remembrance that the eyes of God were fixed upon them (Dan. xiii. 9). Give me, said someone who was solicited to do what was wrong, give me a place where God does not see me, and I will do what you propose to me. No, says St. Augustine, a soul which is deeply impressed with the truth that God beholds it as though it were alone in the world, that He hears all it says, and puts all down in the great book by which it will be judged, will never sin. There is no temptation over which a lively faith in this divine presence does not triumph; no vanity or ill-temper which it does not correct; no weakness which it does not sustain; and after a fall, no sin for which it does not inspire contrition. *I have sinned against Heaven and before thee,* said the prodigal son. This thought confounds it, because if to sin against God be an evil, to sin in the presence of God is a monstrosity of which few men would be capable if they thought of it. So true is it that the thought of the presence of God is a preservative against sin.

SECOND POINT.

The Exercise of the Presence of God is a Powerful Means of Sanctification.

God Himself taught Abraham this truth by the words: *"Walk before Me and be perfect"* (Gen. xvii. i), and He confirmed it by those other words of Solomon:

"In all thy ways think on Him, and He will direct thy steps" (Prov. iii. 6). In point
of fact, the exercise of the presence of God attracts graces upon the soul which
is faithful to it; this thought augments its faith, strengthens its hope, enkindles
it with love, in such a way that henceforth it does nothing except from love.
By means of this holy exercise it learns to know God better every day, and He
appears to it in such beauty that it feels a disgust for everything else, will love
nothing except Him, and exclaims with the saints: *God is my all.* At every action
it says: God sees me, God hears me; He considers all I do, all I say, all I think
(Prov. v. 21), and under the empire of this reflection, it necessarily does all things
well; like a soldier, who in the sight of his prince is easily brave, and a servant,
who under the eyes of his master is easily faithful. If you desire to do well all that
you do, says St. Basil, you must represent to yourself that God is contemplating
you; then you will adore Him, you will love Him, you will thank Him, you will
do everything for Him and in the best possible manner; all your actions will be
supernatural and your days full of merits. You will live with God by conversing
with Him; you will live in God by reposing in Him; you will live by God, who
will make Himself the food and the life of your mind and your heart, and from
that time you will be perfect.

Resolutions and spiritual nosegay as above.

NINETEENTH SATURDAY AFTER PENTECOST

Summary of the Morrow's Meditation.

We will continue to meditate upon the advantages of the exercise of the presence of God, and we shall see: 1st, that therein is the strength of the Christian; 2nd, that therein is his joy. We will then make the resolution: 1st, to place our happiness in keeping ourselves in the presence of God, applying ourselves to it without intensity of thought, but with the expansion of a heart which delights in God, and which rejoices in such august society; 2nd, to restrain the dissipation of our senses and the wanderings of our mind. Our spiritual nosegay shall be the words of David: *"I remembered God and was delighted"* (Ps. lxxvi. 4).

Meditation for the Morning.

Let us adore God, present everywhere; let us lovingly abase ourselves in His immensity, as in a vast ocean which penetrates us with its essence; let us rejoice to be in Him through a necessity of our being, in common with all creatures, and with this object in view let us render to Him our homage of adoration, of praise, and of love.

FIRST POINT.

The Exercise of the Presence of God is the Strength of the Christian.

Man, of himself, is nothing but weakness and misery. Temptations stronger than us environ and pursue us (Ps. cxiv. 3). Often discouraging thoughts besiege us; often the trials of life make us despair and overcome our virtue. But we have only to unite ourselves to God, to see Him at our side offering us His graces here below, with His recompenses in a future life, and who only awaits a word from our heart to protect and defend us, and immediately courage and confidence will be renewed ; we shall feel ourselves to be strong with the strength of God, and we shall sing with the Psalmist: *"The Lord is my firmament, my refuge, and my deliverer. My God is my help, and in Him will I put my trust. My protector and the horn of my salvation and my support. Praising, I will call upon the Lord, and I shall be saved from my enemies"* (Ps. xvii. 3 *et seq.).* Ivy left to itself simply clings to the ground, but attached to a tall tree it rises to lofty heights; it is a faithful image of the soul which walks with God; it triumphs over the devil, the world, and the flesh, without any temptation having power to shake it, or any passion getting the upper hand of it. If we examine our conscience, we shall see that our faults and our weaknesses proceed only from the dissipation in which we live, which delivers us up like a defenseless city to all the assaults of the enemy.

SECOND POINT.

The Exercise of the Presence of God is the joy of the Christian.

I have had moments of cruel anguish, the holy king David tells us; my soul would not receive any consolation. *"I remembered God and was delighted"* (Ps. lxxvi. 4). *"In the day of my trouble I sought God, with my hands lifted up to Him in the night, and I was not deceived"* (Ibid. 3). *"I set the Lord always in my sight: for He is at my right hand, that I be not moved. Therefore my heart hath been glad and my tongue hath rejoiced"* (Ps. xv. 8, 9). Let us make the experience ourselves. When we are in trouble it is an inexpressible consolation for us to represent God to ourselves as being at our side, and to pour forth into His paternal heart our afflictions. When we have joys they are a thousand times sweeter when they are poured into the heart of God and enjoyed for God. When we feel ourselves to be forsaken and, as it were, abandoned in this place of exile, it is sufficient to remember that we are not alone, that we have God with us; God the Father, who calls Himself the God of all consolation (II. Cor. i. 3); God the Son, who so loved us as to die for us; God the Holy Ghost, who calls

Himself the Paraclete or the Consoler of souls, and their more than maternal providence, which loves us, which wills us nothing but good; and at this thought the heart is consoled. Lastly, in whatever position we may be, there is ineffable joy and, as it were, a foretaste of paradise in thinking that we live in God, in God who is infinitely good, infinitely beautiful, infinitely perfect. Filled with these sweet remembrances, the heart dilates, it feels that God alone is all, it loves Him and is loved by Him; what more does it want to make it happy? *"Let the just feast,"* exclaims David, *"and rejoice before God, and be delighted with gladness:"* they are in the presence of God (Ps. lxvii. 4). Nothing can trouble a heart which maintains itself in the presence of God, and says to itself with faith, I am in God, my best friend, my protector, and my defense; in God, who watches over me as though I were alone in the world and He had nothing else to think of; in God, the delight and the paradise of hearts; in God, the sovereign good; I possess Him, and I am full of happiness.

Resolutions and spiritual nosegay as above.

Twentieth Sunday after Pentecost

The Gospel according to St. John, iv. 46-53.

"There was a certain ruler whose son was sick at Capharnaum. He having heard that Jesus was come from Judea into Galilee, went to Him, and prayed Him to come down and heal his son, for he was at the point of death. Jesus therefore said to him: Unless you see signs and wonders you believe not. The ruler saith to Him: Lord, come down before that my son die. Jesus saith to him: Go thy way, thy son liveth. The man believed the word which Jesus said to him and went his way. And as he was going down his servants met him, and they brought word saying that his son lived. He asked therefore of them the hour wherein he grew better. And they said to him: Yesterday at the seventh hour the fever left him. The father therefore knew that it was at the same hour that Jesus said to him: Thy son liveth; and himself believed, and his whole house."

Summary of the Morrow's Meditation.

We will meditate tomorrow upon the gospel for the day, and we shall learn from it: 1st, to profit by the moment of grace; 2nd, to profit even by the delay of grace after we have asked for it. We will thence derive the resolution: 1st, never to resist the inspirations of grace, and to allow ourselves to be led in everything by the Spirit of God; 2nd, instead of being discouraged when grace is not given us immediately in answer to our prayers, to persevere in our requests with confidence and a renewal of fervor. Our spiritual nosegay shall be the words of the Psalmist: *"I will hear what the Lord God will speak in me"* (Ps. lxxxiv. 9).

Meditation for the Morning.

Let us adore Our Lord giving us in the gospel two instructions of the greatest importance with regard to the use we ought to make of His grace. Let us bless Him for these lessons, which He wills to communicate to us for the guidance of our life, and let us ask of Him grace to profit by them.

FIRST POINT.

The Importance of Profiting by the Moment of Grace.

There are three reasons which show us this: 1st. *The moment of grace, once past, never returns.* This is what the gospel of the day teaches us, by the example of the great personage of Galilee whose son was dangerously ill. He had no sooner learnt the arrival of Jesus Christ in the country than, without losing a moment, he went in search of Him. If he had not profited by the visit of the Saviour to Galilee, he would perhaps never have seen or known Him. God attaches His graces to times, seasons, places, and objects, to a number of circumstances which but rarely coincide. Not to profit, then, by grace is to expose ourselves never again to receive it. 2nd. *The moment of grace is often decisive in regard to our salvation.* If, in fact, the officer of our example had not profited by the journey of Jesus Christ, his son would have died. Whence comes it that we persevere so long in tepidity, or perhaps in a worse state still? Is it not that we allow to pass, without profiting by them, moments of decisive graces, such as the grace of a retreat or a mission, certain inspirations, certain sentiments of remorse? 3rd. *When we profit by a moment of grace, God grants us others, and greater ones, which we did not expect.* The officer of our gospel thought of nothing less than of obtaining his own conversion and that of his family, yet Jesus Christ granted it to him at the same time as the cure of his son. *He believed,* says the gospel, he and the whole of his house. Let us admire this goodness of Our Lord, and let us thank Him for so often, when we have profited by His graces, giving us immediately new ones. Let us consider, on the other side, that God gives us graces at every moment. All our days are filled with them; and yet we are so poor, so weak, so miserable, we allow these moments of grace to pass. Let us fear this misfortune, and let us determine to be henceforth more faithful to them.

SECOND POINT.

How to Behave when Grace is Delayed after we have Asked for it.

If grace often forestalls us, God also often retards it, and does not grant it immediately after we have asked for it. Then we must submit peacefully, Solomon has told us (Ecclus. ii. 3). God has promised us His help and He loves us. If, then, He sometimes delays to grant our petitions and seems to repel us, it is because of His loving designs in regard to us. He wishes to try us, to augment our faith, to increase our merits, to make us grow in patience. Let us adore His designs and bless Him at all times. In days of trial let our confidence be reanimated. It is to perseverance in prayer that God has promised His help, and perseverance is only exercised when God delays. Let us say to Him in our troubles, Yes, my God, it is just because Thou dost delay to grant my prayers that I trust Thou wilt do so, and the more Thou dost repel me, the more will I cast myself with greater ardor into Thy arms. Let us learn from the officer of our gospel to redouble, then, our fervor. He did not stop to justify himself when Jesus Christ reproached him. Without paying -any attention to it, he earnestly begged Our Lord: O Lord, come down to my house ere my son die. And he was heard, and we also shall be heard.

Resolutions and spiritual nosegay as above.

Twentieth Monday
after Pentecost

Summary of the Morrow's Meditation.

We will meditate tomorrow upon three practices of the presence of God, which are: 1st, to take pleasure in the divine presence; 2nd, to do everything with the object of pleasing God; 3rd, to converse with God by means of frequent ejaculatory prayers. We will then make the resolution: 1st, to be faithful to these three practices; 2nd, often to withdraw our thoughts from creatures in order to fix them upon God. We will retain as our spiritual nosegay the words of the Blessed Virgin: *"My soul hath rejoiced in God my Saviour"* (Luke i. 47).

Meditation for the Morning.

Let us adore the Holy Spirit inspiring the holy king David with continual attention to the presence of God (Ps. xxiv. 15), and enabling him to find a delicious joy in this exercise—a joy, as it were, of paradise (Ps. ciii. 34). Let us ask of Him a share in this grace, according to the advice of the Wise Man: Let nothing hinder you from being always attentive to God (Ecclus. xviii. 22).

FIRST POINT.

To take Pleasure in the Presence of God, the First Condition of the
Holy Exercise on which we are Meditating.

This complaisance in the presence of God is the sweet joy of a son living in the society of a beloved father. It is a happiness to think of him; he looks at him lovingly, whilst continuing his work and performing his duties. It is a simple and affectionate remembrance; there is no eagerness and no intensity in it; an interior look of the heart towards God, full of peace and sweetness accompanied by an ardent desire to please Him. *"To Thee have I lifted up my eyes, who dwellest in heaven. Behold, as the eyes of the servants are upon the hands of their masters, so are our eyes unto the Lord our God"* (Ps. cxxii. 1, 2). It is an enjoyment experienced by the soul in the ineffable beauty and the infinite perfection of the Supreme Being, present with us and in us; it is a calm attention to the interior words which He may will to address to us; we receive them with gratitude, we retain them with love, we feed on them, we are penetrated with them. It is an abandonment of the whole of one's self to the good pleasure of God. All for Thee, all for Thee, O my Treasure and my All, I desire nothing but Thee (Ps. xxx. 16). It is to be perpetually contented with God, whatever He may do, in abandonments as well as in consolations, in reverses as well as in prosperity. We are alone with Him in the little heaven of our soul, St. Teresa says: we there enjoy Him at our ease, we contemplate Him lovingly, remaining at His feet like Mary, sister of Martha, and offering ourselves to Him as a victim of love to be sacrificed to all that He wills. Let us make this sweet experience.

SECOND POINT.

To do Everything with a View to Pleasing God, the Second
Practice of this Holy Exercise.

An excellent way of walking in the presence of God is to do everything with the object of pleasing Him; it is that which the Apostle recommends in the words: *"Whether you eat or drink, or whatsoever else you do, do all to the glory of God"* (I. Cor. x. 31). We begin this exercise the first thing in the morning when we awake: I rise, Lord, in order to please Thee; Thy good pleasure is mine, I desire no other. We dress ourselves in these dispositions, we continue in them the whole day, repeating at each action, Lord, all to please Thee. The whole of my happiness consists in accomplishing Thy will. Provided that I please Thee, I am content (Acts ix. 6; Ps. lxxii. 25). At night, before going to sleep, we repeat once more: *"Info Thy hands, O Lord, I commend my spirit ... In peace in the self-same I will sleep, and I will rest"* (Ps. iv. 9; xxx. 6). Thus during the night as well as during the day our whole life is spent in the continual accomplishment of the good pleasure of God. We can 3ay, with Jesus Christ: *"I do always the things that please Him"* (John viii. 29), or like the spouse in the Canticle: "My *beloved to me and I to him"* (Cant. ii. 16); and if we fall into any fault, we are not disgusted, but unite ourselves more intimately with God, like the little child, who, led by the hand of its mother, holds it faster after he has had a fall. Are we faithful to this practice?

THIRD POINT.

Speaking to God by Means of Frequent Ejaculatory Prayers,
a Third Practice of the Presence of God.

Ejaculatory prayers are like spiritual wings wherewith the soul flies to God, unites itself to Him, and lives a paradisiacal life in Him. By means of it, it speaks to its God, as though it saw Him with the eyes of its body, saying to Him, for example: I adore Thee, great God; I love Thee, infinite Goodness; I admire Thee, adorable Union of all perfections. Thanks for Thy blessings. Pardon my faults and innumerable negligences. Help me by Thy grace to love Thee better. When shall I go to Thy paradise in order that I may love Thee more there? Oh, how I long to enter into it! I am drawn downward by my evil nature and drawn upward by the desire to love Thee. *"Lord, I suffer violence"* (Is. xxxviii. 14), have pity on me. *"Woe is me, that my sojourning is prolonged"* (Ps. cxix. 5). In order to console itself for not loving God as much as it desires to do, the soul offers to Him in a spirit of love each one of its actions, of its words, and of its thoughts: All for Thy love, O my God! nothing except for Thy love! To these different considerations, upon which it dwells more or less according to the attraction it feels in them, may be added a thousand other subjects of pious colloquies with which the Spirit of God inspires it. "I have a great deal to do today," a holy soul said; "my God is in me, waiting for me; we have innumerable things to say to each other. I will unite myself to Him, I will listen to Him (Ps. lxxxiv. 9), and if He is silent, or if I remain before Him without being able to say a word, I will ask Him to teach me how to speak to Him (Luke xi. 1). I will tell Him that I love Him, that I desire to love Him always more and more; I will repeat it without ceasing, and my repetitions, far from being displeasing to Him, will be agreeable, He is so good and so paternal!"

Resolutions and spiritual nosegay as above.

Twentieth Tuesday
after Pentecost

Summary of the Morrow's Meditation

We will meditate tomorrow upon a sixth effect of the love of God, which is zeal for His glory, and we shall see: 1st, that this zeal is obligatory; 2nd, what are its characteristics. We will then make the resolution: 1st, to prevent, by all the means in our power, above all by our good example and our advice, offences against God and wrongs done to religion; 2nd, to give to good works, in so far as it shall be possible, our co-operation and our money. Our spiritual nosegay shall be the words of St. Ignatius: *"To the greater glory of God."*

Meditation for the Morning.

Let us adore Jesus Christ in the immense zeal with which He burned for the glory of His Father. It was the supreme object of all His labors, of all His mysteries, of His Church, of His sacraments: His life and His death tended to nothing but the establishment in the world of the kingdom of God, of making Him to be known, served, and loved by the whole earth, so great was the zeal which devoured Him (Ps. cxviii. io). Let us admire, let us praise, let us bless this incomparable zeal.

FIRST POINT.

The Obligation of being Zealous for the Glory of God.

It is as impossible for us to love God and not to take an interest in His glory as it would be impossible for a son not to be sensitive with regard to the honor of his father, to the injuries which lower him or the glory which raises him. When divine love is really seated in the heart, it bears with it therein a great desire to see God known, loved, and served; a profound grief at beholding offences committed against so good a Master, and a devouring zeal to bring back to Him sinners who have abandoned Him. If then iniquities, overflowing like torrents the face of the earth, find us insensible; if all the wrongs done to religion, all the sufferings of the Church, do not weigh down our souls beneath their immense burden, we ought to strike our breast, and with sighs and weeping say: Miserable creature that I am, I fancied that I loved God, and I find that I do not love Him! David at the sight of the prevarications of men bursts into tears, is dried up with suffering, falls down fainting (Ps. cxviii.). Jeremias feels a sacred fire boiling the very marrow of his bones and cannot contain it, because he has heard the blasphemy of many (Jer. xx. 10). In the New Law, thousands of apostles, missionaries, heroic women, sacrificed some their country and their family, others their repose and their property, some even their own life, in order to make God served and loved by childhood, by youth, by all the ages of life. Ah, how well those great souls knew how to love! It was because they said every day with a heart that was holily jealous for the honor and glory of God: O Father, who art in heaven, may Thy name be exalted, sanctified, and blessed! May Thy reign be established over all hearts and dominate every other affection! May Thy will be everywhere respected, everywhere loved upon earth, as it is in heaven! Let us examine whether our zeal bears any resemblance to the zeal of these great souls, if we have not preferred our repose, our interests, a life of comfort to the greater glory of God; whether we feel, down to the very bottom of our hearts, the wrongs committed against the Church and against religion, so that we can say with the Psalmist: *"The reproaches of them that reproached Thee have fallen upon me"* (Ps. lxviii. 10).

SECOND POINT.

The Characteristics of Zeal.

1st. True zeal is active; it cannot inflame a heart without showing it exteriorly by works. Seeing with what ardor, with what a spirit of proselytism, the wicked labor to ruin souls, and to spread everywhere their dreadful doctrines, even at the cost of great sacrifices, the soul which loves cannot bear the idea of doing less for what is good than the wicked for what is evil. In consequence it seeks for and puts in use all kinds of means for making God known and loved; it is happy to seize upon all opportunities for gaining souls; and the loss of its possessions, *of* its repose, even of its life, would seem to it to be a gain, if at that price it could make one heart more upon earth to love the Lord. 2nd. True zeal is insatiable. The more it sees of good to be done, the more it desires to do, and it never says: It is enough. It would, if it could, spread itself over the whole earth, to make God to be loved and honored everywhere, saying with St. Francis Xavier: *"As long as I knew that there was a corner upon earth where God is not loved I should not have an instant of repose."* 3rd. True zeal is gentle and prudent. Spite of its great desire that God should be loved, it knows how to contain itself, and it never does anything hastily. Its language is always moderate, its steps only taken after reflection; gentleness and prudence always preside over its acts and open to it the door of the heart. Are these the characteristics of our zeal?

Resolutions and spiritual nosegay as above.

TWENTIETH
WEDNESDAY AFTER
PENTECOST

Summary of the Morrow's Meditation.

We will meditate tomorrow upon zeal for the salvation of souls, and we shall see: 1st, how God loves souls; 2nd, how this love of God for souls obliges us to have zeal in order to gain them. We will then make the resolution: 1st, to use all the means in our power to bring back to God our relatives, friends, or acquaintances who have abandoned religious practices; 2nd, to labor at this holy work by means of our prayers, of our words, of our good examples, above all by the example of a good disposition, which is so well calculated to make religion loved. We will retain as our spiritual nosegay the words which the Acts of the Apostles make use of in regard to St. Paul: *"His spirit was stirred within him, seeing the city wholly given to idolatry"* (Acts xvii. 16).

Meditation for the Morning.

Let us adore Jesus Christ as a model of the zeal with which we ought ourselves to burn in order to gain souls for God. Let us listen to Him, crying to us from His cross that He thirsts for souls, that we may thereby understand the great desire He has to save them. Let us admire Him living and dying for so noble an aim, and let us ask Him to permit us to share in His zeal.

FIRST POINT.

How God Loves Souls.

A soul, says the Holy Scripture, is to God as a sigh of His heart, a breath of His own life (Gen. ii. 7). It is His image, because in creating it He impressed upon it the figure of His substance and marked it with His seal. It is the end of all His works in time, for it was for it that He did everything on the earth and in the heavens. It is in His decrees the companion of His eternity, for He desires to live eternally with it; to take in it His everlasting delight, to pour forth into it His immense glory; and He has such a desire for its society that on a certain day, the soul having separated itself from Him and sold itself to the devil, He did not hesitate to send His eternal Son here below to redeem it, not with all the riches of heaven and all the treasures of the earth, which would have been in His eyes an insufficient ransom, but with the very blood of His adorable Son, shed to the very last drop. The soul thus redeemed He makes His abode of delight, the member of the mystical body of His Son, the temple of His Holy Spirit Then, foreseeing that spite of so much devotedness to it, this soul would be still unfaithful to Him, He wills that His Son should remain on the earth throughout all ages, to redeem for Him at the price of His blood, by the ministry of priests, all the souls which after having quitted Him desire to return to Him. At the same time, He gave His Holy Spirit the mission to watch over these souls, to recall them when they had wandered away, and to pursue them until their return. What miracles in this love of God for souls! What a world of mysteries, and how our hearts ought to bless our infinitely good God who works them!

SECOND POINT.

How this Love of God for Souls Obliges us to have Zeal to Gain them for Him.

When we see a friend filled with an ardent desire to obtain something that is good, and we are able to obtain it for him, friendship obliges us to do everything in our power to put him in possession of it. If, then, we truly love God, we cannot refuse Him the whole of our zeal to gain for Him souls, by which He so greatly desires to be loved. What! we flatter ourselves that we love God, and yet we neglect the souls which are as a sigh of His heart, that is to say, the object of His tenderest love! We flatter ourselves that we love God, and we leave His living image in the dirt, without giving ourselves the trouble of lifting it up out of it! We flatter ourselves that we love God, and we will not labor to gain for Him souls of which a single one is dearer to Him than all imaginable worlds; souls for which He has made everything, the universe, its laws and its miracles; souls destined to praise Him eternally, to be the object of His delight in heaven, the abode of His glory; souls, lastly, which He desires to have as friends, in searching for which He has worked so many miracles, which He has bought at so great a price! We flatter ourselves that we love God, and we look coldly upon a soul dyed in the blood of Jesus Christ drowned in the pit of vice, a member of His mystical body become the member of a prostitute, the temple of the Holy Ghost occupied by the idol of Dagon, without our taking any means to remedy this terrible state of things! We flatter ourselves that we love God, and we are indifferent to the salvation or the loss of souls for which Jesus Christ remains on earth exposed to so many outrages, for which He immolates Himself every day upon all the altars; which He pursues by so many exterior and interior graces; to which, lastly, He holds out unceasingly His arms, in order to press them, on their return, to the bosom of His mercy! Should we look upon as a friend a man who, seeing us hastening in search of some good thing, were to refuse the services by means of which he might obtain it for us? Now, would it be possible for God to content Himself with a love with which men would not be contented? No, doubtless; and so have thought all the saints who devoted themselves with so much zeal to the salvation of souls; laymen and priests, all ought to labor therein. Ecclesiastical history shows us a simple slave converting the whole nation of the Iberians. Let us enter into ourselves; do we find that we have this zeal for the salvation of souls, this ardent thirst to save our perishing brothers?

Resolutions and spiritual nosegay as above.

TWENTIETH THURSDAY AFTER PENTECOST

Summary of the Morrow's Meditation.

We will continue tomorrow to meditate upon zeal for the salvation of souls, and we shall see: 1st, that to labor to save souls is in itself a wholly divine work; 2nd, that to neglect to labor at it is to be wanting towards Jesus Christ. We will then make the resolution: 1st, to make use of all the means in our power in order to convert sinners; 2nd, never to be discouraged in regard to this work, and never to despair of the salvation of anyone. We will retain as our spiritual nosegay the words of St. Paul: *"We are God's coadjutors"* in the great work of the conversion of souls (I. Cor. iii. 9).

Meditation for the Morning.

Let us adore Jesus Christ on the cross, adjuring us to help Him to save the souls for which He died. Let us bless Him for permitting us to help Him in so great, so divine a work, and let us offer Him our aid with all our heart.

FIRST POINT.

To Labor to Save Souls is a wholly Divine Work.

To withdraw a soul from sin and to gain it for God is more than to render liberty to whole provinces; it is more than to conquer the universe; it is an essentially divine work; it is the work of Jesus Christ, who came to earth for its sake alone.

In order to perform it He divided it into two parts, one of which He took upon Himself and the other He imposed on us. As His share of it, He ascended the cross, and there shed the whole of His blood; there He closed hell, opened heaven, merited for the world faith to know the truth, grace to do what is right, and He instituted the sacraments in order to communicate to all men the fruits of His death. As to the other share, He reserved it for men, whom He thus called to the distinguished honor of being His helps, His coadjutors, and, together with Him, of being the saviours of the world. The blood shed upon the cross can save the world, but it will be only in so far as other men will make the value of it to be felt by the faithful, and will apply the merits of it to them. Through Him heaven has become accessible to all men, but they will only enter into it in so far as other men will show them the way thither and will open to them the gates of it. Through Him faith was brought to earth, but the present will be of use only in so far as other men teach it to those who are ignorant. Through Him grace was given to the world to do what is right; but what is right will be done only in so far as other men will deliver the doctrines to make it known, the exhortations to make it loved. The sacraments are an inexhaustible source of riches and spiritual blessings, but this treasure will profit the world only in so far as other men will induce sinners to receive it. It is thus that man has been established to be the helper and coadjutor of Jesus Christ in the great work of salvation. What a glory for us! and could God do us a greater honor? It is for us to appreciate it and show ourselves worthy of it by seizing upon all the means in our power for laboring for the salvation of our brethren and bringing their hearts to God.

SECOND POINT.

To Neglect to Labor for the Salvation of Souls, in so far as is Possible to each one of us, is to be Wanting to Jesus Christ.

If God has established us as His helpers in the work of the salvation of souls, it is doubtless in order that we should labor with Him. In proportion as we refuse or give Him our help, it will be decided by us whether such or such souls, with which we have relations, shall be saved or damned; that is to say, whether for them the blood of Jesus Christ shall have been shed utterly in vain, His labors rendered useless, His sacraments sterile, His graces of no avail, heaven lost, redemption a failure. Now, to cause a work which cost the Son of God so dear to be lost through our negligence, and in spite of His love to allow souls so dear to Him to perish, when by means of a little good will and zeal we might save them, is a terrible responsibility for us. Ah! all the wounds of Christ cry out to us: Be zealous; it will be in vain for us to have been opened for this soul, if you have no zeal. All His blood cries out to us: Be zealous; it will have been in vain that I shall have been shed for this soul, if you have no zeal. The whole of His heart cries out to us: Be zealous; it will have been in vain that I shall have loved this soul, if you have no zeal. O Lord, all these cries go to my heart. I would not refuse an enemy who might ask of me a service on his deathbed; how could I refuse Thee, who art the best of friends, who from the summit of Thy cross, as though it were Thy deathbed, adjures me to help Thee to save the world? I hear Thy apostle calling out to me on his side: *"And through thy knowledge shall the weak brother perish, for whom Christ hath died? Now, when you sin thus against the brethren, you sin against Christ"* (I. Cor. viii. 11, 12); and at the last day He will demand of you an account of His blood, which has remained useless through your fault. O unfaithful steward of the blood of a God, what a chastisement will fall upon your head! But, Lord, I will not draw upon myself this reproach. I will endeavor to gain souls by my counsels, my example, and my prayers.

Resolutions and spiritual nosegay as above.

TWENTIETH FRIDAY AFTER PENTECOST

Summary of the Morrow's Meditation.

After having meditated upon the love of God and its effects, it will be most suitable to meditate now upon the love of Jesus Christ, His amiable Son. We will consider: 1st, how amiable Jesus Christ is; 2nd, what our hearts owe to Him. We will then make the resolution: 1st, often and lovingly to consider all that is amiable in the person of Jesus Christ, in order that we may. rejoice in it and find our happiness in dwelling upon it; 2nd, often during the day to make acts of love towards our divine Saviour. Our spiritual nosegay shall be the words of St. Paul: *"If any one love not Our Lord Jesus Christ, let him be anathema"* (I. Cor. xvi. 22).

Meditation for the Morning.

Let us adore the great love which the Eternal Father bears His Son. He makes of this dear Son the object of His complaisance; He gives Him all that He has and all that He is; through consideration for Him He bears all our defects, pardons our sins, listens to our prayers, and presents us with His graces. What homage and what thanksgivings ought we not to render to a Father who is so full of love for the most amiable of all sons! He is the most perfect model of the love which we ourselves owe to Jesus Christ.

FIRST POINT.

How Amiable Jesus Christ is.

Evidently Jesus Christ, considered as God, is infinitely amiable, since in that title is contained all perfection and all holiness, all that ravishes the saints and angels in heaven. Full of grace and of truth, the beginning and the end of all things, the center of all good, He is the eternal love of the Father, His joy, His beatitude, His delight considered as Man-God, He is amiable in all the states through which His holy humanity has passed. Amiable in the womb of His mother; He thinks therein of us, He prays therein for us, He treats respecting our reconciliation with His Father, and even then His eyes are preparing to cast upon us looks of kindness, His ears to listen to us, His tongue to instruct us, His feet to seek the wandering sheep, His hands to help us, His arms to embrace us, His blood to flow for us, His body to be sacrificed for us, and His heart gives itself to us whilst asking us for ours. Amiable in the crib; He suffers there, He weeps there, He humbles Himself there for us. Amiable in His Epiphany; He therein appears to us as our God and our King. Amiable in His Presentation; He therein offers Himself to His holy Father as our victim. Amiable in His hidden life; He thereby teaches us labor, humility, obedience. Amiable in His public life; He passed through it doing all things well (Acts x. 30). Amiable at the Last Supper; He there institutes the Eucharist, the greatest miracle of His love, and He therein begs His Father to give us His throne (John xvii. 24). Amiable at Gethsemani; He there sheds for us His tears and His blood. Amiable before His judges; He receives blows as being a blasphemer, He is scourged as being an impious man, crowned as a fool, condemned as a wretch, and all that was in order to save us. Amiable on Calvary; He allows Himself to be crucified there for our love, He prays there for His executioners, He gives us His own mother, even as He had given us His own Father, that we might be His sisters and brothers of one and the same parents; lastly, He dies of love, with His arms stretched out to embrace us, His head bent down to give us the kiss of peace, His breast and His side open to receive us. Amiable in His resurrection; He gives us thereby the warrant of our own resurrection. Amiable in His ascension; He goes to prepare a place in paradise for us, and, like the eagle exciting its little ones to imitate its flight, He invites us to follow Him. Amiable in the mystery of Pentecost; He therein sends us His Holy Spirit, the substantial love which consoles, which aids human weakness, and produces in us good prayers and good works. Amiable at the right hand of His Father; He is there our Mediator, our Advocate, our Pontiff, our King. Amiable, lastly, in His tabernacles; He is therein heaven and earth for us, the food of our soul, the summary of all the mysteries of love (Ps. ex. 4, 5). O God, Thou dost ravish my heart! Why have I not the heart of the seraphim with which to love Thee?

SECOND POINT.

What our Hearts Owe to Jesus Christ.

We owe it to Him, 1st, to love Him as our God and Sovereign Lord. As our God, we ought to love Him above all things, more than all creatures, more than ourselves, and our hearts should be constantly filled with the highest joy at the thought of His greatness and all the perfections which He possesses. As our Sovereign Lord, we owe Him the obedience of a servant, the fidelity of a subject, the dependence of a slave, and true joy for His supreme dominion over us, which gives Him the right of life and death over our whole being. We owe it to Him, 2nd, to love Him as our Saviour and our Master. As our Saviour, we ought to do everything and suffer everything through gratitude for what He willed to do and suffer for our salvation. As our Master, we owe it to Him to conform our life to His instructions, to His holy maxims, and to long that such excellent teaching should be spread throughout the whole world. We owe it to Him, 3rd, to love Him as our Chief and our Shepherd. As our Chief, we ought to receive from Him the principles and the rule of our conduct, and expose all that we are and have in order to guard His glory, in the same way as the members expose themselves to preserve the head. As our Shepherd, who feeds us with His own blood, we ought to listen to His voice, follow Him, and be ready to give our blood for His love. We ought, 4th, to love Him as our Father, the Spouse of our souls, and our All. As our Father, we owe Him a love of tenderness, of respect, of gratitude, and we ought to fear nothing so much as to displease Him. As the Spouse of our souls, we ought to espouse all His interests, desire nothing but what He wills, and place all our happiness in being inseparably united to Him in time and in eternity. Lastly, as our All, we owe it to Him to fill our hearts with Him alone, and to pour forth in Him alone all our affections. Let us here examine ourselves. Do we regret to have hitherto loved Him so little, and do we resolve to love Him better henceforth, and to prove our love to Him by our acts?

Resolutions and spiritual nosegay as above.

TWENTIETH SATURDAY AFTER PENTECOST

Summary of the Morrow's Meditation.

We will meditate tomorrow upon the love of Jesus towards us, and we shall see: 1st, how unworthy we were of it; 2nd, to what an extent He has loved us, spite of our unworthiness. We will then make the resolution: 1st, often to protest to Our Lord, by fervent acts of love, that we love Him, and that we desire to love Him always more and more; 2nd, to offer Him the homage of all our actions, of all that we have, and of all that we are, not wishing to do anything but for Him, to possess nothing except for Him, and to see only Him in the persons whom we love. Our spiritual nosegay shall be the words of St. John: *"Let us love God, because God hath first loved us"* (I. John iv. 19).

Meditation for the Morning.

Let us adore Jesus Christ as the passionate lover of our souls, who carried love for us to its very last excess (Ephes, ii. 4); who made for us all that exists, sacrificed Himself, spent Himself entirely for us. Let us render Him all the homage of which our heart is capable.

FIRST POINT.

How Unworthy we were of the Love of Jesus Christ.

O my God, if it be true that love is greater in proportion as it sets forth from the loftiest summit and descends to the lowest abyss, how unworthy, then, was I to be loved by Thee! When I contemplate Thee in the highest heavens, where Thou dost reign; when I gaze at the vast extent of the firmament which Thou hast set forth as a magnificent tent above my head, and the countless stars Thou hast sown therein, even as the laborer sows seed in his field, and the whole universe, which was for Thee but as the playing of Thy fingers, I fall down abased and confused in the presence of so much greatness. When I tell myself that all the nations are in Thy presence as though they were not, that with three of Thy fingers Thou dost sustain the globe and balance the mountains, that Thou dost send the thunder, and it goes, and on its return it says, Behold me (Baruch iii.), I cannot overcome my astonishment that a God so great should lower His affections to me, and that He should will to love me, I who am so infinitely below Him. O prodigy which will be the astonishment of the heavens during all eternity! and what am I, then, that I should be loved by so lofty a majesty? I am a worm of the earth, crawling in the dust of this lower world; a nothingness which lives only by means of a borrowed existence; less still than that, a sinner by origin, a child of wrath by nature; less than that even, a sinner by malice, an abyss of misery and corruption, capable of all evil, if grace does not hold me back; and a God so great, so holy, loves a creature so vile in every respect; a God who is an abyss of majesty, of greatness, of independence, loves a rebel nothingness, an abyss of baseness, of indigence, and of sin! O love which dost bring distances together, which triumphs over contrasts! And even this is not all. Jesus Christ completely foresaw that we should respond to His love only by coldness, by the indifference which does not care for it, by the ingratitude which thinks of it without being thankful, by other sins which crucify Him afresh, and spite of these He has loved us so much. O mystery of love!

Jesus Loving.

SECOND POINT.

How Jesus Christ has Loved us Spite of our Unworthiness.

He has loved us: 1st, with an anticipated love which dates from all eternity (Jer. xxxi. 3), and which is anterior to all merit on our part; 2nd, with a gratuitous love: He possessed in Himself the plenitude of all good, and without any self-interest on His part, without any merit on our part, He conceived for us a love of preference which made Him go and seek us from out of nothingness, choose us out of a number of possible creatures who would have made a better use of existence than we have done, amongst so many millions of infidels to make of us Christians, amongst so many millions of Christians to make of us Catholics, and amongst so many millions of Catholics to surround us with special graces of salvation. He has loved us, 3rd, with an infinite love. We should here have to traverse a whole world of miracles; and heaven and earth, and the order of nature and the order of grace, all is full of the love of our God, all cries out to us to love Him. Amongst so many marvels, the crib, the cross, the altar, cry out louder than all the rest, *Behold how Jesus Christ has loved us!* Let us listen to these voices in the silence of our soul, and let us respond to them by all the ardor of love.

Resolutions and spiritual nosegay as above.

TWENTY-FIRST SUNDAY AFTER PENTECOST

The Gospel according to St. Matthew, xviii. 23-35.

"At that time Jesus said: The kingdom of heaven is likened to a king who would take an account of his servants. And when he had begun to take the account, one was brought to him that owed him ten thousand talents. And as he had not wherewith to pay it, his lord commanded that he should be sold, and his wife and children and all that he had, and payment to be made. But that servant falling down, besought him, saying: Have patience with me, and I will pay thee all. And the lord of that servant being moved with pity, let him go, and forgave him the debt. But when that servant was gone out he found one of his fellow-servants that owed him an hundred pence, and laying hold of him, he throttled him, saying: Pay what thou owest. And his fellow servant falling down, besought him, saying: Have patience with me and I will pay thee all. And he would not, but went and cast him into prison till he paid the debt. Now his fellow servants seeing what was done, were very much grieved, and they came and told their lord all that was done. Then his lord called him and said to him: Thou wicked servant, I forgave thee all the debt, because thou besoughtest me; shouldst not thou then have had compassion also on thy fellow-servant, even as I had compassion on thee? And his lord being angry, delivered him to the torturers until he paid all the debt. So also shall My heavenly Father do to you, if you forgive not every one his brother from your hearts."

Summary of the Morrow's Meditation.

We will meditate tomorrow upon the gospel of the day, and we shall thereby learn: 1st, what are our duties in regard to the justice of God; 2nd, our duties towards His mercy. We will then make the resolution: 1st, to recall to ourselves, when we are speaking, that divine justice will demand from us an account of all our words, and when we act, that it will require an account of each one of our acts; 2nd, to act towards our neighbor in the same spirit of mercy and endurance which God exercises toward us. We will retain as our spiritual nosegay the words of Our Lord: *"Be you merciful, as your Father also is merciful"* (Luke vi. 36).

Meditation for the Morning.

Let us adore Our Lord Jesus Christ under the figure of the king of which our gospel speaks; a just king, who requires from his officers an exact account of the goods he has committed to their stewardship, but also a merciful king, who grants forgiveness to whoever asks it of him, on condition that he himself pardons others. How greatly Jesus Christ deserves through this double title all our homage! Let us render it to Him from the bottom of our heart.

FIRST POINT.

Our Duties toward the Justice of God.

We ought to forestall it, to fear, and to satisfy it. 1st. To forestall it, by always keeping our conscience pure, because, like the master of our gospel, this adorable justice will one day cite us to appear before its tribunal; there we shall have to render to it an account of every action, of every word, of every thought, of the employment of our time, of the use of our talents, of our graces, of our possessions; and we must always keep this account ready, because at any moment death may demand it from us. Alas! we hardly ever think of iit! We live as though we had to render no account of anything to anyone, and as though it were due only to ourselves. We should act very differently if we were to say: I am before the eyes of my Judge to whom I shall have to render an account of this action! How much more discreetly should we speak if we said to ourselves: God is there; He is listening to my words and will require an account of them. 2nd. We ought to fear the justice of God.

"If is terrible," says St. Paul, *"to fall into His hands"* without being ready.
The king, our gospel tells us, *"look away from the unfaithful servant all his possessions;"* that is to say, God will take away from the sinner all his possessions, whether of riches, of grace, of glory, even of nature itself; He will cast him into *"outer darkness;"* God will condemn the sinner to the dreadful darkness of hell; He will deliver up the sinner to devils, who in order to torment him will make use of all they possess of intelligence, of strength, and of rage; lastly, *"He will cast them into the darkness, hands and feet bound"* that is to say, these miserable men will not be able to take one step or perform one single action which will enable them to escape from it; that is to say, their misery will be eternal.

These chastisements are doubtless severe, but it was necessary they should be so, because if the fear of so great an evil did not restrain the passions, there would neither be righteous men on earth nor any saints in heaven; every one, yielding to his evil nature, would be damned: Now there is nothing more worthy of God than to have made it a necessity, as it were, for us to be happy, and in a manner forced to enter into paradise. O my God! hitherto I had not understood it. Thanks for hell; it is the creation of Thy love as well as of Thy justice; enable me to fear it with the salutary fear which is the beginning of wisdom. 3rd. We ought to satisfy divine justice; this is what is taught us by the servant of our gospel. He prostrates himself at the feet of his master (Matt, xviii. 26): let us humble ourselves in the same way before God. It is the first satisfaction demanded by His justice. Then, again, the servant prays earnestly (Ibid.), he prays with confidence (Ibid.), he prays with a sincere will to repair the past by means of a better life (Ibid.). Let us act in the same way and we shall obtain pardon.

SECOND POINT.

Our Duties towards the Mercy of God.

We ought, 1st, to love it, for is it not infinitely amiable, this mercy of a God who, offended everywhere, at every moment, by all kinds of persons, and in all kinds of ways, bears everything in silence, and heaps blessings even on those who offend Him; this mercy which might have visited us with death when we were in a state of mortal sin, which has borne with us up to the present day, in which He offers us pardon with His paradise, and conjures us to accept both the one and the other? Touching goodness, symbolized by the king in the gospel, who had pity on his servant and allowed him time in which to pay his debt! (Matt. xviii. 27.) We ought, 2nd, to have confidence in the divine mercy. Oh, how will they understand the goodness of God who mistrust it, are discouraged, give way to grief and exclaim: Heaven forsakes me; I shall not be saved! Let us better understand God and His mercy. In the service of so good a God, he who wills it may be saved; it is sufficient to will it. Whatever may be our wretchedness, we ought always to have confidence and courage, to strive against obstacles, and to look upon it as certain that we shall be saved if we will to be saved. Whatever reverses God may send us, let us remember that He strikes only to save. 3rd. We ought to imitate the mercy of God in our relations towards our neighbor. The servant in the gospel, after having obtained pardon himself, would not forgive his fellow-servant; the king hears of it, sends for him, and retracts the favor accorded to him. "I *had pity upon you,*" he says to him, *"ought not you also to have pity on your fellow-servant?" "Thus,"* says Jesus Christ, *"will your heavenly Father do towards him who does not forgive his brother from the bottom of his heart."* There is therefore no forgiveness for him who does not forgive, for him who retains any resentment for wrongs inflicted on him. God bears all our sins without revenging Himself, without being carried away by anger, without even showing that He is displeased. It is to teach us that we must not be so sensitive to the ill that is done us, or that we imagine to be done us, or be impatient, angry, vindictive, implacable, often for a trifle ; that we must, on the contrary, be good, gentle, indulgent, merciful, like our heavenly Father, and, like Him, to feel great pity for the miseries of humanity in the person of our brethren.

Resolutions and spiritual nosegay as above.

Twenty-first Monday after Pentecost

Summary of the Morrow's Meditation

After having seen how amiable Jesus Christ is and how loving, we will excite ourselves: 1st, to love Him as the saints loved Him; 2nd, we will study what, should be the way in which to testify our love. We will then make the resolution: 1st, often to ask Our Saviour for His love; 2nd, to perform all our actions in a spirit of love, and to accept all crosses as testimonies of this love. Our spiritual nosegay shall be the words of St. Paul: *"The charity of Christ presseth us"* (II. Cor. v. 14).

Meditation for the Morning.

Let us adore the immense, eternal, infinite love of God the Father for Jesus Christ. He loves Him more than all creatures put together; He loves Him with a love which is the Holy Spirit Himself, God like Him, with a love which is the beginning and end of all His divine operations, since it is for the love of Jesus that everything has been created, that He preserves all, governs all, vivifies all in heaven and on earth, in the order of nature and in the order of grace. Let us rejoice to see Jesus so much loved, and let us desire to love Him in our turn with all our strength.

FIRST POINT.

The Example of the Saints Invites us to Love Jesus.

There is nothing more powerful than the example of the saints to induce souls
to love Jesus Christ. Let us therefore excite ourselves to love Him as did the
Blessed Virgin, whose heart burned with ineffable ardor for her divine Son, like
the angels, who love in Jesus their king, their lord, and their master; like the
patriarchs and the prophets, who supplicated for Jesus of the heavens (Is. lxiv.
i), of the earth (Ibid. xlv. 8), of God Himself (Ibid. xvi. 6); like David and Isaias,
who summoned Him by the most ardent desires; like the prophet Micheas, who
exclaimed, *"I will look towards the Lord, I will wait for God my Saviour"* (Mich.
vii. 7); like Habacuc, who sang, *"I will joy in God my Jesus"* (Habac. iii. 18);
like Solomon, who said in his canticle: *"Thou art fair, my Beloved, and comely"*
(Cant. i. 15). Let us look at the saints of the New Testament, who were still more
admirable; the just Joseph, with his paternal love for Jesus; St. John Baptist, the
true burning lamp, with flames of holy love; St. Peter, saying to the Saviour,
"Thou knowest all things; Thou knowest that I love Thee;" St. John the Evangelist,
a furnace of love; St. Paul, suffering in his heart a martyrdom of love; the martyrs,
victims of their charity for Jesus; St. Augustine, drawing from his heart such
overflowing of love as these: *"O love, which burns always, inflame me; may I be
all fire for Thee" (Conf,* lib. x., c. xxix.); St. Romuald and St. Bernard, melting
into tears of love; St. Francis of Assisi, a living brazier of love; St. Philip Neri,
only by means of a miracle bearing the violence of the charity which beats in his
heart and breaks one of his rribs; St. Ignatius of Loyola, St. Aloysius Gonzaga,
St. Stanislaus Kostka, burning here below with the love of the seraphim. And
what shall we say of the love of so many holy virgins—of a Teresa, with her heart
pierced with love by the arrow of a seraphim; of a Catharine of Siena, receiving
in her body, as the price of her love, the stigmata of the Passion of the Saviour;
of a Magdalene of Pazzi, complaining in these words to Jesus Christ: "O Lord, if
Thou dost not interfere, the excess of Thy love will make me die. I cannot bear
its ardors. O Love, how little art thou loved! Who will enable me to make all
the nations of the earth understand how Thou dost deserve to be loved!" O my
soul, wilt not thou be touched by so many beautiful examples, and will they not
make thee resolve to live henceforth only for the love of Jesus?

SECOND POINT.

How we ought to Testify our Love for Jesus Christ.

We ought to testify it to Him in our exercises of piety, in our actions and our sufferings. 1st. In our exercises of piety. Love ought to make us fly to them with joy as to the delicious moment of our union with Jesus, when we are able to pour forth our heart into His and to ask Him for His love for ourselves and for all men. When we employ ourselves in the reading of pious books, what delight to listen to the love which speaks to us, and to treasure up His sweet words! When we present ourselves at the sacred tribunal, what a consolation for us to cast ourselves, like the prodigal, upon the breast of the best of fathers, and to promise to love Him more and more! When we sit down at the holy table, what delight to identify ourselves with Jesus and to be able to say: *"My Beloved to me and I to Him. ... I found Him whom my soul loveth: I held Him, and will not let Him go"* (Cant. ii. 16; iii. 4). 2nd. In our ordinary actions, how sweet it is to do everything for Jesus, as being our last end; to do all like Jesus, as being our model; to do all with Jesus, as being our help! When we converse, we speak of Jesus, at least from time to time, and we endeavor always to imitate His goodness, His gentleness, His discretion. When we are alone, we unite ourselves with Jesus, solitary, silent, and then more united than ever to God His Father. When we are at table, we imitate the temperance and the modesty of Jesus taking His meals together with Mary and Joseph. Lastly, in the employment of our time, we endeavor, like Jesus, to make the most holy use of every moment 3rd. In suffering, we unite ourselves with Jesus suffering (I. Pet. iv. 13). We say to Him as did the sister of Lazarus, *"Lord, he whom Thou lovest is sick"* (John xi. 13), and we take Him as the rule of our conduct: the patience, the meekness, the obedience, the simplicity, the humility of the Saviour, above all His abandonment to the will of God in health or sickness, life or death.

Resolutions and spiritual nosegay as above.

TWENTY-FIRST TUESDAY AFTER PENTECOST

Summary of the Morrow's Meditation

After having meditated during several weeks upon the love of God, we will meditate tomorrow upon love towards our neighbor, and we shall see what are the two commandments which Jesus Christ has given us. The first is this: *"Love your neighbor as yourself."* The second, which is much more exalted, is contained in these words: *"A new commandment I give unto you, That you love one another as I have loved you"* (John xiii. 34). We will then make the resolution: 1st, to treat our neighbor with great consideration, whoever he may be; 2nd, never to do to any one what we should not desire he should do to us, and to do to others what we should be very glad for them to do to us. We will retain as our spiritual nosegay these words of the gospel: *"Thou shall love thy neighbor as thyself ... A new commandment I give unto you, That you love one another as 1 have loved you"* (Matt. xxii. 39; John xiii. 34).

Meditation for the Morning.

Let us adore Jesus Christ imposing upon us the precept of loving one another. He is a good father who delights to see his children bound together by the sweet bonds of reciprocal charity, in such a manner that they form but one heart and one soul. Whence results amongst all men the mutual debt of charity; a debt, says St. Augustine, from which we are never free, and which we owe always, even after having paid it. Oh, how amiable Jesus is in this commandment, and how well He merits all our praise and all our adoration!

FIRST POINT.

Jesus Christ Commands everyone to Love his Neighbor as himself.

Let us weigh the sense of these words: We ought to love our neighbor as ourselves; that is to say, we ought never to do to another what we would not they should do to us (John iv. 16), and we should do to him all that we should be glad he should do for us (Luke vi. 31); that is to say, that it is not sufficient not to wish ill to our neighbor: we must also wish him good, rejoice when anything pleasant happens to him, be sad when what is grievous happens to him, as though it had happened to ourselves; that is to say, we must be ready to render him a service, to give him help and assistance when we can; to be careful in avoiding all that may displease him, whether in conversation or in our behavior; we should conceal his faults, excuse and diminish them as much as possible, and turn away the conversation as much as possible when others speak of them; that is to say, finally, we must interest ourselves charitably and zealously in all that concerns him, above all, in his salvation, rejoice over the graces he receives, weep over the faults he commits, and deem ourselves happy if we can do anything for the good of his soul. These duties are so deeply impressed upon us that we cannot fail in them without reproaching ourselves and without feeling that we are doing wrong. Let us here examine ourselves. Is it thus that we have loved our neighbor? Do we feel no hatred for any one, no resentment, no aversion? Do we love all men from the bottom of our heart? Are we inclined to give everyone a pleasant and amiable welcome, and to render service to all? We, who are so sensitive with respect to everything which relates to ourselves, do we understand how much we deceive ourselves in fancying we love our neighbor as ourselves, if we do not show him any interest, and if we treat him only with cold indifference?

SECOND POINT.

Jesus Christ Commands us to Love one another as He Himself has Loved us.

Ah. how much more does this commandment say than did the first! Jesus Christ
has loved us: 1st. As God; and who could express what love and tenderness and
mercy there is in the heart of God towards His creatures? Made after the likeness
of a God who is essentially good, infinitely good, we ought to seek to be good
like Him in our sentiments, our acts, and our words. 2nd. Jesus Christ has loved
us as Man-God; and who could conceive to what extent He has carried this love,
He who has never done any harm to any one, but who traversed the earth doing
good and giving to all a kind reception (Acts x. 38); He who, after having led
a life wholly of charity, suffered, through love, all that it was possible to suffer,
and died of love; He, lastly, who, after eighteen centuries, still continues upon
the altars His life of love and of sacrifice? O Lord Jesus, how much, then, ought
we to love our brethren! What love could be tender enough, strong enough,
generous enough to approach to Thine? Is there an injury we ought not to be
ready to forgive, any sacrifice we ought not to be ready to make? Is there any
kind of ice or of coldness which ought not to melt, any bitterness which ought
not to be softened, any repugnance which ought not to disappear, at the sound
of these words: *"A new commandment I give unto you, That you love one another
as I have loved you"?*

Resolutions and spiritual nosegay as above.

Twenty-First Wednesday After Pentecost

Summary of the Morrow's Meditation

We will meditate tomorrow upon the first characteristic of the love of our neighbor, which is that it is supernatural. We shall see: 1st, what it is we must understand by the supernatural love of our neighbor; 2nd, in what respect this love differs from a simply natural love. Our resolution shall be: 1st, to treat everyone with consideration and kindness, from love for God, whom we ought to see and love in our neighbor; 2nd, to be on our guard against all purely natural affections which do not accomplish the precept of charity, and which are, in addition, very dangerous. Our spiritual nosegay shall be the words of St. John: *"Dearly beloved, let us love one another, for charity is of God"* (I. John iv. 7).

Meditation for the Morning.

Let us go to the heart of Jesus as to a furnace of charity, there to fill ourselves with the spirit of this virtue. True charity is not of this world, it is entirely heavenly; Jesus Christ brought it down to us from heaven, and the great desire of His heart is that it should be diffused in all hearts. Let us offer ourselves to Him, that He may infuse and inflame us with it.

FIRST POINT.

What is to be Understood by Supernatural Love for our Neighbor.

Supernatural love is a pious affection of the soul by which we love our neighbor in God and for God. It is not a product of our own nature, which is not capable of anything in the supernatural order; it is the product of the Holy Ghost, who alone can form in us a sentiment so pure, so elevated, and so holy (Rom. v. 5). Supernatural in its principle, true charity is so also in its motives. By its means, we love our neighbor not because of his merits or of his fine qualities, but because we love God, and because the love of our neighbor is a necessary and inseparable consequence of the love of God. If I really love God, I ought, 1st, to be happy to give myself to all that He desires, to what He wills, to what will give Him great pleasure. Now God, the common Father of the great family of human nature, desires and wills that all His children should love one another, and form together but one heart and but one soul. His pleasure is to see them all linked together in the sweet bonds of reciprocal charity; and to exclude a single individual from this family affection would be to offend Him. If I really love God, I ought, 2nd, to love His friends, who are very dear to Him, to love His children, whom He loves as though they were His other selves. Now, all without exception are friends of God; friends whom He has loved to the extent of delivering up His Son to death in order to save them, and whom His Son loved to the extent of dying for them. All are His children; they have the right and on them is incumbent the duty of saying, *"Our Father, who art in heaven."* Not tenderly to love a single one of these children of God is to wound the good Father in the apple of His eye. If I really love God, I ought, 3rd, to love His resemblance and His image made by His own hand, and not by the hand of another. Now such are all men (Gen. vi. 21). If I really love God, I ought, 4th, to love the members of Jesus Christ His Son, who form with our divine Saviour but one body, of which He is the head. Now such are all men, and to such an extent that Jesus Christ has said: *"As long as you did it to one of these My least brethren, you did it to Me"* (Matt xxv. 40), and I will recompense it as such, if it be good, or I will punish it as such, if it be evil. If I really love God, I ought, 5th, to love all whom He has given me as brothers and as coheirs of His kingdom. Now such are all men; all are My brethren both on My Father and My Mother's side; on My Father's side, because all are, like Me, children of God; on My Mother's side, because all are, like Me, children of the Church and of the Blessed Virgin;

all are co-heirs of the kingdom of heaven; we are all called upon to sit in glory, upon an immortal throne, and to glorify God throughout eternity, with one same voice and one same heart. O my God, it is then very true that Thy love and the love of my neighbor are inseparable. We deceive ourselves if we imagine that we love Thee if there be a single man upon earth whom we do not love for Thee. Oh, how beautiful it is, how noble and sublime, that supernatural charity which is one and the same with the love of God; how well suited it is to elevate the soul, to inflame the heart, to inspire it with generous devotion and with the desire of great sacrifices. Let us here examine ourselves. Do we love our neighbor with this supernatural love?

SECOND POINT.

How Supernatural Love Differs from Natural Love.

1st. Simply natural love with all the acts which it inspires has no merit in regard to heaven; God gives a recompense only to what is done for Him and with a view to pleasing Him. Alas! how many good works are lost because they are inspired by a purely natural sentiment and without any thought of God! 2nd. Natural love is often nothing more than egotism. We love those who please us by their sympathetic disposition, who are agreeable to us because of their amiable manners, their witty and lively conversation, or from whom we hope to receive some service or other. Alas! pagans love one another after this fashion, but it is not to love like a Christian. 3rd. Natural love is often nothing more than worldly politeness, the complaisance of a kind heart, the goodness of an affectionate heart, a pure form of good breeding, but it is too often inconstant as is caprice, variable as is the temper. 4th. It is a love which is partial and exclusive; it is only given to those who are acceptable to us, others are treated with carelessness, coldness, disdain. 5th. It is a love which is often very dangerous; it converts itself into an intimate friendship, which softens the heart, disgusts it with God, with piety, and with its duties, and leads it sometimes to the commission of the greatest evils, and of which it has no idea, because it looks upon ill-regulated affections as being charity. Let us examine our conscience with regard to all these characteristics of purely natural love.

Repositions and spiritual nosegay as above.

Twenty-first Thursday after Pentecost

Summary of the Morrow's Meditation.

We will meditate tomorrow : 1st, upon the excellence of the supernatural love which we owe to our neighbor; 2nd, on the marks by which we may recognize it. Our resolution shall be: 1st, never to speak of the absent except to say what is good respecting them; 2nd, always to treat both those who are present and those who are absent with the same consideration which we should show to Jesus Christ Himself. Our spiritual nosegay shall be the words of St. Peter: *"Before all things have a constant mutual charity among yourselves"* (I. Pet. iv. 8).

Meditation for the Morning.

Let us adore Our Lord Jesus Christ several times reiterating the precept of charity towards our neighbor. He gives it us often Himself; He repeats it to us by His beloved disciple, by His apostles and evangelists, and there is nothing in the whole of the Holy Scriptures which is more recommended to us; it is a proof of the ardent desire He has to see all of us filled with the spirit of charity. Let us thank Him for having given us by this sole precept the means of satisfying all the others, since it is written: *"He that loveth his neighbor hath fulfilled the law"* (Rom. xiii. 8).

FIRST POINT.

The Excellence of Supernatural Charity.

"If I speak with the tongues of men and of angels, and if I should have prophecy and should know all mysteries and all knowledge; and if I should have all faith so that I could remove mountains; and if I should distribute all my goods to feed the poor, and if I should deliver my body to be burned, and have not charity, it profiteth me nothing" (I. Cor. xiii. 1-3). This charity, which dominates all, is a virtue so high that it is modelled upon the Blessed Trinity itself. Holy Father, said Jesus Christ, in His discourse after the Last Supper, I pray Thee that all My disciples may be one through charity, even as we are one by nature (John xvii. 22); that all their hearts may be one, as Thou, My Father, art in Me and I in Thee (Ibid. 21). Holy Father, I conjure Thee once more, grant that they may be all one, and that the love which unites me to Thee may pass into their hearts to unite them to one another (Ibid. 23, 26.) How beautiful these words are! how well suited to exalt the excellence of charity! Jesus Christ, by conforming Himself to this sublime teaching, is so identified and made one with us, that He declares that He looks upon what we do and say to the least of His children as done and said to Himself. O marvelous invention of a God to force men to love Him! He covers in a manner with His sacred person every Christian, to receive the good or the evil done to him, and thereby He elevates, ennobles, and renders charity divine, because, in accordance with this saying, to love, to oblige, and be kind to our neighbor is to love, to oblige, and to be kind to Jesus Christ Himself. What a consolation for a heart which loves so amiable a Saviour, and at the same time what a beautiful recompense does not Jesus Christ give to him by whom He considers Himself to be obliged! This it is which explains how a glass of water given to a poor man is worth an eternal recompense to him who bestows it. On the other hand, to be wanting in charity towards our neighbor is to be wanting towards Jesus Christ; to treat our neighbor harshly, to wound or to mock at him, is to treat Jesus Christ harshly, to wound and to mock at Him; to be cold and disagreeable to our neighbor is to be cold and disagreeable to Jesus Christ (Matt. xxv. 40). How dreadful! Let us here examine ourselves and see if Jesus Christ has reason to be content with the manner in which we have treated Him in the person of our neighbor.

SECOND POINT.

The Marks by which we shall be Able to Recognize whether our Love is
Supernatural.

1st. Supernatural love embraces all men without exception or distinction, because by loving Jesus Christ in our neighbor it finds Jesus Christ to be equally amiable in all men. Consequently, it acts towards all with the same benevolence, without permitting itself to have too much complaisance and affection for some and aversion and coldness for others; it is respectful towards all without giving a preference to any one, without ever giving any one cause to complain or conceiving bitterness against any. 2nd. Supernatural love is disinterested; it loves, it obliges, it testifies esteem and friendship, even when it does not receive any advantage by it; in that respect it is very different from egotistical love, which obliges a person only in so far as it feels it to be its interest to do so; it is cordial even towards those who have been disobliging and have treated it ill. 3rd. Supernatural love looks before anything else to what has regard to the salvation of its neighbor, desiring nothing so much as to gain him over to piety, and seizing every opportunity in its power to disgust him with the world and to lead his thoughts to eternity, his mind towards Christian truths, and his heart towards the practice of the gospel. 4th. Supernatural love loves purely for God, without any thought of talents, of cleverness, of birth, of good breeding, of a sympathetic disposition, of conformity of inclinations, and it is even a pleasure for it to love those who have nothing amiable about them, because it is then all the more sure to love purely for God and to have a real supernatural and meritorious charity; whilst this assurance is wanting when it is natural inclination alone which leads us to love. Do we recognize in ourselves these marks of supernatural love?

Resolutions and spiritual nosegay as above.

— · —

TWENTY-FIRST FRIDAY AFTER PENTECOST

Summary of the Morrow's Meditation.

We will meditate to-morrow upon the second characteristic of charity, which is benignity (I. Cor. xiii. 4), and we shall see that we owe: 1st, to God; 2nd, to our neighbor; 3rd, to ourselves, to maintain always within us the spirit of benignity. We will then make the resolution: 1st, to exercise great watchfulness over ourselves, in order to repress movements of impatience and fits of bad humor; never to speak or to act under the influence of emotion, and to wait until we have attained to calmness; 2nd, to endeavor to be kind and amiable to everyone, and to be cordial and affable in our behavior. We will retain as our spiritual nosegay the words of the Apostle: *"The servant of God must be mild towards all men"* (II. Tim. ii. 24).

Meditation for the Morning.

Let us adore Our Lord under the amiable title of *"Lamb of God,"* which St. John gives Him (John i. 36), and by which the prophets had designated Him in the early ages. I will show Myself to the world, He says in Jeremias, with the gentleness of the lamb (Jer. xi. 19). Let us thank Him for this beautiful example, and let us ask Him to enable us to imitate Him.

FIRST POINT.

We Owe it to God always to Maintain within us a Spirit of Benignity.

The first lesson that I have come to give you upon earth, said Jesus Christ, is
that you must be meek (Matt. xi. 29). Be gentle as lambs (Luke x. 3), He said to
His apostles. If your heart is not disposed to be benignant towards the least of
your brethren, do not approach My altar until you have reconciled yourself to
him (Matt. v. 24). If you are struck on one cheek, offer the other; if your tunic is
taken from you, give up your mantle, rather than enter into disputes in which
benignity will be compromised. To this language of precept Our Lord adds the
language of example, to which every Christian must be subjugated under pain
of losing his salvation. The whole life of Jesus Christ presents us with nothing
but an example of benignity. He is gentle in His infancy in the crib; He is gentle
in His adolescence in the midst of the doctors of the law; He is gentle during
the thirty years He passed with Mary and Joseph; He is gentle during the three
years of His mission, even in the midst of His apostles, who have no education
and no manners; He is gentle towards sinners, and His relations with them are
full of kindness and mercy. Let the Pharisees be scandalized and call Him the
friend of sinners, He does not diminish on that account His kindness towards
them; and this gentleness converts the Samaritan, touches Zacheus, brings back
Magdalene, and pronounces words of forgiveness over the adulterous woman.
He is meek in His Passion, gentle towards Judas who betrays Him, towards His
enemies who accuse Him, towards His executioners who crucify Him. What a
magnificent example, and, consequently, what a magnificent precept!

SECOND POINT.

We Owe it to our Neighbor always to Maintain within us a Spirit of Benignity.

All men, said St. Vincent de Paul, have this in common, that they desire
to be treated with kindness; they do not like any one to display ill-temper
towards them, or to speak to them harshly. There is no affection possible if
our conversation be not seasoned with tenderness, benignity, and gentleness;
if the tone of voice, instead of being fraternal, is rough, dry, and austere; if
the manners, instead of being kind, amiable, and gracious, are brusque and
accompanied by ill-temper; if, when a reproach has to be addressed to any
one, it is made with bitterness and passion, and the words are forgotten of St.
Francis de Sales, who said that reprimands are bitter fruits which cannot be
digested unless they are enveloped in gentleness. Oh, how much evil in families

and in the relations of society springs from impetuous outbursts, fits of bad humor, impatience which cannot endure contradiction. Everything in life can be done by gentleness, says St. Francis de Sales, nothing by force; rudeness spoils all, closes the heart, engenders hatred and obstinacy. We may, says Bossuet, constrain and force creatures inanimate and devoid of reason, but the human heart is not ruled so much by power as it is managed by art; it is led by skill, and gained by kindness; there is nothing therein which can be subjected to force, power has nothing to govern; there is no other resource but to study men and the manner in which to gain them over, by asking ourselves: How should I wish to be treated if I were in their place ? And the answer would certainly be: I should like to be spoken to kindly, and to be treated in the same way, and to have esteem and affection always shown me. I should like to see in others the cordiality and serenity of expression which touches and consoles, the agreeable and smiling manner which gives pleasure, the grace, the openness, the charming simplicity which seems to offer its heart and to ask for ours in return. Is it thus that we have treated our neighbor?

THIRD POINT.

We Owe it to Ourselves always to Maintain a Spirit of Benignity.

As soon as we lose the spirit of gentleness we lose the calmness and self-control of reason; we speak no longer the language of duty, but the language of ill-temper and of passion; the soul is disquieted, it possesses itself no longer, it does not measure either what it says or what it does; and in this state it always says things which are to be regretted. The soul which quits the paths of gentleness has neither wisdom to enable it to conduct itself aright, nor vigilance to watch over its words, nor attention to itself to regulate the motions of its heart The man who is gentle, on the other hand, invariably exercises self-control, and can say, like the holy king: *"My soul is continually in my hands "* (Ps. cxviii. 109). His interior is like a beautiful sky which no cloud obscures, which no wind troubles, and where all is done by the light of reason and of faith.

Resolutions and spiritual nosegay as above.

— · —

Twenty-First Saturday After Pentecost

Summary of the Morrow's Meditation.

We will meditate tomorrow upon the advantages of meekness, and we shall see that, possessed of this virtue, we can do everything: 1st, in regard to the heart of God; 2nd, in regard to that of our neighbor; 3rd, in regard to our own. We will then make the resolution: 1st, to repress, even when we are alone, the very least movements of impatience, of haste, and of discontent which try to rise within us; 2nd, to behave towards everyone with kindness, and to speak kindly to all. Our spiritual nosegay shall be the words of Our Lord: *"Learn of Me, because I am and humble of heart, and you shall find rest to your souls"* (Matt. xi. 29).

Meditation for the Morning.

Let us adore the infinite goodness of God, so greatly celebrated in the Holy Scriptures: "Thou, *O God, art sweet and mild, and plenteous in mercy"* (Ps. lxxxv. 5). Thou callest Thyself Father, Shepherd, Lamb, names which express nothing but sweetness. I admire, O my God, I praise, I bless, I love Thy infinite sweetness, and I ask of Thee a share in it.

FIRST POINT.

With Meekness we can do Everything in Regard to the Heart of God.

Meekness is the cherished virtue of God, and that which He beholds with the most complaisance in a soul; by its means our prayers are always favorably received before His throne (Jud. ix. 16). He abases the proud sinner down to the ground, but He sustains meek souls (Ps. cxlvi. 6); He gives them His grace (Prov. iii. 34); He raises and saves them (Ps. cxlix. 4). Moses was listened to by God because of his meekness (Num. xii. 3), and through it he also obtained the grace of holiness (Ecclus. xlv. 4). The whole of the Jewish people, desiring to obtain from God the cessation of His anger, begged it of Him because of the meekness of David (Ps. cxxxi. i). A meek heart recalls to God the image of His Son, who was meekness itself; and, if Raguel melted into tears on perceiving in Tobias the image of his old and virtuous friend (Tob. vii. 2), could God help loving and kindly receiving the suppliant who bears impressed upon his soul the most striking characteristic of Jesus Christ, namely, meekness? Therefore, the gospel assures us that the meekness with which we treat others will be the measure of the kindness with which God will treat us (Matt. vii. 2; Mark iv. 42); and is not this a very consoling truth ?

SECOND POINT.

With Meekness we can do all Things in Regard to our Neighbor.

We can do anything with the heart of a man if we treat him with meekness. The apostles converted the world because they made proof of admirable meekness on all occasions and in regard to everyone (Titus iii. 2). Meekness dissipates prejudices, does away with repugnances; it commands by praying, it corrects by conjuring; dissimulating the want of consideration and the outrages inflicted by others, it causes them to be repaired by a superabundance of attention and of zeal, which its charms call forth. It makes itself loved by all, even by the worst men, because, instead of bruising the bent reed or quenching the flax which still burns, it receives every one with kindness, speaks tenderly, visits with charity and pities those who suffer. If it has advice to give, reproaches to make, it does all in so kind and amiable a manner, with so visibly loving a heart, that it is felt that it is solely affection, the desire for good, by which it is inspired, and then resistance is but seldom made to it. It redresses errors without wounding him who has made the mistake, it cures the heart without making it suffer; sometimes, even, it persuades by silence in the same way as it charms by speaking. Hence the words spoken by a holy Father, that nothing is difficult to meek men, any more than to those who are humble. There is that in meekness to gain hearts which there is in Providence to rule the world. Providence never abandons anything; it does not allow even a hair to fall from our head without its permission, but it rules everything by such gentle action that we hardly feel it. It leads the march of events by a gradation which is so insensible that it generally escapes our observation, and its strength is in its very meekness. It is thus that meekness governs so powerfully the human heart that it leads it where it will, and that in so sweet a manner that the empire which it exercises is hardly felt at all.

THIRD POINT.

With Meekness we can do Everything in Regard to our own Heart.

As long as we maintain our soul in a state of meekness and calmness, we are masters of our passions, and we govern them easily, because then we observe without any difficulty all their movements, and because the powers of our soul not being distracted about other things, we can direct them against the passions. Impatience, that ebullition of weakness angry with its powerlessness, drags us along of itself; but meekness, which is the calmness of strength, renders easy to us the perfection of patience, of charity, of humility, of abandonment to the divine will, of confidence in God, of all the virtues. He who possesses himself always will soon be perfect.

Resolutions and spiritual nosegay as above.

Twenty-Second Sunday after Pentecost

The Gospel according to St. Matthew, **xxii. 15-21.**

"Then the Pharisees, going, consulted among themselves how to ensnare Him in His speech. And they sent to Him their disciples with the Herodians, saying: Master, we know that Thou, art a true speaker, and teachest the way of God in truth, neither carest Thou for any man: for Thou dost not regard the person of men. Tell us, therefore, what dost Thou think, Is it lawful to give tribute to Caesar or not? But Jesus, knowing their wickedness, said: Why do you tempt Me, ye hypocrites? Show Me the coin of the tribute. And they offered Him a penny. And Jesus saith to them: Whose image and inscription is this? They say to Him: Caesar's. Then He saith to them: Render, therefore, to Caesar the things that are Caesar's, and to God the things that are God's."

Summary of the Morrow's Meditation.

We will meditate tomorrow upon mutual forbearance, which is the third characteristic of charity, and of which Jesus Christ, in the gospel of the day, gives us a beautiful example. We shall see: 1st, that this mutual forbearance forms an essential portion of the precept of charity; 2nd, that God makes of it a special law incumbent on us; 3rd, that justice itself obliges us to observe it. Our resolution shall be: 1st, to bear with the defects and the wrongs done us by our neighbor without complaint and without reproaching him for them, and, above all, in a manner calculated to humble him; 2nd, not to take any notice of his mistakes or his blunders, but, on the contrary, not to seem to perceive them, when we have not the mission to reprove them. Our spiritual nosegay shall be the words of St. Paul: "*We ought to bear the infirmities of the weak, and not to please ourselves*" (Rom. xv. i).

Meditation for the Morning.

Let us adore the patience of Our Lord in the gospel of the day. His enemies, who were bent on His destruction, addressed to Him this insidious question: "*Is it lawful to pay tribute to Caesar?*" If He answered Yes, He would be odious to the people, who pretended, as being the people of God, not to owe anything to Caesar; if He said No, He would be odious to the prince whose authority He did not recognize. Jesus Christ bears with patience and meekness the perfidy of those who thus question Him; He is not angry and He calmly makes them an answer full of divine wisdom: a beautiful example well worthy of our admiration and our praise, and teaching us to bear with calmness and in peace the malice of men. Let us offer Him our thanksgivings.

FIRST POINT.

Mutual Forbearance is an Essential Precept of Charity.

These two things are so closely linked together that, without mutual forbearance, no charity would be possible and we must efface the precept from the gospel, for every man here below has his defects and his imperfections; there are no angels except in heaven; if you do not bear with them, union is broken and charity disturbed. Every man has his own temperament; inclinations and characters are not the same; opinions and ideas contradict one another: wills come in contact, tastes vary. Now, amidst so many diverse or contrary elements, the fusion of hearts in such a manner as to form but one heart and one soul, as charity commands, is only possible in so far as we bear with one another, that we remember we all of us have our weaknesses, and that we suffer charitably and patiently (II. Thess. iii. 5) all that shocks us, all that displeases us, and all that does not harmonize with our tastes or our humor. Without this endurance, the fusion of hearts would be as impossible as the fusion of water with fire, of light with darkness, and there would necessarily be divisions, quarrels, and discord. The experience of every day attests it; and thou, O holy charity, thou who art so beautiful a virtue, who dost form the charm of our exile, the consolation of our sorrows, thou wouldst disappear from the earth. What a misfortune, and what ought we not to endure in order to prevent it!

SECOND POINT.

God has made a Special Law of Mutual Forbearance.

Doubtless God, in commanding charity, commanded forbearance, since the one cannot exist without the other; at the same time, He attaches to it such an importance that He makes of it a special law. *"We ought,"* says St. Paul, *"to bear the infirmities of the weak"* (Rom. xv. 1). If we ought, it is not a favor that we do them, it is a duty that we fulfil; it is a debt which we acquit.

"Bear ye one another's burdens," continues the Apostle, "and *so you shall fulfil the law of Christ"* (Gal. vi. 2). He seems to reduce the whole of the gospel to this sole precept; therefore, He takes pleasure in developing it. Bear with one another, he says, *"in all humility,"* which excludes sensitiveness and prejudices; "in *all mildness and patience,"* which excludes murmurs and reproaches, antipathies and impatience, with regard to the displeasure which others cause us; *"in charity"* (Eph. iv. 2), which teaches us to treat our neighbor as we desire to be treated ourselves. It is an amiable law, well worthy of the common Father of all men; a law of benevolence and indulgence, which takes under its shield all kinds of miseries, and does not permit itself to entertain any contempt for weakness, or to indulge in any derision for mistakes, or in censures for even faults when we are not commanded to reprove them; a law to which is attached our dearest interests, since it is written that God will be indulgent to our faults only in proportion as we are indulgent to the faults of our brethren (Luke vi. 38). Whence St. Chrysostom concludes that if we do not bear with our brethren, God will not bear with us; if we do not sympathize with others, God will not sympathize with us; and we ourselves subscribe to this law when we say, *"Forgive us our trespasses as we forgive those who trespass against us"* that is to say, be indulgent to my faults in the same proportion as I am indulgent to the faults

of others : words which are as a sentence of death in the mouth of whoever pronounces them with a heart embittered against his brother. If he were taken at his word, a flame from heaven would come and devour him alive.

THIRD POINT.

Justice itself Makes Mutual Forbearance incumbent on us.

Who is there, in fact, who does not feel in his own case the need of a law of forbearance, of that law which is a protector of human weakness? Now, if we wish that it should be observed in regard to us, would it not be strange injustice not to observe it in regard to our brethren? We complain of the imperfections of our brethren; but are they not obliged to bear with ours? of their characters and dispositions; but have we not our caprices? of their vivacity and rudeness; but does a sharp speech never escape our lips? of excuses with which they cover up their faults without ever allowing that they commit them ; but is not this also our history, to the extent that we come to imagine that we are less bad, sometimes even that we are better, than others? He alone who is without sin could throw a stone at them (John viii. 7). As for us, it ill becomes us to desire perfection in others to such a point as not to be able to bear a spot or imperfection in them. Let us here examine our conscience; how do we bear with our neighbor's faults, his too gay or too melancholy disposition, his temperament, which is too easy-going or too austere; his manners, which are too slow or too quick? Instead of excusing and sheltering our neighbors, their mental or corporal infirmities, their want of good breeding, their want of talent, their frivolity, their obstinacy, their blunders, what is defective in their pronunciation, in their behavior, in their deportment, have we not often ridiculed them? How do we bear with the importunity of such and such persons, the complaints of the afflicted or the sick; lastly, all that we have to suffer from various individuals?

Resolutions and spiritual nosegay as above.

Twenty-Second Monday after Pentecost

Summary of the Morrow's Meditation.

We will meditate tomorrow upon two other characteristics of charity, which are: 1st, to devote ourselves to our neighbor to the extent of making sacrifices in order to oblige him; 2nd, to include in this devotedness even our enemies. Our resolution shall be: 1st, never to refuse our neighbor the good services we can render him, even if we must make some sacrifices; 2nd, to pardon all the evil he does us, and be reconciled to him as soon as possible. Our spiritual nosegay shall be: *"Charity seeketh not her own and is not provoked to anger"* (I. Cor. xiii. 5).

Meditation for the Morning.

Let us adore Jesus Christ teaching us by His example to devote ourselves to our neighbor, even to our enemies. He loved all men, even the most ungrateful among them, even the greatest sinners, to the extent of delivering Himself up to torments and death for their sake. Let us thank Him for so much love, and let us ask Him to give us grace to imitate Him.

FIRST POINT.

Charity Carries Devotedness to its Neighbor even to Sacrifice.

The laws of purely human friendship themselves impose upon men the obligation of devoting themselves to making sacrifices for the good of their brethren; for what man would look upon another as his friend if he were to limit his friendship to the condition of not putting himself out of the way in order to render a service? With still greater reason, Christian charity, so superior as it is to natural friendship, the charity moulded upon the precept of the Lord, *"Love one another as I have loved you"* (John xiii. 34), ought to raise itself to the height of making sacrifices; sacrifices of comfort and pleasure, sacrifices of fortune and even of life in certain cases. We ought to be ready, said St. John to the faithful, to sacrifice in order to serve our neighbor all that we have, all that we are, and our own life even if it were necessary, seeing that Jesus Christ, our model, sacrificed His life for us. *"I most gladly"* says St. Paul to the Corinthians, *"will spend and be spent myself for your* souls" (II. Cor. xii. 15). In conformity with these holy doctrines and these beautiful examples, the primitive Christians sold their possessions, and laid the price at the feet of the apostles, to distribute according to the needs of each; and in the following centuries we see some spending their fortune in alms and good works, others sacrificing their lives to go and evangelize idolatrous nations, others spending their days in hospitals and in taking care of the sick, in instructing children in schools in barbarous countries, in redeeming captives, or in their own country solacing all kinds of misfortunes. Let us here examine our conscience. Do we possess a charity which carries us to the length of making sacrifices, which does not spare either time or trouble or money for the good of its neighbor? Does not selfishness sometimes close our heart to compassion, our hand to alms?

SECOND POINT.

Charity includes even our Enemies in its Devotedness.

The devotedness of charity embraces all men without exception, even those who hate us, who have wounded us by their words or their acts, and who have done us the greatest injuries; for we are all children of God, all members of one and the same body, of which Jesus Christ is the head; and Jesus Christ does not intend that His members should be divided, and should hate one another, and He looks upon as done to Himself what is done to the least among them. This love of our enemies even possesses this advantage, that we are surer of loving them with a supernatural and meritorious love, whilst our love towards our friends is exposed to the danger of being purely natural and devoid of merit. As to the practice of this precept, four words in the gospel teach it clearly to us: *"Diligite—benedicite—orate—benefacite"* (Matt. v. 4; Luke vi. 27, 28). Love those who are your enemies, never say anything but what is good of them, pray for them, render them services when you have an opportunity. 1st *Love them;* that is to say, never permit any leaven of animosity or aversion, of vengeance or of bitterness, against them to exist in your heart; do not be content with simply wishing that no evil should happen to them, but be ready to be reconciled to them as soon as possible, and do not hesitate to make the first advances, even should they be your inferiors, even should they be more in the wrong than you. Lastly, feel for them a sincere affection, have for them a loving heart, and profit by all opportunities of doing them a service. 2nd. *Never say anything but what is good of them;* that is to say, never complain of them, or of the injuries they have done you; on the contrary, say all the good you can of them. 3rd. *Pray for them*; that is to say, if they have faults or are in the wrong, implore for them the grace which corrects and sanctifies, pity them and beg of Heaven to make them better; if they are in trouble, pray to God to have pity on them and to raise them from the state into which they have fallen. 4th. *Render services to them at every opportunity:* aid them with your advice, your counsels, your credit, with even your purse if necessary, and forestall their needs if they dare not ask you to do so. If they persist in remaining your enemies, continue to love them, as did St. Paul, when he said to the Corinthians: *"Even though you love me less in proportion as I love you more, I most gladly will spend and be spent for your souls"* (II. Cor. xii. 15). Is it thus that we conduct ourselves towards our enemies?

Resolutions and spiritual nosegay as above.

TWENTY-SECOND TUESDAY AFTER PENTECOST

Summary of the Morrow's Meditation.

We will meditate tomorrow upon a sixth characteristic of charity, which is, to be tender and compassionate. We shall see: 1st, how essential to charity is this characteristic; 2nd, how contrary to it is the opposite vice of harshness. We will then make the resolution: 1st, to pity all the afflicted, and to console or solace them to the utmost of our power; 2nd, to avoid hard words, a severe or haughty demeanor, and to be, on the contrary, frank and kind towards all, and to be pleasant and cordial in our behavior. Our spiritual nosegay shall be the words of the Apostle: *"Put ye on the bowels of mercy, benignity, humility, modesty, and patience"* (II. Cor. iii. 12).

Meditation for the Morning.

Let us admire the tenderness with which Jesus Christ loved men and pitied all their woes; how He wept over the death of Lazarus, and mingled His tears with those of Martha and Mary; how He wept over the ruins of faithless Jerusalem; how tender He was towards John His apostle, who delights to call himself the disciple whom Jesus loved (John xxi. 27). Oh, how well these beautiful examples teach us always to be tender and compassionate toward our neighbor! Let us thank our amiable Saviour for so useful a lesson.

FIRST POINT.

We ought to have a Heart full of Tenderness and Compassion for our Neighbor.

True charity is sensitive, respecting everything our neighbor feels, whether it be good or evil; it weeps with those who weep, and rejoices with those who rejoice. It suffers with all who suffer, whether they be present or absent, known or unknown, friends or enemies, neighbors or persons who are far distant, because in all it sees the members of the same body of which it forms a portion; and as in the human body no member suffers without all the other members being filled with compassion for it (I. Cor. xii. 26), as the foot cannot be wounded without the arm being immediately stretched out, the knee bending, the eye-opening wide, and, in a word, the whole body setting to work to be of use to it, so true charity gives a tender and compassionate heart towards all who suffer. A pagan philosopher has said: *"I am a man, and all that interests men cannot be foreign to me"* (Terence). The Christian, with much stronger reason, ought always to be tender towards his neighbor, even as Jesus Christ was, and to have for all bowels of mercy and kindness; it is the text of the law (John xiii. 34; xv. 12; Coloss. iii. 12). He ought always to receive with kindness, with an open expression of face, and with evidence of sincere affection, whoever confides to him his troubles. Every individual will be treated by God in the same way as he has himself treated others (Luke vi. 38). Now we all of us stand in immense need of God treating us with compassion and not with harshness. This is why, even if our brother were our enemy, if he were a great criminal, although the law would have the right to condemn him, we never have the right to rejoice over his misfortunes, or to look at him with an air of triumph. As soon as he has become unfortunate, he has a right to our interest, to our consideration, to our affectionate compassion. If he is in need, we ought to feel how hard it is to suffer cold and hunger when our equals are beside us and perfectly fed and clad; we ought, consequently, to forgive him **for** looking at us with envy. If he has vices, we ought, instead of judging him with inflexible severity, to gain him over to religion by being indulgent and amiable toward him. It is so beautiful, the tender pity which looks with affectionate compassion on all who suffer, all who are sick, in trouble, or in a state of inferiority. It is what has been admirably understood by the Christians of all centuries. St. Paul collects alms, and travels more than three hundred leagues to take the money to the poor at Jerusalem. In 261 the Christians of Alexandria devoted themselves to those stricken by pestilence who had been their persecutors; every house was a hospital, every Christian a sick-nurse. In 379 St. Basil at Cesarea; in 400 St. Fabiola at Rome; in 407 St. Chrysostom at Constantinople, founded hospitals. In the sixth century, St. Remi forms the first establishment of Penitents at Rheims; in 650 St. Landry establishes the Hotel-Dieu at Paris, and the Nuns died there in 1348, through nursing those who are a prey to the pestilence, and the extinct community is immediately renewed. In 850 Robert, Archbishop of Mayence, feeds more than three hundred poor; and in the seventeenth century what did not St. Vincent de Paul do? What have not numerous souls filled with tender and compassionate charity done since then, and what do they not do every day? It is in the presence of such spectacles that unfortunate men, consoled, at finding themselves treated with such tender respect by those who are above them, feel their hearts to be filled with gratitude, and they understand why the rich is rich, why the man who occupies a place of dignity is great. Instead of following these rules, do we not imitate the hard men of whom the prophet Amos speaks, who are indifferent to the sufferings of their brethren? (Amos vi. 6.)

SECOND POINT.

Harshness is wholly Contrary to Charity.

To be wanting in consideration to a man stricken by misfortune is of all kinds of baseness the most unworthy. *"Laugh no man to scorn in the bitterness of his soul,"* says the Holy Ghost, *"for there is one that humbleth and exalteth, God who seeth all"* (Ecclus. vii. 12). To sadden any one who is afflicted by harsh words, by an unkind manner; to look down on an inferior, upon someone we do not know from the height of our grandeur; to speak to him in a haughty and austere way, and to be curt and cross in our behavior, is cruelty unworthy of a Christian who is speaking to his brother. Even if he had been wanting to us in some respect or other, it is ignoble vengeance to refuse to do him a service, not to wish to speak to him or recognize him; or if we are obliged to do so, to address him rudely, with a sharp tone of voice and a cold expression of countenance, to rejoice when he does not succeed in his projects or falls into affliction. True charity behaves in a very different manner; it is indulgent to those who are in the wrong, it is tender to those who suffer or who are in affliction, it makes itself all things to all men (I. Cor. ix. 22): poor with those who are poor, infirm with those who are infirm, ignorant with those who are ignorant.

Resolutions and spiritual nosegay as above.

TWENTY-SECOND WEDNESDAY AFTER PENTECOST

Summary of the Morrow's Meditation.

We will meditate tomorrow upon a seventh characteristic of Christian charity, which is indulgence, and we shall see : 1st, that we ought never to think evil of our neighbor unless the evil be proved; 2nd, we ought never to speak evil of him unless the evil be known, or there is some useful reason to induce us to speak of it. We will then make the resolution: 1st, to entertain, in regard to our neighbor, an indulgent disposition which will make us delight in always thinking well of him, and to correct the critical or censorious spirit in which we indulge; 2nd, to watch over all our words, in order not to allow a single one to pass our lips which may wound charity, or which we would wish should not be said of us. Our spiritual nosegay shall be the words of St. James: "*If any man offend not in word, the same is a perfect man*" (James iii. 2).

Meditation for the Morning.

Let us adore Our Lord repeating several times in the gospel the precept of charity. It is a proof of the great desire He has to see us avoid all that may wound this divine virtue; it is the condemnation of the license which we so often permit ourselves to commit in thinking and speaking evil of our neighbor. Let us thank Him for the kind sentiments He has for us all.

FIRST POINT.

We ought never to Think Evil of our Neighbor unless the Evil be Proved.

"Charity," says the Apostle, *"thinketh no evil"* (I. Cor. xiii. 5). Far from allowing ourselves to indulge in unfavorable judgments in regard to our neighbor, to suspect his intentions and his defects, it delights in thinking all the good that is possible in regard to him. It only believes the evil which is incontestably proved of him; and even, unless our position obliges us to conduct ourselves in a different manner, it conceals it, excuses it, and believes as little as possible of it. Very different are the critical, censorious spirits who are always ready to think evil and to give an evil interpretation to everything. They are presumptuous men, who think themselves wiser and better informed than others, who set up a tribunal within themselves, whence they judge everything, cut everything short, pronounce sentences without appeal respecting both persons and things. They do not think anything good except what they have done themselves, and cast blame in full measure upon everything that is done and said by others. Hence such numerous evils springing up in society and in families; forgetfulness of respect towards superiors, of consideration towards equals, and of those sweet relationships of charity and mutual esteem which form the charm of life; such persons can do nothing but discredit others, and lower them by rash judgments, not remembering that rash judgments, in serious matters, are a mortal sin. Therefore, God has a horror of these universal censors, who fancy that they alone are possessed of wisdom and common sense; He curses them (Is. v. 21). Have we not many reproaches to address to ourselves on this head? Are we not easily led to think evil of our neighbor, to conceive suspicions of him, to form rash judgments, and to give vent to them in our conversations?

SECOND POINT.

We ought Never to Speak Evil of our Neighbor unless the Evil be Known, and unless we have some Useful Reason for Speaking of it.

To speak evil of our neighbor, or to calumniate him, is a vice which excites the hatred of God (Rom. i. 30). It is an evil which St. Paul declares to be as worthy of reprobation as is theft (I. Cor. vi. 10). It is even something worse than theft, because the reputation which the calumniator takes away is of a much higher order and is worth far more than all the treasures which are stolen by a thief. Lastly, it is an ignoble product of the worst kind of propensities, and of what propensities! Sometimes it is of pride, which fancies that it raises itself in proportion as it lowers others, and which flatters itself interiorly to be, or to make itself believed to be, better than those who are calumniated; sometimes it is a low kind of jealousy, which tries to obscure the splendor of everything which effaces it, and thinks others worthy of blame only because they are praised; at other times it is concealed hatred, which sheds upon words the bitterness hidden in the heart; a miserable vanity, which endeavors to make itself valued at the expense of others, and is very glad if, with enough malice to calumniate, it joins enough of wit to give pleasure; a harmful weakness, which cannot keep back a single word; a cold piece of barbarity, which strikes a person who is absent: considerations which led St. Augustine expressly to forbid this vice at his table by means of an inscription engraved upon the wall. Let us examine whether we have the same horror of calumny that this great saint entertained. There are very few, even amongst Christians, says St. Paulinus, who completely uproot the habit of this vice out of their heart. "It might be said that many people cannot say anything but what is evil of their neighbor, and that no conversation has any charm for them unless some one or other is torn to pieces, some reputation or other immolated" (St. Paulinus, *Ep. ad. Celant.*). Are we not of that number?

Resolutions and spiritual nosegay as above.

Twenty-second Thursday after Pentecost

Summary of tbc Morrow's Meditation.

We will meditate tomorrow upon an eighth characteristic of charity, which is benevolence, and we shall see: 1st, in what this benevolence consists; 2nd, the reasons which render it obligatory on us. We will then make the resolution: 1st, to endeavor to make all who surround us happy, and to endeavor always to give pleasure to our neighbor; 2nd, to forget ourselves to the point of making the joys of another our joys, his troubles our troubles. Our spiritual nosegay shall be the words of the Apostle: *"Let everyone please his neighbor unto good"* (Rom. xv. 2).

Meditation for the Morning.

Let us adore Our Lord Jesus Christ teaching us by His apostle to love one another reciprocally as brethren, and to be full of amiable intentions towards one another (I. Pet. i. 22). Let us thank Him for such loving advice, and let us propose to ourselves to profit by it.

FIRST POINT.

Characteristics of Christian Benevolence.

This benevolence, as the name itself indicates, consists in wishing all kinds of good things to our neighbor, to obtain for him, in fact, all the good things we can, and in this manner, as far as is possible, to make all those who surround us happy. St. Paul, in his first epistle to the Corinthians (I. Cor. xiii. 4, *et seq.),* admirably describes the characteristics of this benevolent charity. Charity, he says, is patient and gentle, full of reserve and of circumspection, that it may offend no one ; it never speaks harshly, or answers with bitterness, or demands arrogantly. Far from being jealous or envious, it wishes others all possible happiness, and does not rejoice any less in their success than in its own advantages. Far from wounding others from caprice or bad temper, it proceeds in everything with a wisdom and a moderation which arranges for the best all that has to be arranged. Far from giving offence by pretentiousness, it is full of deference, and is the first to give honor to whom honor is due. It has so little ambition and cares so little for its own interests that it forgets itself and finds its happiness in whatever advantages others possess over it. Whatever may be the displeasure which is caused to it, it is obliging towards every one, and thinks only of the evil which might have been inflicted upon it. It is filled with joy when it sees its brethren making progress in virtue, and it is a great grief to it to see any one under the empire of vice. It endures everything rather than be wanting in kindness in the smallest things; it believes all the good it can of its neighbor, and has no difficulty in deferring to the opinions of others. Always ready to judge its brethren favorably, it never despairs of the reformation of any sinner whatever. Lastly, rather than be the occasion of discomfort to others, it cheerfully bears all kinds of burdens without even complaining or allowing its fatigue to be perceived. Let us examine ourselves as to whether we possess all these characteristics of Christian benevolence.

SECOND POINT.

The Reasons which render Benevolence a Law incumbent on us.

1st. Our neighbor is a child of God. Now let us suppose that a great monarch has confided to us the care of his child, the heir to his throne, conjuring us to be prodigal of good offices towards him, and promising to recognize them by all the munificence in his power, and even by a throne, with what zeal and kindness should we not treat such a child! Now a child of God is very different from the child of a monarch; heavenly recompenses are very different from all earthly recompenses, and very preferable to all thrones. 2nd. Our neighbor is a living image of Jesus Christ, another Jesus Christ, so much so that Our Lord counts as done to Himself what is done to the very least of His children. Now what benevolence is there not due to this adorable Saviour? 3rd. We ought to love our neighbor as Jesus Christ loved us (John xiii. 34; xv. 12). Now what was the benevolence of Jesus Christ towards us? 4th. We ought to act towards others as we would wish they should act towards ourselves. Our hearts have need of kindness. If we had all we could wish for, we should be unhappy if we were surrounded by persons who were unkind to us; whilst, on the contrary, if we were in need of a great many things, kind hearts full of delicate attentions would console us in our troubles. 5th. Lastly, if we are kind to others they will be kind to us; our kindness will gain their hearts, and divine charity will embellish our existence with its sweetest charms. Let us examine our conscience; have we this spirit of benevolence towards our neighbor? Do we feel pleasure in obliging him every time that an opportunity presents itself, and do we seize upon it with all our heart?

Resolutions and spiritual nosegay as above.

TWENTY-SECOND FRIDAY AFTER PENTECOST

Summary of the Morrow's Meditation.

We will meditate tomorrow upon a ninth characteristic of charity, which is Christian amiability; and in order to form a just idea of it we will study it in Jesus Christ Himself, our adorable model, and we shall see how amiable He was: 1st, in His character; 2nd, in His manners; 3rd, in His language. We will then make the resolution: 1st, to treat everyone with perfect urbanity, without ever allowing ourselves to give way to a word or to conduct which shall not be in accordance with the most exquisite politeness; 2nd, in particular to exercise a strict surveillance over our temper, in order to repress outbursts and hastiness. Our spiritual nosegay shall be the words of Solomon: *"A man wise in words shall make himself beloved" (Ecclus.* xx. 13).

Meditation for the Morning.

Let us adore Our Lord Jesus Christ showing Himself amiable in everything: in His character, His manners, His language. He does not content Himself with not giving pain in any way, but He desires to give pleasure and be amiable in every respect For if St. Paul says, *"I in all things please all men "* (I. Cor. x. 33), he immediately adds: It is from Jesus Christ that I have learnt this science: *"Be ye followers of me, as I also am of Christ"* (Ibid. xi. 1). Let us thank our divine Saviour for so useful a lesson.

FIRST POINT.

Jesus Christ is Amiable in His Disposition.

In this adorable Saviour there was no ill-humor, none of those fits of bad temper which cause it to be said of some persons, that in order to be well received we must choose the proper moment. In Him there was a serenity of disposition that nothing could trouble; He is the same when He is blamed as when He is praised, when He is insulted as when He is honored, when the people wish to stone Him as when they wish to make Him king, when the crowd presses upon and hustles Him (Luke viii. 45) as when He is alone in the desert or on the mountain. What a beautiful example for us, above all for persons subject to bad temper, who are the dishonor of devotion, angels in church and disagreeable at home! Are we not of this number?

SECOND POINT.

Jesus Christ is Amiable in His Manner.

Jesus Christ, even if He had not been God, would still have been the most upright, the most amiable, the most courteous man that ever lived. A heavenly modesty shone in all His person; there was nothing somber or melancholy in His features, nothing hasty or turbulent, nothing flighty or frivolous in His manners (Is. xlii. 4). He was characterized by a serenity full of ease and grace, a kindness in the expression of His eyes, an amenity in His deportment, a frankness in the expression of His face, a genial and amiable manner, which always gave pleasure. During the first thirty years of His life He carried His courtesy towards Mary and Joseph to the point of deferring to all their wishes and condescending to all their desires (Luke ii. 51). At the epoch when He made His appearance in the temple in the midst of the doctors, He did not speak in the tone of a master, as He certainly had the right to do; but He listened, He questioned, He who had nothing to learn; and if He spoke it was only after having been invited to do so. During the three years of His mission He was faithful to the rules of courtesy and good breeding; visiting the mother-in-law of St Peter, who was sick; Martha and Mary, who were in affliction; making Himself little with the little, and knowing how to show His grandeur at the table of the Pharisee; lastly, His conduct was such, in every circumstance, that from nothing more than His example and His maxims there might be drawn up a set of perfect rules of Christian civility. Whence we may conclude that not to be always amiable in our manners, always pleasant and polite, is a great defect even in the eyes of faith, since it is to depart from the model which is obligatory upon all Christians.

THIRD POINT.

Jesus Christ is Amiable in His Conversation.

The prophet beheld Him in the coming ages so full of grace in all His words that His lips seemed to distil amenity and sweetness (Ps. xliv. 3); and the gospel, confirming the prophecy, relates that the words which flowed from His mouth were so kind, so amiable, so gracious, that the people marveled at it (Luke iv. 22). Never a contentious word, never any dispute (Matt. xii. 19), never a harsh or wounding speech, never a quick or angry word except against the profaners of the temple, against hypocrites and great men who abused the authority they possessed. He was, of all men, the wise man who makes himself amiable in all that he says (Ecclus. xx. 13), the good man who has on his tongue a superabundance of sweetness and of grace (Ibid. vi. 5). Is it thus that we speak? Do we measure our words in such a manner as never to give pain to our neighbor, and to render him, on the contrary, happy in his relations with us? Is our conversation equally removed from the affected elegance which is unpleasant, and from the frivolous language ill-suited to an educated man, and still less to a good Christian? Is it composed only of good and suitable language which tends to infuse into the souls of our hearers a sweet joy and the love of virtue?

Resolutions and spiritual nosegay as above.

TWENTY-SECOND SATURDAY AFTER PENTECOST

Summary of the Morrow's Meditation.

We will continue to study Christian amiability in Our Lord, and we shall see how amiable He was: 1st, in family life; 2nd, towards inferiors and the afflicted; 3rd, towards those who had faults; 4th, towards His enemies. We will then make the resolution: 1st, always to be amiable, attentive, and kind in the family circle; 2nd, always cordially to receive little children, the poor, and the afflicted; 3rd, to treat the faults and the wrongs done to us by others with nothing but kindness and charity. Our spiritual nosegay shall be the words of the Apostle: *"I in all things please all men, not seeking that which is profitable to myself"* (I. Cor. x. 33). *"Be ye followers of me as I also am of Christ"* (Ibid. xi. 1).

Meditation for the Morning.

Let us adore Our Lord, so amiable towards all men. He may well say like the Apostle : I strive to be amiable to the little as well as to the great, to the poor as well as to the rich, to those who are afflicted as well as to those who rejoice, to persons who have innumerable faults as well as to the most perfect, to my enemies as well as to my friends (I. Cor. x. 33). Let us thank Him for such universal amiability and let us render Him all our homage.

FIRST POINT.

Jesus Christ is Amiable in Family Life.

Jesus Christ lived a family life as an inferior during thirty years, and as a master during three. As an inferior, He always honored God His Father in those whom He obeyed; as a master, He always spoke with gentleness, reproved without ill-temper, commanded by entreating. Whether as inferior or as master, He neglected nothing whereby to render all around Him happy. It is thus that He teaches us the family life, which is the safeguard of morals, the protector of virtues, and that He teaches all the members of a family to embellish each other's existence by a reciprocity of affection and delicate attentions. He teaches fathers and mothers to make their homes happy; children to show gratitude, respect, and love to the authors of their being, to console and gladden their old age by their amiable words and manners; servants to cherish and faithfully serve their masters, and masters to see in those who serve them brethren and sisters in Jesus Christ. Is it thus that we conduct ourselves?

SECOND POINT.

Jesus Christ is Amiable towards Inferiors and the Afflicted.

He is amiable towards little children; He calls them to Him, caresses them, presses them to His breast, places His hands on them and blesses them. He is amiable towards the poor; He is born, He lives and dies in their condition; to render it honorable and more endurable, He mixes with them as though He were one of them. He evangelizes them before other men, and declares that He looks upon as done to Himself all the good that is done to them, and as refused to Himself all that is refused to them; He takes from amongst them the chiefs of His Church to govern kings and nations here on earth, and to judge them at the last day as His assessors. He is amiable towards the afflicted; *"Come to Me, all you that labor and are burdened, and I will refresh you"* (Matt. xi. 28), He says to them; He feels the woes of others as though He suffered them Himself (Mark viii. 2), and He weeps at Bethania with the relatives and friends of Lazarus (John xi. 35). Let us examine our conscience; are we, like Jesus Christ, amiable towards childhood? It is being perverse to despise or grieve it unjustly, and it is being absurd to try to form it to virtue through anger or blows. Are we amiable towards the poor? They are already sufficiently unhappy, without being made more so by a reproachful tone, by ill-tempered or contemptuous words; these kind of speeches embitter them; they feel that it is cruelty to make them pay for alms by humiliation. Nothing, on the contrary, consoles them more than to be treated with consideration. A kind word, says the Holy Spirit, is worth more to them than the gift they receive (Ecclus. xviii. 15, 16). Are we amiable towards the afflicted? Misfortune is a sacred thing. There is no baseness more odious than that of being wanting in consideration towards an afflicted brother, as there is no delight greater for a kind heart than to alleviate the pain of those who suffer.

THIRD POINT.

Jesus Christ is Amiable towards those who have Faults.

He lived three years with twelve fishermen, people of no education, without refinement or good breeding, and their want of manners did not anger Him; He never treats them with mortifying words or an act calculated to give pain. He suffers everything from them without making them suffer anything, without allowing to escape Him, with regard to even those whom He knew would deny Him, betray, or abandon Him, one word or one glance which would wound them. He lives in the midst of them, less as their master than their servant, to teach us to be amiable even towards those who displease us by their character by their wrong-headedness, or the vices of their heart. And we, who despite all our faults expect that others should be amiable towards us, by what right do we require that others should be without defects in order that we should be amiable towards them?

FOURTH POINT.

Jesus Christ is Amiable to His Enemies.

They overwhelm Him with insults, call Him a Samaritan and a man possessed by the devil, and He calmly answers them, "*Which of you shall convince Me of sin?*" (John viii. 46.) They want to stone Him, and He contents Himself with saying to them, "*Many woodworks I have shown you; for which of those works do you stone Me?*" (John x. 32.) Judas betrays Him with a kiss, and He calls him His friend (Matt. xxvi. 50). Herod delivers Him up to public derision; the soldiers scourge Him and crown Him with thorns; the people declare Him to be worse than the robber and the homicide Barabbas; His executioners crucify Him, and in the midst of all His enemies, who are so unjust and so barbarous, He does not allow a look, a word, a gesture, expressive of displeasure to escape Him. Alas! is it thus we treat our enemies? The least offence excites in us coldness, antipathies, desires of vengeance, rancors, an odious mixture of pride and baseness. Let us examine our conscience upon so important a point of Christian morals.

Resolutions and spiritual nosegay as above.

TWENTY-THIRD SUNDAY AFTER PENTECOST

The Gospel according to St. Matthew, ix. 18-26.

"And it came to pass that as Jesus was speaking these things unto John's disciples, behold a certain ruler came up, and adored Him, saying: Lord, my daughter is even now dead; but come, lay Thy hand upon her, and she shall live. And Jesus, rising up, followed him, with His disciples. And behold a woman who was troubled with an issue of blood twelve years came behind Him, and touched the hem of His garment. For she said within herself: If I shall touch only His garment, I shall be healed. But Jesus turning and seeing her, said: Be of good heart, daughter, thy faith hath made thee whole. And the woman was made whole from that hour. And when Jesus was come into the house of the ruler, and saw the minstrels and the multitude making a rout, He said: Give place, for the girl is not dead, but sleepeth. And they laughed Him to scorn. And when the multitude was put forth, He went in, and took her by the hand. And the maid arose. And the fame hereof went abroad into all that country."

Summary of the Morrow's Meditation.

We will meditate tomorrow upon the gospel of the day, and we shall learn from it: 1st, to have recourse with confidence to God in all our troubles; 2nd, not to put any confidence in creatures. Our resolution shall be: 1st, not to count upon human means in order to get out of the difficulties in which we find ourselves; 2nd, to call God to our aid by fervent and persevering prayers, accompanied by humility at the sight of our miseries, and of confidence at the sight of the divine mercies. Our spiritual nosegay shall be the words of Ecclesiasticus: *"No one hath hoped in the Lord and hath been* confounded" (Ecclus. ii. 11).

Meditation for the Morning.

Let us adore Our Lord curing the sick who have recourse to Him and thereby teaching us that it is to Him we must have recourse in the troubles of life. Let us adore His power, let us bless His goodness.

FIRST POINT.

We ought in all our Troubles to have Recourse to God with Confidence.

The gospel of the day shows us, first, a prince of the synagogue, who, plunged into grief by the death of his daughter, aged twelve, comes to Jesus, prostrates himself at His feet, and adores Him as the master of life and of death. *"Lord,"* he says, *"my daughter is even now dead; but come, lay Thy hand upon her, and she shall live."* Could there be more faith in the power of the Saviour, more confidence in His goodness? Therefore his faith and confidence were not deceived; Jesus takes the young girl by the hand, and she rises. The cure is sudden, complete; all are forced to recognize how good it is to confide in the power and the goodness of Jesus, and how, sensible as He is to our afflictions, He compassionates all our sufferings. The same day a person attacked by a serious infirmity, not daring to present herself to the Saviour, so unworthy does she deem herself to speak to Him, followed Him behind, mingling in the crowd where she tried to hide herself, and saying to herself, *"If I shall touch only the hem of His garment, I shall be cured."* Jesus, to whom the secrets of all hearts are known, heard this interior language; and touched by so much humility on the one side, and such lively faith on the other, and such entire confidence in the weakest of means, the simple contact of His garment, He turns round and says to her: *"Be of good heart, daughter, thy faith hath made thee whole,"* and at that moment she was cured. What a marvelous effect of prayer uttered with humility and confidence! Humility without confidence is useless;

confidence without humility is presumption; humility and confidence joined together are all-powerful over the heart of God. Happy those who take these holy dispositions to Mass, to Communion, to visits to the Blessed Sacrament, where we have something better far than the garment of the Saviour, since we have therein His body, His blood, His soul, and His divinity!

SECOND POINT.

If Dependence can be Placed upon the Support of Creatures; it is Deceptive.

The prince of the synagogue had his daughter's room filled with relations, friends, mourners, players on instruments, and a crowd of persons who had gathered together to console him. But what could they do to alleviate his grief? Men, said Job, *"are all troublesome comforters"* (Job xvi. 2), and all human means, without God, are powerless to cure our afflictions. Therefore, the Saviour made all the multitude leave the room. He had no need of the help or concurrence of any witness. He alone was sufficient for the work He willed to do, and He proved it in a high degree by raising from the dead the youthful daughter of the prince of the synagogue. He did not show this any the less plainly in suddenly curing the poor woman who followed Him. She had had recourse to a great number of doctors, who had tried many remedies; all had been useless. Then she addresses herself to Jesus with faith and confidence, and immediately she is cured. So true it is that in God alone must we place our confidence; not, doubtless, that we must disdain human aid, it would be tempting God not to have recourse to it; but whilst employing it we must feel that it will be of efficacy only in proportion as it pleases God to bestow it, and that He will give this efficacy only in proportion to the measure of our confidence in His power and goodness.

Resolutions and spiritual nosegay as above.

Twenty-third Monday after Pentecost

Summary of the Morrow's Meditation.

After having meditated for so long a time on our duties towards God and our neighbor, we will now meditate upon our duties towards ourselves. We will commence by Christian modesty, and we shall see that it is a duty imposed upon us: 1st, by respect for the presence of God; 2nd, the edification of our neighbor; 3rd, the interests of our salvation. We will then make the resolution: 1st, to hold modesty in great esteem, as being a virtue of great importance; 2nd, to observe this virtue not only in public and under the eyes of men, but also in private and when we have no other witnesses but God. Our spiritual nosegay shall be the words of the Apostle: *"Let your modesty be known to all men. The Lord is nigh"* (Philipp, iv. 5).

Meditation for the Morning.

Let us adore the modesty of Our Lord conversing upon earth. This virtue had in Him charms which ravished men and angels, and which made Him to be recognized, even in the midst of His abasement, as the God of sovereign majesty (St. Bernard). Let us offer to Him in this state our homage of adoration, of praise, and of love.

FIRST POINT.

Respect for the Presence of God Imposes upon us the Duty of Christian Modesty.

Modesty does not consist only in the outward expression of the face, or in what is visible exteriorly in the manners and tone; that would be only a pharisaical virtue, which under a beautiful outside might hide a very different interior. All real virtue has its essential principles in the heart, and the exterior ought only to be the reflection, as it were, of the piety existing within. In conformity with this principle, modesty, rightly so-called, is the respect due to the presence of God, inspiring man with a serious demeanor, such as he ought to maintain under the eyes of so lofty a majesty. God sees me, the man of faith says; He looks at me night and day, in solitude as well as in society, outside as well as inside the house (III. Kings xvii. 1). At all times His eye follows the whole of my person and my behavior (Prov. xvi. 2); in all places He sees me, whether I do evil or whether I do good (Ibid. xv. 3). I must therefore always and everywhere observe the perfect modesty, the irreproachable decency, which is proper to such august society (Philipp, iv. 5). If a glance of the eyes of God makes the earth tremble, shakes the pillars of hell, seizes the angels with holy fear, how could I, when He is beholding me, allow myself to indulge in frivolity, in buffoonery, in loud laughter, which is wanting in dignity? God beholds me! The witness of my actions, He will be the severe judge of them and will make me render an account of my unmeasured language, of the license I have permitted to my eyes and the want of modesty in my manners. God beholds me! This thought made the holy bishop of Geneva observe so much modesty that an indiscreet eye examining him at a moment when a man, imagining himself to be alone, sometimes allows himself to indulge in a more free and easy behavior, found that he was always an exact observer of the rules of the most austere decency, as well in secret as in public. The Lord beheld him, and he looked upon such an august presence as more worthy of respect than all mankind put together.

SECOND POINT.

The Edification of our Neighbor Requires of us Perfect Modesty on our Part.

Every man, says the Scripture, has received from God the mission to labor for the salvation of his neighbor (Ecclus. xvii. 12). Now, it is only in edifying him by our modesty that we can each of us fulfil this divine mission. All cannot preach, but we can all edify. A modest and recollected countenance makes the dissipated soul return to duty, stops it in its ramblings, reproaches it for its frivolities, recalls it to the care of its salvation, to compunction for its faults, and to holy desires for heaven. Witness St. Lucian, the mere sight of whom converted the pagans; a St. Bernardine, whose mere presence inspired all his companions with recollection; a St. Francis of Assisi, who had only to walk along the streets in order to make every one turn to God, and to withdraw sinners from their wanderings. *"To be modest is to preach virtue,"* he said. St. Ambrose had said before him: *"The sight of a just man is a remedy for the ills of the soul, and what is there more beautiful than to have only to show one's self in order to do good"* Is it thus that we labor for the salvation of our brethren? Do we take care to regulate our exterior so well that all who see us are edified?

THIRD POINT.

The Interest of our own Salvation makes Modesty incumbent on us.

There exist between the exterior and the interior intimate relations, which, according to the testimony of Solomon, make the one to be known by the other (Ecclus. xix. 26). The deportment, the laugh, the manners, enable us to know what the man is (Ibid. 27). Behold the child of Belial, the Holy Spirit says; you will have it in your power to see into the bottom of his heart by means of his exterior alone, like those who look into the water and see their face distinctly reflected in it; he is vain and uneasy, he walks with a ferocious kind of air, he turns his eyes in every direction, he is constantly moving his feet, gesticulating with his hands (Prov. vi. 12, 13). Exterior immodesty puts the soul in great peril, for this poor soul is like a besieged city, open to all the assaults of the enemy, without walls, without gates, without defense (Prov. xxv. 28). The senses, says the Holy Spirit, are the gates whereby evil enters into the heart. If modesty keeps these gates closed, the heart feels itself to be safe; if they are left open, defeat is certain, according to the words of the prophet: My eye has delivered up my soul a prey to my enemies (Lam. iii. 51).

And that is truer today than ever, when so many dangerous objects are presented to the sight, when the dress and the manners of so many persons seem to conspire to seduce and ruin souls.

Resolutions and spiritual nosegay as above.

TWENTY-THIRD TUESDAY AFTER PENTECOST

Summary of the Morrow's Meditation.

We will meditate tomorrow on the advantages of modesty, and we shall see that this virtue is: 1st, the charm of society; 2nd, the path of perfection. We will then make the resolution: 1st, henceforth to hold modesty in greater esteem, and no longer to look upon it as the portion of simple, scrupulous, timid persons, who do not know how to conduct themselves in society; 2nd, to observe modesty in our eyes, by depriving ourselves of looking at what we have no need to see; in our manner of walking, by never taking hasty, precipitous steps; in our conversations, by willingly deferring to the opinion of others, when conscience permits. Our spiritual nosegay shall be the words of the Apostle: *"Put ye on therefore, as the elect of God, the bowels of modesty"* (Coloss. iii. 12).

Meditation for the Morning.

Let us adore Jesus Christ under the figure of the wise man whom the Holy Spirit represents to us as wearing modesty painted on the features of his face (Prov. xvii. 24). It was sufficient to see our divine Saviour in order to recognize that there was in Him something more than a man. In fact, the saints tell us that modesty is a ray, and as it were a reflection, of the Divinity. Let us render our whole homage to the Man-God for so ravishing a modesty.

FIRST POINT.

Modesty is the Charm of Society.

Who, in fact, has not experienced when in the society of a modest man a pure and intimate pleasure which has something of heaven itself in it? Who has been able to prevent himself from feeling inexpressible delight in looking at the modesty of his countenance, and of his eyes, and the propriety of his behavior? It is difficult to please everyone, it has often been said: this privilege has been reserved for a modest man. There is in him an inexpressible something which captivates esteem, which charms the heart, and pleases the most exacting. The mere sight of him gives pleasure; his manners, equally distant from affected politeness and vulgar rusticity, are at once simple and amiable, and we see that it is his heart alone which has taught them to him. His conversation is genial, humble, tranquil; he does not indulge in arguments of disputes, because, very different from men of a presumptuous frame of mind, who consider that their opinion decides everything, he is reserved in pronouncing an opinion. If he does give an opinion, it is with simplicity and without being attached to it; he does not endeavor to make his own ideas prevail, and he prefers to allow himself to be conquered by yielding with gentleness rather than to be triumphant by means of disputing obstinately. He does not belong to the class of great talkers who seem to desire that no one should speak save themselves alone, any more than he belongs to the opposite class of taciturn persons who, by their ill-regulated silence, are a weariness to others. He has none of the pretension and self-sufficiency which aims at domineering, at making itself to be listened to, and gain esteem. Looking on himself, on the contrary, as the last of all men, he feels within himself and he outwardly testifies all kinds of considerations and of amiabilities towards his brethren; in his eyes they are the holy children of God and he is their servant, who ought to do everything to make himself agreeable to them. Hence his words, which are seasoned with goodness and gentleness; his manners, which are full of grace and amenity. This is how modesty is rendered the ornament of all the virtues, the honor of religion, the link of charity between men, and the charm of society. At what point have we arrived in the practice of so beautiful a virtue?

SECOND POINT.

Modesty is the Pathway of Perfection.

The masters of the spiritual life represent perfection as a height which we reach
by three degrees. In the first we expiate past sins; in the second we form ourselves
to virtue; in the third the soul, detached from all things, unites itself to God, its
principle and its end. Now it is by modesty that we pass through these three
degrees, 1st. We expiate by it past sins. Without having recourse to hair-shirts,
modesty is of itself a magnificent penance; it is a universal mortification which
affects all the senses, the eyes, the tongue, the behavior, the deportment; it is a
mortification possible to all kinds of persons, a mortification which does not
injure the health, which does not exhaust the strength, which does no harm
either to the head or the lungs; a mortification which is practicable in all places,
private or public, sacred or profane; at all times, at night as well as during the day,
in company as well as in solitude; a mortification which is always wise, wherein
excesses need not be feared ; a mortification, lastly, of the most sanctifying kind,
which fashions the soul to the great law of abnegation, by accustoming it to fight
against seeking after its own comfort, the frivolity and license of its fancies. 2nd.
By modesty we rise to all the virtues, according to the saying of the Holy Ghost:
The fruits of modesty are the fear of God, spiritual riches, and a perfect life
(Prov. xxiii. 4). The first fruit of modesty: the fear of God, for it disposes the soul
to reflect upon God and upon itself, to the order and wisdom which regulate
words and movements with perfect discretion; the second fruit of modesty:
spiritual riches, which are a more lively and actual faith, a greater confidence,
a more ardent charity; lastly, modesty has, as its last fruit, a perfect life, because
a modest exterior favors interior recollection and purity of soul, whilst, if the
senses are not under control, the soul is like a house open to all passers-by,
with continual goings out and goings in, the entrance of exterior objects which
dissipate, and the goings forth of the heart to exterior objects to attach itself to
them and to become sullied by the contact (St Gregory). 3rd. We unite ourselves
to God by modesty. The eyes being cast down to the ground, says St. Bernard,
cause the heart to rise to heaven; and the less we occupy ourselves with outward
things, the more easy it is for us to occupy ourselves with God within. It is then
that we enjoy Him, that we fill ourselves with Him, that we live in Him, leaving
below ourselves all creatures, with their tumult and agitation, which distract us
from God (Ps. lxxv. 3).

Resolutions and spiritual nosegay as above.

TWENTY-THIRD WEDNESDAY AFTER PENTECOST

Summary of the Morrow's Meditation.

From meditations upon modesty, we will pass to meditations upon the holy virtue of purity, which is as the sister of it, and we shall see: 1st, the esteem and love we ought to have for this virtue; 2nd, the care with which we ought to preserve it. We will then make the resolution: 1st, to watch constantly over our heart and over our senses, in order preciously to guard the treasure of purity within us; 2nd, carefully to avoid all that may expose us to lose it. We will retain as our spiritual nosegay the words of the Saviour: *"How beautiful and honorable is the chaste generation with glory"* (Wis. iv. 1.)

Meditation for the Morning.

Let us adore the singular esteem and the great love of Our Saviour for purity. He loved this virtue so greatly that He willed to be born of a virgin mother, to have as His adopted father St. Joseph, who was a virgin, and as His beloved disciple the virgin disciple. Let us admire, let us praise, let us bless such sentiments, and ask of Him a share in them.

FIRST POINT.

The Esteem and Love we ought to have for Purity.

Purity is a wholly divine virtue, which "makes *him who preserves it an angel, and him who loses it,*" says one of the Fathers, *"a demon."* It so enchants the heart of God, that He loves pure souls as His spouses (Prov. xxii. 11). He overwhelms them with His graces and His favors, reserves for them His tenderest caresses, His most intimate communications (Matt. v. 8). In heaven they will have a special place, side by side with the angels (Apoc. xiv. 4), and they will sing an ever new song which they alone will be able to sing (Ibid. 3). Could the Holy Spirit tell us more plainly that nothing in the world equals the excellence and the value of purity? (Ecclus. xxvi. 20.) Do we hold it in this high esteem?

SECOND POINT.

The Care we ought to Take in Order to Preserve Purity.

If there be nothing in the world more precious than this virtue, there is also nothing easier to lose and more difficult to recover once it is lost. It is like a well-polished mirror which the slightest breath tarnishes; like a lovely flower, but so delicate that a nothing fades it; like a precious crystal of infinite price, but which is very fragile; like a treasure carried in a vessel of clay which it is easy to break (II. Cor. iv. 7). Whence it follows that we ought to neglect nothing in order to preserve or prevent the loss of it. We ought not to care what it may cost us to obtain so great a possession, neither frequent and fervent prayers, attention to ourselves to put away from our imagination dangerous ideas and reveries, from our mind immodest thoughts, from our heart carnal affections; nor the abstaining from tender and sentient affections with persons of an opposite sex, however holy and spiritual they may be; nor the keeping a restraint over the senses, especially the eyes. We must flee as far as possible from everything in which there is any danger, keep ourselves away from the slightest temptations, because, on the one hand, the poison which corrupts purity is so subtle that it insinuates itself into the heart with extreme facility, and, on the other hand, the weakness and malignity of the flesh are very much inclined towards it; we must, lastly, avoid the least faults which have regard to this matter, because all of them are of extreme consequence; we must do and suffer nothing which has even the shadow or the appearance only of impurity, and keep ourselves in a continual state of self-distrust, without ever reassuring ourselves by our experience in the past, because he who has not fallen for a long time is always exposed to the danger of falling again (St. Jerome, *Ep. ad Nepot.*). Do we bring all these precautions to bear in relation to the preservation of this precious virtue?

Resolutions and spiritual nosegay as above.

Twenty-Third Thursday After Pentecost

Summary of the Morrow's Meditation.

After having meditated upon the excellence of purity and the care we ought to take in order to preserve it, we will meditate upon the horrible vice which is its opposite, and we shall see: 1st, that it is supremely odious to God; 2nd, that it does man an incomparable evil. We will then make the resolution: 1st, to be on our guard against all dangerous occasions, above all against idleness and too great freedom in the use of our eyes; 2nd, to send away the temptation at the very instant that it presents itself, not by combating it in a direct manner, but by making a diversion. Our spiritual nosegay shall be the words of St. Timothy: *"Keep thyself chaste"* (I. Tim. v. 22).

Meditation for the Morning.

Let us adore the infinite holiness of God, supremely detesting sin, and amongst all sins pursuing the sin of impurity with special hatred. Let us at the same time adore His justice, visiting the vice of impurity with His most terrible chastisements, often even in this life, but above all in hell. Let us render our most fervent homage to His holiness and His justice.

FIRST POINT.

Impurity is Supremely Odious to God.

Of all vices it is the one which excites in the highest degree the horror and the vengeance of God. It is the vice which buried the human race beneath the waters of the deluge (Gen. vi. 3), which made fire from heaven descend upon Sodom and Gomorrah, and which still every day calls down upon earth so many private misfortunes, so many public calamities. No vice, in fact, is more opposed to the infinite purity of God; none more directly profanes His temple and His dwelling, seeing that our bodies are temples of God wherein His holy Spirit dwells (I. Cor. iii. 16), and that by communion they become living ciboriums, tabernacles animated by the Holy Eucharist; a horribly profanation against which the Holy Spirit has pronounced the anathema: *"If any man violate the temple of God, him shall God destroy"* (I. Cor. iii. 17). No vice attacks in a more direct manner the very person itself of the Incarnate Word, since these bodies which we soil, which we cast into the foulest mud, are as the members of Jesus Christ (I. Cor. vi. 15); none more deeply insults the Divine Majesty, because the man who is impure, putting into the balance God and infamous pleasure, gives the preference to all that is most filthy and vile over God. No vice, lastly, is more opposed to the divine plan, because God has given us a wholly spiritual soul, His image and resemblance, that it might live the life of angels here below, and enjoy the delights of His love, making in this way, as it were, its novitiate for the life of heaven; and behold, by means of this impure vice we degrade the image of God, we drag His image in the mud, we plunge into filthy pleasures the soul which was created to enjoy the pure delights of paradise and to be absorbed in the contemplation and love of the divine perfections. What an overthrow of the divine designs! No, we shall never be able to conceive what horror impurity excites in the heart of God. Let us pray to Him to infuse into our soul something of this supreme horror.

SECOND POINT.

Impurity Causes Man an Irreparable Evil.

We might first say that it injures his body, because it exhausts and wears out its strength, makes it grow old and die before the natural term of existence, and often occasions the sudden deaths which are as a clap of thunder; but, independent of this reason, impurity makes a man vile in his own eyes and takes from him self-respect, which is the pathway leading to all the vices; it withers all right sentiments in the heart; there is no more filial piety, no more compassion for misfortune, no more nobility of soul, nothing elevated and generous in this degraded heart. It engenders disgust of prayer, of virtue, of all duties, of God Himself. It makes charity die within the soul, and substitutes for it a cruel egotism which has no bowels of compassion, kills hope, which it replaces by the desire of annihilation, and destroys even faith, the pure doctrine of which is incompatible with corruption of the heart (Ps. xiii. 1). Lastly, of all the vices, once the habit of it is contracted, it is the most incurable. Can there then be anything more dreadful for man than impurity? Is it thus that we detest it?

Resolutions and spiritual nosegay as above.

Twenty-third Friday
after Pentecost

Summary of the Morrow's Meditation.

After having excited ourselves to love purity by means of the two preceding meditations, we will meditate tomorrow upon what we must avoid in order to acquire or preserve this virtue. We must avoid: 1st, an idle, sensual life; 2nd, dangerous society and dangerous resorts. Our resolution shall be: 1st, always to be usefully occupied, not losing time in useless thoughts and daydreams, and to embrace the manly and virile life which disdains a sensual existence; 2nd, to abstain from all social relations calculated to expose to danger and to soften the heart. Our spiritual nosegay shall be the words of St. Paul: *"We have the treasure of chastity in earthen vessels"* (II. Cor. iv. 7).

Meditation for the Morning.

Let us adore Jesus Christ in the beautiful characteristic the Church gives Him in her litanies: *"Jesus, lover of chastity."* It is He who came from heaven to bring this virtue to the earth, a virtue which until then had been but little appreciated; it is He who has enabled us to understand the excellence of it, and who by His grace inspires His children with courage to embrace it Let us unite ourselves with all the chaste souls in heaven and on earth in rendering Him homage.

FIRST POINT.

In Order to be Pure we must Avail an Idle and Sensual Life.

Our nature is so inclined to evil in consequence of our original depravity, that it cannot escape from it except by dint of not thinking of it; and the only means whereby not to think of it is to be absorbed in occupations which will distract us from it (St. Bernard). Hence the words of St. Augustine: *"If the devil finds you always occupied he will not be able to do anything against you."* A sensual life is as much opposed to purity as is an idle life. Nothing corrupts the heart so much as the effeminate delicacy which is always wishing to flatter the senses. The flesh is a slave which is kept in order only by weaning it from all delicacies and treating it with severity, and the more severe we are towards ourselves, the more mortified and penitent we are, the easier it is to keep ourselves pure. Satan, says St. Antony, fears nothing so much as watchings, fastings, the privations of voluntary poverty. Woe, then, to those who make of their body an idol for which they are always endeavoring to obtain all kinds of enjoyments, flattering the sense of touch by the softness of their couch and the fineness of their clothing, the sense of smell by perfumes and scented water, which the saints call the baits of voluptuousness (Clement of Alex.), the sense of hearing by profane and effeminate songs, the sense of sight by the reading of romances, theatrical pieces, and other writings of the same kind, by looking at statues and engravings which are wanting in decency, upon the features, the figure, and the dress of persons of the opposite sex, contrary to the example of Job, who said: *"have made a covenant with my eyes, that I would not do so much as think upon a virgin"* (Job xxxi. i); the sense of taste by seeking after good cheer, which St. Ambrose calls *"the aliment of voluptuousness,"* which St. Jerome styles *"the triumph of passion"* *(Ep.* xxxiii.), which St Ephrem declares to be *"the enemy of chastity"* {De Cast.), and which, lastly, St. Isidore of Seville calls *"the focus of vice."*

SECOND POINT.

In Order to be Pure we must Abstain from Dangerous Society and Dangerous Resorts.

Solitude is the asylum of chastity, and Jesus Christ ordinarily attracts to it pure souls. The world, on the contrary, is a center of corruption; its spectacles, its assemblies, its diversions, its fetes, and its long soirees invite the poison of impurity to enter into the soul by all the senses. All that is seen there, all that is heard, all that is done, softens and corrupts the heart, and not even the holiest of persons escape the pestilential influence (St. Jerome, *Ep.* xxiii.). If, then, we wish to keep ourselves pure, let us fly these assemblages as much as possible. Let us do still more: let us avoid tete-a-tete conversations with persons of an opposite sex; it is then that the devil makes the third in the company, and inclines us to take liberties, because no one sees us. Let us avoid laughing, joking, and playing the amiable with them, and let a holy gravity, a sweet modesty in words and manners, a restraint kept over our eyes, and gestures forbidding familiarity season our relations. To dispense with these rules given us by the saints, who were the first to observe them, not considering themselves to be able to keep their virtue intact without taking these precautions, would be a temerity which would ruin us, even as it has ruined numerous others. Let us here examine ourselves; do we really believe in the necessity of these rules, and are we disposed to conform ourselves to them?

Resolutions, and spiritual nosegay as above.

Twenty-third Saturday after Pentecost

Summary of the Morrow's Meditation.

After having seen what we must avoid in order that we may acquire or preserve purity, we will meditate tomorrow on what must be done, and we shall see that we must: 1st, be humble; 2nd, frequent the sacraments; 3rd, pray. We will then make the resolution: 1st, to have a great mistrust of ourselves, and not to expose ourselves to peril; 2nd, often to approach the sacrament of penance and of the Eucharist; 3rd, to be faithful in performing our meditation every morning, and to have a great devotion to the Blessed Virgin. Our spiritual nosegay shall be the counsel given us by Our Lord: "Watch *ye and fray, that ye enter not into temptation*" (Matt. xxvi. 41).

Meditation for the Morning.

Let us adore Our Lord declaring to us in the gospel that there is a class of devils which we cannot overcome except by mortification and prayer (Matt. xvii. 20). This class of devils are above all the devils of impurity. Let us thank Jesus Christ for this warning and let us ask of Him grace to conform ourselves to it.

FIRST POINT.

In Order to de Pure we must be Humble.

Pride, says the Holy Ghost, is the precursor of all kinds of evils. *"Pride goeth before destruction, and the spirit is lifted up before a fall. Before destruction the heart of a man is exalted"* (Prov. xvi. 18; xviii. 12). It is because the proud man does not distrust his weakness, he does not watch over himself and his dangers. God, in order to confound him, abandons him to shameful passions (Rom. i. 26); He withdraws His grace from him, and leaves him to his own weakness, whether from hatred of pride or in order to give him a lesson respecting his weakness without succor from on high: this made St. Augustine say that it was useful for the proud to fall (St. Augustine, *Serm.* lvi. *in Matt.*), that they might be brought back by experience to a knowledge of themselves. But if pride be the cause of our ruin, humility saves us (Gregory Great, *in Job* xxvi. 19). On the one hand, humility makes us watch over ourselves, avoid occasions, and pray; on the other hand, God, who loves humble souls, protects them, defends them, and renders them, as it were, impeccable. Thus, humility is a sure guardian of purity; it is like its sister and inseparable companion.

SECOND POINT.

In Order to be Pure, we must Frequent the Sacraments.

There is nothing better than frequent confession to prevent or correct relapses into impurity. A fault, if it be not promptly confessed, engenders another. The tempted soul has need to be sustained in the strife by the counsels of the confessor and by the grace of the sacrament, otherwise it becomes discouraged, allows itself to be cast down, and is soon conquered. Frequent confession offers it a preservative against relapses, whether on account of the salutary shame attending the self-accusation, whether in the exhortations of the confessor, which raise their courage and point out the means to be taken, whether in the good resolutions which are made, whether in vigilance which is roused, whether, above all, in the grace of the sacrament. These are facts founded upon experience. Holy Communion is not less useful; for the Eucharist, say the saints, is the corn of the elect and the wine which makes virgins to germinate (Zach. ix. 37); it deadens the fire of concupiscence; it gives the soul a delicious pleasure in purity; it develops therein the love of Our Lord, and in consequence a horror of all that offends Him, above all of the vice which is most opposed to His divine holiness, in such a manner that the more we feed ourselves with the bread of angels, the more we are led to embrace an angelical life, raised above the senses and the flesh.

THIRD POINT.

In Order to be Pure, we must Pray.

"I knew" says Solomon, *"that I could not otherwise be continent, except God gave it"* (Wis. viii. 21), and it is prayer which obtains it. It is above all meditation which, at the same time that it brings down to men help from on high, fills the mind so entirely with good thoughts, the heart with holy suggestions, that the tempter finds no longer any place there in which his evil thoughts can enter. With prayer and meditation chastity is assured, without it it is in peril (Gregory of Nyssa, *Oral.* i.). God willingly listens to souls which come and ask Him for the gift of purity, because it is asking Him for what most delights His heart. The Blessed Virgin does not receive with less benevolence the prayer addressed to her on this subject She takes particular care of souls who place their purity under her care; she has an affection for them, whether because they have the same tastes as she has, whether because, her Son having a special love for purity, she desires to see all Christians possessed of this virtue. Therefore, the saints have pointed out devotion to Mary as being one of the great means of acquiring and preserving purity; hence it is that the Church places upon our lips this beautiful prayer: "In comparable virgin, sweet above every creature, make us pure, sweet, and chaste. Grant that a perfectly pure life may lead us to heaven, where we shall enjoy the happiness of seeing and loving Thy divine Son."

Resolutions and spiritual nosegay as above.

Twenty-fourth Sunday after Pentecost

The Gospel according to St. Matthew, xxiv. 15-35.

"At that time Jesus said to His disciples: When you shall see the abomination of desolation, which was spoken of by Daniel the prophet, standing in the holy place: he that readeth let him understand. Then they that are in Judea let them flee to the mountains. And he that is on the housetop let him not come down to take anything out of his house; and he that is in the field let him not go back to take his coat. And woe to them that are with child and that give suck in those days. But pray that your flight be not in the winter or on the Sabbath. For there shall be then great tribulation, such as hath not been from the beginning of the world until now, neither shall be. And unless those days had been shortened, no flesh should be saved; but for the sake of the elect those days shall be shortened. Then if any man shall say to you: Lo, here is Christ, or there, do not believe him. For there shall arise false Christs and false prophets, and shall show great signs and wonders, insomuch as to deceive (if possible) even the elect. Behold I have told it to you beforehand. If, therefore, they shall say to you: Behold He is in the desert, go ye not out: Behold He is in the closet, believe it not. For as lightning cometh out of the east, and appeareth even into the west: so shall also the coming of the Son of man be. Wheresoever the body shall be, there shall the eagles also be gathered together. And immediately after the tribulation of those days the sun shall be darkened and the moon shall not give her light, and the stars shall fall from heaven, and the powers of heaven shall be moved. And then shall appear the sign of the Son of man in heaven; and then shall all tribes of the earth mourn; and they shall see the Son of man coming in the clouds of heaven with much power and majesty. And He shall send His angels with a trumpet, and a great voice; and they shall gather together His elect from the four winds, from the farthest parts of the heavens to the utmost bounds of them. And from the fig-tree learn a parable: When the branch thereof is now tender, and the leaves come forth, you know that summer is nigh. So, you also, when you shall see all these things, know ye that it is nigh, even at the doors. Amen I say to you, that this generation shall not pass till all these things be done. Heaven and earth shall pass, but My words shall not pass."

Summary of the Morrow's Meditation.

We will meditate tomorrow upon the end of the world, of which the gospel of the day speaks to us, and we shall see: 1st, that the end of the world may arrive for us at any moment; 2nd, that the world, for the very reason that it does pass away, ought to be as nothing to us. We will then make the resolution: 1st, not to attach ourselves to anything whatever here below, or to worldly possessions which we shall soon have to quit, or to the esteem of men who will soon forget us; 2nd, always to place in the topmost line the interests of our salvation and of our eternity, and to look upon all the rest as secondary and accessory only. We will retain as our spiritual nosegay these words of Holy Writ: *"The fashion of this world passeth away, and only the grave remaineth"* (I. Cor. vii. 31; Job xvii. 1).

Meditation for the Morning.

Let us adore the eternal God beholding all the generations passing by the foot of His throne, and being lost in eternity, even as the waters of a river cast themselves into the ocean. Yes, verily, O Lord my God, everything passes away, *"but Thou art always the self-same"* (Ps. ci. 28). Thou alone art just, because Thou alone art eternal (Hymn, *Gloria in excelsis).* To the immortal King of ages be honor and glory forever and ever!

FIRST POINT.

The End of the World may Arrive for us at any Moment.

The world will end for us at our death, and death may seize upon us at any moment, as well in youth and in the maturity of our strength as in our declining years and in old age. People die when they least expect it, and we are not sure of one single moment of enjoyment. Each may say to himself: It is possible that death may strike me in the place where I am, and that I may be carried from here to the grave; it is possible that death may interrupt the action in which I am engaged and that I may not finish it, may steal me away from the present hour, of which I may not see the end. Night and day with its sword suspended over my head, it only awaits a word from God to let it fall; at this very moment I may be no more, and everything to which I am attached may be taken away from me forever. Now, in such a position, how can we allow our hearts to become attached to possessions which, more fragile than glass, may be broken in our hands at any moment? How can we torment ourselves to amass a fortune, honors, knowledge, when we know that after many labors, violent desires, anxious hopes, at the moment when we count upon enjoying all these things death may seize upon the too confident possessor, and cast him into eternity? O vanity of vanities! O nothingness of the goods of this world! O blindness of the heart which attaches itself to them!

SECOND POINT.

The World, for the Sole Reason that it Passes Away, ought to be as Nothing to us.

The time of enjoyment, were it as certain as it is uncertain, would lose all right to any interest for the very reason that it must end. The human heart has need of a possession infinite in its duration as well as in its perfections, and that death cry, "*We must one day quit all and descend into the earth*" is for the man who reflects a thunderclap, as it were, which breaks down all his attachments and all his ties. Everything which charmed him until now is no longer anything more to him than a quicksand which gives way under his feet, than a shadow which passes, smoke which is dissipated, and he no longer has anything but vain chimeras in his joys, because they are fugitive; in his pleasures, because they are temporary; in his hopes, because they are fragile.

The longest life, when it has passed away, is no more than a dream of the night of which only a confused idea remains in the morning; it is an arrow which we have hardly seen pass us, a flash of lightning which disappeared almost at the same moment that we saw it, a vapor which a breath of wind dissipated, a speck, an atom. Now is such a little space in the course of ages worth so much anxiety in order to fix ourselves in it, so much eagerness to be honored therein, to be great, rich, happy? I pass along like the traveler in the desert, who at night pitches his tent, and in the morning taking it up goes into another world; shall I be so unreasonable as to be anxious and so attach myself to it for the short night that I have to spend in the desert of life? I go away like the waters of a river whose waves push each other onward; could I have the weakness to attach myself to the banks which I hardly touch whilst passing them by? I see that all around me portends speedy ruin; that death changes, overthrows, casts down, destroys, and drags everything into the abyss of eternity; could I be so foolish as to attach myself to these fragile supports which fall before me or with me, to desire to fix myself where nothing is fixed, where all perishes from one day to another? What folly! And yet do I not indulge in this weakness?

Resolutions and spiritual nosegay as above.

Twenty-Fourth Monday After Pentecost

Summary of the Morrow's Meditation.

We will continue tomorrow to meditate upon the world, and we shall see: 1st, how entirely opposed is the spirit of the world to the spirit of Jesus Christ; 2nd, that we can only be Christians in so far as we renounce the spirit of the world and embrace the spirit of Jesus Christ. We will then make the resolution: 1st, to regulate the whole of our external conduct as well as our internal sentiments upon the spirit of Jesus Christ, often asking Him what He would think in our place; 2nd, not to take any notice of the opinions of the world, and to take as our motto: *"Do what is right and let people talk."* Our spiritual nosegay shall be the words of St. Paul: *"Be not conformed to this world"* (Rom. xii. 2).

Meditation for the Morning.

Let us adore Our Lord teaching us by His apostle that we have not received the spirit of the world, but the spirit of God (I. Cor. ii. 12). He reveals to us thereby the great opposition which exists between these two spirits, and how we ought to empty ourselves of the spirit of the world, if we wish to be filled with the spirit of God. Let us thank our divine Saviour for such useful advice.

FIRST POINT.

The Opposition which Exists between the Spirit of the World and the Spirit of Jesus Christ.

1st. The spirit of the world leads us to esteem gold and silver, splendor and magnificence, luxury in clothing and furniture, profane amusements, public assemblies, theatres, and the thousand things which amuse the children of men. The spirit of Jesus Christ, on the contrary, leads us to fly from splendor and grandeur, to love simplicity and poverty, to keep at a distance, as far as we can, from everything that tends to dissipation, to despise what the world esteems, to esteem what it despises, to flee what it seeks after and to seek what it flees from, to love what it hates and to hate what it loves. 2nd. The spirit of the world, placing our happiness here below, leads us to do and suffer anything to gain possession of the false goods of this world; and dominated by this passion, neither lying nor vice, stops us, nor the sacrifice of our repose and of our health which is required of us. The spirit of Jesus Christ, on the contrary, placing our happiness in heaven, leads us to despise, as a vanity unworthy of an immortal soul, all that does not tend to it, and to esteem, to seek, and do all we can to render the possession of it surer and more complete. 3rd. The spirit of the world, counting sin as little provided that amusement is secured, precipitates itself unscrupulously into every occasion of sin. The spirit of Jesus Christ, on the contrary, placing duty and innocence before everything, leads us to flee from danger, to pray, to watch over little occasions as well as great ones, in order to be equally faithful in all things. 4th. The spirit of the world is only pride, independence, and love of domination; it commands arrogantly, it strives to supplant every rival and to revenge every affront. The spirit of Jesus Christ, on the contrary, is nothing but humility, gentleness, obedience, patience, forgiveness of injuries and outrages. Let us judge ourselves by these considerations and see what spirit animates us.

SECOND POINT.

We can only be Christians in Proportion as we Renounce the Spirit of the World and Embrace the Spirit of Jesus Christ.

The Holy Ghost has said so in formal terms: *"If any man have not the spirit of Christ, he is none of His"* (Rom. viii. 9). *"We have received not the spirit of this world, but the spirit that is of God"* (I. Cor. ii. 12). *"Love not the world, nor the things which are in the world"* (I. John ii. 15). *"Whosoever will be a friend of this world becometh an enemy of God"* (James iv. 4). The world is incapable of receiving the spirit of God, and Jesus Christ excludes it from His prayers (John xiv. 17; xvii. 9). If, then, we cannot quit the world, we ought at least to live in it as though we were not of it, to be on our guard against its spirit, its prejudices, its errors, its vices, and prefer to all these pleasures a good conscience, a wise mediocrity, virtuous frugality, evangelical simplicity, Christian modesty, fervent piety, lively faith, a sweet confidence in Providence, and the love of God, one act of which is worth more than a thousand worlds.

Resolutions and spiritual nosegay as above.

TWENTY-FOURTH TUESDAY AFTER PENTECOST.

Summary of the Morrow's Meditation.

As the spirit of the world, upon which we meditated this morning, is formulated in maxims which pass for incontestable axioms, we will consider tomorrow in our meditation: 1st, how false these maxims are; 2nd, how every Christian ought to love and prefer to them the maxims of Jesus Christ. Our resolution shall be: 1st, not to count as anything the maxims of the world; 2nd, always to take as the rule of our conduct the maxims of Jesus Christ. Our spiritual nosegay shall be the words of the gospel, that Jesus Christ is the sole master whose teachings we ought to follow: *"Neither be ye called masters, for one is your master, Christ"* (Matt, xxiii. 10).

Meditation for the Morning.

Let us adore Jesus Christ, the Eternal Truth, descended from heaven to earth to enlighten every man coming into the world (John xiv. 6; viii. 12; i. 9). Let us thank Him for having come to make this sweet and blessed light shine in the midst of the errors which cover the world (John i. 5). We can never bless Him sufficiently.

FIRST POINT.

The Falsity of Worldly Maxims.

The best proof of the falsity of these maxims is that they are in direct opposition to the maxims of the Eternal Truth, which is Jesus Christ. For, 1st, the world says: "If honors present themselves to you, refuse them not; if they do not come to you, then seek them. A man can neither have a mind nor a heart if he acts differently. Happy he who is honored, applauded, and who marches forward to glory; miserable he who drags along an obscure life and without splendor." Jesus Christ says, on the contrary: "Happy are the humble; happy are those who are persecuted for justice' sake; happy those of whom a great deal of evil is said, if they suffer with patience and resignation ; happy those who do not blush at practicing religion and at being confounded with the common herd, knowing how to understand that because many vulgar men are upright and just, uprightness and justice do not thereby cease to be worthy of elevated minds." 2nd. The world says: "A man must be insensible not to love pleasures and not to enjoy them when he can. Happy those who wish for them, who laugh, who amuse themselves, and whose days and nights are spent in enjoyment; unhappy is the man who is in affliction." Jesus Christ says on the contrary: "Happy are those who suffer and who weep, because a day will come in which their tears will be changed into joy; and woe to you who laugh and have your consolation in this world, because your laughter will be changed into cries of grief and into gnashings of teeth." 3rd. The world says: "A man must be a fool to love poverty and prefer it to riches. Happy the rich man who wants for nothing and obtains all that he desires; who sits down every day at a splendid table, and can satisfy all his tastes; who has numerous servants eager to forestall his desires and execute his will; who inhabits beautiful palaces fitted with all the inventions of effeminacy and luxury; who rambles over his vast domains in his leisure moments, whilst saying to himself: All this belongs to me." Jesus Christ says on the contrary: "Woe to ye rich who have your enjoyments in this world, because it is written that the wicked rich man died and was buried in hell; but happy the poor who know how to bear privation and poverty, because the kingdom of heaven belongs to them." 4th. Lastly, the world says: "A man must make himself happy here below at all costs; that is his great affair." Jesus Christ, on the contrary, says: "Your great, your only affair is to save yourself. Happiness is not for this present life; it is for the future life. It will serve you nothing to gain the whole universe if you lose your soul."

Such are the contrary maxims of Jesus Christ and of the world; they cannot be both of them true. Either the world deceives itself or Jesus Christ deceives Himself; the world may choose to say that Jesus Christ is wrong, that His cross is folly. *"Thou art beside thyself"* said a great man of the world to St. Paul (Acts xxvi. 24). Dare we say the same?

SECOND POINT.

The Christian ought to Prefer to the Maxims of the World, and to
Love above all else, the Maxims of Jesus Christ.

In bygone days the world bowed before the words of a pagan philosopher—Aristotle. On hearing the simple words, *The master has said so,* everyone submitted. How much more ought we to be docile to the words, *Jesus Christ has said so.* Jesus Christ has said: It is happiness to be humbled, to be poor, to suffer. Therefore, that saying is true, and I believe in it as much as in the existence of a God in three persons, as much as in the Incarnation and Redemption, for Jesus Christ is not less credible in regard to moral truths than in regard to speculative doctrines. The world, which is beside me, will act, speak, and think differently; but what signifies to me the speeches and the acts of a madman when I am sure of following the Eternal Truth? I will therefore be entirely Thine, O my God, without dividing myself between Thee and the world, between Thy cross and pleasure, between grace and nature (Matt. viii. 19). But here, O my Lord, a reflection which I am making confounds me. I enter into my conscience, I cast a glance upon my past. If I believe these truths, wherefore then, in suffering and privation, have I allowed murmurs, discouragements, such words of incredulity as these to escape me: God is not just to make me suffer in this way? Wherefore then, on seeing the prosperity of the wicked and the enjoyments of those who seem to traverse the pathway of life without having any crosses to bear, has this cry escaped my lips: How happy they are and how I would like to be in their place! Pardon, O Jesus! I have been incredulous in regard to Thy word, which told me that the cross is a happiness, poverty a blessing, contempt and humiliation a glory! It consoles the afflicted, it makes the rich to be detached, it inclines him to be charitable and generous, it moderates the passions. O God, increase my faith (Luke xvii. 5).

Resolutions and spiritual nosegay as above.

TWENTY-FOURTH WEDNESDAY AFTER PENTECOST

Summary of the Morrow's Meditation.

With a spirit and maxims of so contrary a kind, as has been shown by our preceding meditation, it is evident that Jesus Christ and the world must follow very different paths. We will meditate tomorrow: 1st, in what these two paths differ; 2nd, that the path of Jesus Christ is the only one that every Christian ought to follow. Our resolution shall be: 1st, often to ask ourselves: How would Jesus Christ do this, that we may do it in the same manner; 2nd, often to assure Him that we desire, like Him, to tread ambition under foot, together with the desire to amass riches and to enjoy them, and following His example, to lead a modest, simple, and unpretentious life. Our spiritual nosegay shall be the words Our Saviour said of worldly men: *"Let them alone, they are blind"* (Matt. xv. 14).

Meditation for the Morning.

Let us adore Jesus Christ as the sole way which leads to heaven (John xiv. 6). Let us thank Him for having come on earth to show us this way, by walking in it the first, and inviting us to follow Him (Matt. viii. 22). Let us render Him, with this object in view, all our homage.

FIRST POINT.

The Difference between the Path Followed by the World and the Path Followed by
Jesus Christ.

The path followed by the world is wide and spacious, men walk in it at their
ease, and think of nothing else except of not being annoyed and of indulging
in pleasures; it is a miserable path in which men are fed upon illusions and
cradled in frivolous hopes, in which they follow, as the whole of their gospel,
the torrent of the world and of custom, believing that it suffices not to do worse
than others. Dreadful torrent, says St. Augustine, who can resist thy current?
Wilt thou never be dried up, and until when wilt thou drag the children of Eve
into hell? *(Conf.,* lib. i. c. xvi.) Carried away by this current, men die without
having obtained what they were pursuing, or, if they obtain it, they enjoy it for
a short time only; and even during this short lapse of time, the fear of losing it
or the desire for something more takes from it all the charm they had hoped to
find in it. And what is still more to be deplored, where men are so unhappy who
have chosen this path, they walk with eyes shut to what will happen later on,
that they may only dwell upon the enjoyments of the moment, looking upon
time as everything and upon eternity as nothing; and what is the height of the
evil, they will not hear it spoken of; the least word capable of arousing their
attention in regard to the eternal future which follows the present life irritates
them and excites repulsion. Oh, how much better is the way of Jesus Christ!
It is true that it is narrow and demands restraint, that in it we cannot do what
pleases us, and we must often do what we dislike; but, on the other hand, how
contented is the heart; the conscience renders testimony that we are doing what
is right; we find ourselves therein in the society of all that is virtuous and holy;
the angels assist and guide us; Jesus Christ walks at our head, and God shows us
His paradise as the certain goal of our journey; the way is safe and clearly traced;
it leads to happiness through trial, to victory by combat, to the eternal home
by the rapid passage of exile. That many ill-instructed men do not enter this
path may be easily conceived, but that Christians who know that Jesus Christ
is their God, that His religion is the sole true religion, do not walk openly in it,
that they are ashamed to show themselves in it, because they are afraid of some
arrow of mockery which would fall and be spent at their feet without doing
them any harm, that is what is astonishing and which confounds every mind

which reflects, every heart which loves. And yet do we follow the way of Jesus Christ? Let us examine our conscience thereupon.

SECOND POINT.

Every Christian is Obliged to Follow the Way of Jesus Christ.

It is necessary to make a decision; we cannot belong at one and the same time to God and the world. It is impossible to reconcile together the two paths: Jesus Christ with the world, nature with grace, worldliness with devotion, the service of God with self-love and its susceptibilities, with temper and its impetuosities, with self-will and its caprices. Jesus Christ will have nothing to do with such a mixture, nor will the world; and it gives up to ridicule the hearts which are shared between the two, which are not vicious enough to please it nor virtuous enough to command its esteem. Even our own heart will have nothing to do with it, for in this middle state it has none of the consolations of piety; it does not enjoy either the pleasure of belonging to the world or the pleasure of belonging to God. We must, therefore, whether we will it or not, choose between these two paths. Now, can we for a moment hesitate in our choice? The saints preach to us by their example, call upon us to follow them, and urge us to do so. Why should human respect, which had no power over them, make us pause? There are more true pleasures and more real honor in the service of Christ than in the service of the world; even the cross of Jesus Christ weighs less than that of the world; it is accompanied by a heavenly unction which renders it sweet and amiable.

Resolutions and spiritual nosegay as above.

TWENTY-FOURTH THURSDAY AFTER PENTECOST

Summary of the Morrow's Meditation

We will meditate tomorrow upon the false wisdom of the world, and we shall see: 1st, how worthy it is of reprobation; 2nd, how, in fact, God reprehends it. We will then make the resolution: 1st, to let the world do, say, and think as it wills, and to attach ourselves to Jesus Christ as to the sole true wisdom; 2nd, often to consult our adorable Saviour, begging of Him to enlighten us with regard to all that we ought to think, say, or do. Our spiritual nosegay shall be the anathema pronounced by God against the false wisdom of the world: *"I will destroy the wisdom of the wise, and the prudence of the prudent I will* reject" (I. Cor. i. 19).

Meditation for the Morning.

Let us adore the extreme repugnance which Our Lord shows for the false wisdom of the world and the prudence of the flesh. He combats it by His speeches and declares that He will destroy those who take it as the rule of their conduct. Let us receive with respect and gratitude this salutary instruction.

FIRST POINT.

How Worthy the Wisdom of the World is of Reprobation.

To understand this it is sufficient to consider how false it is, for truth is a need of the soul; it is its repose, its nobility, its dignity, the principle of its energy. Falsehood, on the contrary, necessarily incurs its reprobation; he who lies feels that he betrays a duty and lowers himself. Now the wisdom of the world is only falsehood and lies. It is false in its principle, false in its virtues, false in its vices, 1st. In its principle. It sets out from this dictum, that we must, at any cost, seek our happiness in this world; and hence it concludes that we must, when it is necessary in order to reach this end, sacrifice all the rest, provided that we save appearances by dint of concealments, of dissimulation, and of artifices.

Now what can be more false than this principle and the consequences to be deduced from it? 2nd. It is false in its virtues. It humbles itself only in order to rise, affects to be silent only that it may be listened to more attentively, appears to be indifferent to things only in order to obtain them, patient under injuries only through want of power to avenge them, gentle only whilst waiting the moment to burst out, charitable only when it finds it is to its interest to be so, religious only when it is a means of pleasing any one; in everything it is nothing but falsehood and hypocrisy. 3rd. It is false even in its vices. It calls its incredulity strength of mind, its duplicity wise policy and a talent for business, its resentments and vengeances honor and courage, its seductions urbanity and politeness, its perseverance in guilty attachments constancy and fidelity. Can anything more entirely deserve the reprobation of every upright and Christian soul? And yet do we not possess some of its characteristics?

SECOND POINT.

How God Reproves the False Wisdom of the World.

The Holy Ghost calls it, by the mouth of St. James, *"earthly, sensual, devilish"* (James iii. 15). If it be earthly, it is therefore not suitable for heaven; if it be sensual, it is thereby unworthy of a reasonable soul, which ought to have only noble and elevated sentiments; if it be devilish, it is a hellish wisdom, which can lead to nothing but hell. By the organ of St. Paul, the same Holy Spirit calls it a death (Rom. viii. 6); by following it, therefore, we cannot arrive at life. He calls it an enemy of God (James iv. 4); God is, therefore, its enemy. He calls it an irreconcilable enemy of the law of God (Rom. viii. 7); it is, therefore, impossible to save ourselves if we follow its maxims. He treats it as folly (I. Cor. i. 20) and declares that He has been pleased to confound it by taking, in order to convert the world, the instruments which it esteemed to be the most incapable (Ibid. *27 el seq.).* Could God better show us what a horror He has of this pretended wisdom of the world, how severely He reproves and condemns it? Let us thereby learn that we must not take counsel of the world and of its false wisdom in regard to all that we have to do, but consult God in prayer and wise men filled with His spirit.

Resolutions and spiritual nosegay as above.

Twenty-Fourth Friday After Pentecost

Summary of the Morrow's Meditation.

After having seen the falsity of the wisdom of the world, we will meditate tomorrow upon Christian wisdom, and we shall see: 1st, in what it consists; 2nd, what its excellence is. We will then make the resolution: 1st, to see in all things our salvation as the great end to which we ought to make all tend; 2nd, carefully to avoid all that might expose or compromise it Our spiritual nosegay shall be the prayer of Samuel: *"Give me wisdom, that sitteth by Thy throne,"* that it may assist me and do everything with me (Wis. ix. 4 *et seq.*).

Meditation for the Morning.

Let us adore the Holy Spirit teaching us Himself and through the saints the excellence of Christian wisdom, in order to inspire us with the love and the practice of it. He calls it the science of the saints, the life and the peace of the soul, the mistress, the guardian, and the directress of the virtues, without which they are only vices which are useless in regard to salvation. Let us thank this God of goodness and of light for having given us such lofty and precious ideas of Christian wisdom.

FIRST POINT.

In what Christian Wisdom Consists.

It consists: 1st, in proposing to ourselves, in everything and before everything, the glory of God as the first and principal end of all our actions, and to look upon all creatures and all events as but so many means of attaining this noble end. Jesus Christ Himself gave us this idea of wisdom when He said: *"What doth it profit a man if he gain the whole world and suffer the loss of his own soul?"* (Matt. xvi. 26.) It was to show us that beyond salvation and the glory of God, which is inseparable from it, all the rest is nothing and ought to be counted as nothing. 2nd. Our end being thus laid down, Christian wisdom consists in taking, in order to attain it, the best means, not those which reason or the senses teach us, but those which are revealed to us by the maxims of the gospel and the example of Jesus Christ; consequently, in all things to seek the will of God, which is the rule of all perfection; and as we are never more certain of doing it than when we obey, to love a life of obedience. In things in which the will of God seems to be indifferent, Christian wisdom consists in preferring contempt to honors, poverty to riches, suffering to pleasure, because it was thus that our divine Master acted (Heb. xii. 2). 3rd. The end and the means being thus set down, wisdom says to us: Watch, in order not to let opportunities for putting these maxims in practice slip by; watch for little opportunities as well as great ones, so as to be equally faithful in all; watch over your words, so that you may say nothing but what is discreet; oyer your actions, that they may all be well performed; over your intentions, that they may go straight to God alone; lastly, watch over yourself, that you may never allow yourself to be surprised by the enemy. Let us examine ourselves and see if such be the end and if such be the means which direct the whole of our conduct

SECOND POINT.

The Excellence of Christian Wisdom.

"I called upon God," says Solomon, *"and the spirit of wisdom came upon me. And I preferred her before kingdoms and thrones, and esteemed riches nothing in comparison of her, neither did I compare unto her any precious stone, for all gold in comparison of her is as a little sand, and silver in respect to her shall be counted as clay"* (Wis. vii. 7-9). And, in fact, Christian wisdom is beautiful in

the eyes of God by its innocence of life and the uprightness and candor of its intentions; beautiful in the eyes of men, who cannot refuse it their esteem, and whom it makes to love religion; beautiful in itself, because of its noble simplicity, the elevation of its sentiments, the great virtues which it inspires, and the eternal glory to which it leads. With Christian wisdom we are saved, without it we are damned. With it we are happy, even in the present life; our heart is at peace, our conscience in repose; we enjoy the delicious delights of innocence and of the friendship of God. Without it, on the contrary, there is nothing but affliction and vanity of spirit here below; we are eaten up by remorse, discontented with ourselves; we feel that we are degrading and abasing ourselves, we lose even self-respect at last; it is the greatest misfortune which can befall a man. Oh, how precious, then, is Christian wisdom! Let us ask it of God, that it may preside over all our counsels, all our judgments, all the acts of our life.

Resolutions and spiritual nosegay as above.

Twenty-Fourth Saturday After Pentecost

Summary of the Morrow's Meditation.

After having considered the nature and excellence of Christian wisdom, we will meditate tomorrow upon its signs or characteristics, and we shall see: 1st, what it is in itself; 2nd, what it is in its relations with our neighbor. We will then make the resolution: 1st, often to ask God for Christian wisdom, and to examine ourselves frequently during the day, especially when the clock strikes, to see whether our actions, our words, and our sentiments bear the characteristics of it; 2nd, to maintain ourselves in an habitual spirit of recollection, in which alone true wisdom dwells. Our spiritual nosegay shall be the invocation to the Blessed Virgin, as the seat and throne of true wisdom: "*Virgin most prudent, seat of wisdom, pray for us.*"

Meditation for the Morning.

Let us adore Our Lord filled with the spirit of God, which is a spirit of wisdom, of understanding, and of counsel (Is. xi. 2). Let us admire His constant attention in following, in all His actions and in all His words, the light of divine wisdom, and let us ask of Him grace to imitate Him.

FIRST POINT.

What Christian Wisdom is in Itself.

The Holy Spirit describes it admirably in the epistle of St. James, chapter the third. Above all, he says, it is watchful over itself, that it may always keep itself pure (James iii. 17); it flies occasions which are likely to corrupt it, on that account courageously mortifying its senses, its imagination, its mind, its heart, and keeping itself on its guard against idleness. It is orderly in all things, does everything in the manner which it deems to be the most conformable to the will of God, never anything from caprice; and this makes it live in that heavenly peace which consists in the tranquility of order (James iii. 17). This beautiful, well-ordered life has as its background a perfect modesty in its behavior, its deportment, and its manner of doing everything; a modesty founded upon the respect of the presence of God, and the desire of leading others to what is right; a humble and docile modesty, which delights to obey, to submit to others its judgment and its will, to take counsel and to follow the good advice given to it (Ibid.). It has great respect for the words of the Holy Ghost: *"A wise man shall hear and shall be wiser"* (Prov. i. 5); *"My son, do thou nothing without counsel"* (Ecclus. xxvii. 24); *"Counsel shall keep thee, and prudence shall preserve thee"* (Prov. ii. 11). Let us examine ourselves and see whether we possess these characteristics of Christian wisdom.

SECOND POINT.

What Christian Wisdom is in its Relations towards our Neighbor.

Christian wisdom, the Holy Spirit also tells us by the mouth of St. James, studies to be on a pleasant footing with everyone; with persons who are full of faults, by bearing with them without allowing them to see wherein they are displeasing to it; with the wicked, by trying to bring them over to what is good by its amiable manner of proceeding; with the good, by venerating and cherishing them as the friends of God, rejoicing to see them filled with graces and talents, doing greater things than itself, and excelling in all kinds of virtues; for it does not know the base jealousies which are annoyed by the merits of others and are wounded by the praises given to them. Severe towards itself and indulgent to others, it is ignorant of the spirit of criticism and censure, and is so far from condemning others that it does not even stop to examine their conduct in order to judge them, unless it is obliged to do so (James iii. 17). Lastly, simple in all its relations with its neighbor, it loves candor and frankness, and has a horror of duplicity, slyness, and concealment (Ibid.). Let us examine ourselves by these characteristics and see if we have Christian wisdom.

Resolutions and spiritual nosegay as above.

[Note.—*The meditations which are intended to fill up the weeks until Advent must be taken: 1st, from the last weeks after the Epiphany; 2nd, from the meditations omitted on feast days because the meditation on the feast has taken the place of the current meditation.*

SAINTS

WHOSE FEASTS, BEING ON FIXED DAYS, DO NOT
FOLLOW THE VARIABLE COURSE OF THE LITURGY

September 21st.—St. Matthew

Summary of the Morrow's Meditation.

We will meditate tomorrow on the generosity of St. Matthew renouncing everything for the love of Our Lord; and in order to excite ourselves to imitate him, we will consider that there is: 1st, profit; 2nd, happiness, in depriving ourselves for the love of Jesus Christ. We will thence deduce the resolution: 1st, to mortify ourselves in whatever it costs us the most to renounce; 2nd, to sacrifice to God during the day a part of our joy. Our spiritual nosegay shall be the maxim of the saints: *"Privation is worth more than enjoyment;"* or those other words which the gospel says of St. Matthew: *"Follow Me, and he arose up and followed Him"* (Matt. ix. 9).

Meditation for the Morning.

Let us admire the great detachment of St. Matthew, and his readiness to leave all as soon as God calls him. Neither relations, nor friends, nor attachment to his country, nor consideration of fortune and position, can keep him back. At the first call of Jesus he leaves his bank and his riches, that is to say, his dearest enjoyments, to follow Jesus Christ, who has not whereon to lay His head, who lives by alms, and who promises His disciples nothing but crosses, trials, and persecutions. Let us adore the goodness of Jesus Christ towards this holy apostle, and the efficacy of His word. Let us thank Him for all the graces

He bestowed upon him, and let us abandon ourselves to the Divine Spirit in order to imitate so beautiful an example.

FIRST POINT.

There is Profit in Depriving Ourselves for Jesus Christ.

Jesus Christ declares in the gospel that, even during the present life, he who deprives himself of anything for the sake of His love shall receive a hundred-fold more than he has sacrificed (Mark x. 29, 30), and this hundred-fold, says St. Gregory, is perfection, a fruit of detachment; or rather, it is Jesus Christ who gives Himself as a recompense, says St. Bernard; and that is a possession which nothing in the world can equal, says St. Ambrose. In possessing Jesus Christ we become masters of the whole world; in Him we enjoy all creatures, and all the more advantageously since, possessing them in God, says St. Cyprian, we possess them exempt from inconstancy, anxieties, and all the other miseries which always accompany worldly possessions. Oh, what good reason, then, had St Matthew to quit everything at the first call of the Saviour, in opposition to the example of the young man in the gospel who had great possessions, and went away sorrowful because Jesus Christ had told him that, in order to be perfect, he ought to sell all that he had and distribute it among the poor! He lost everything by not being willing to leave anything, and St. Matthew gained all by quitting all. For he became a saint, an apostle, a man whose name is celebrated throughout all ages, great in all places, great even in heaven, whilst the name of the rich man is forgotten, perhaps it is even unknown in heaven. So true it is that in the service of Jesus Christ privation is worth more than enjoyment.

SECOND POINT.

There is Happiness in Depriving Ourselves for the Sake of Christ.

The joy which St. Matthew had in the service of Jesus Christ was a million times greater than all that which the rich young man of whom we have just spoken could possibly taste in the peaceable possession of all his riches and in the agreeable enjoyment of them. St. Matthew, and all the saints who deprived themselves of everything for the sake of Jesus Christ, would tell us, if they could speak, that their joy was so great, their peace so deep, their consolation so full, that the utmost amount of pleasure which can be felt upon earth does not come near to the smallest drop of their happiness. On the one hand, all created goods inspire them with nothing but disgust; they are a burden from which they are happy to be delivered; on the other side, virtue has so many charms and is possessed of so many attractions in their eyes that the whole universe is as nothing in comparison; the spiritual consolations which God gives in exchange, for temporal enjoyments are so superior that there is no proportion between the one and the other, says St. Cassian (Coll. xxiv. *cap. ullim.*). Let us add that for one person who pleases us and whom we quit, for an amusement which gives us pleasure and which we abandon, God often gives us a hundred persons who interest themselves in us, who endeavor to be agreeable to us, to render us a service when there is an opportunity of doing so, of solacing us in our necessities, and who feel towards us a charity which is all the more generous because it is not founded upon flesh and blood, but upon Jesus Christ, for the love of whom they love us. Oh, how much more happy St. Matthew was in the midst of the faithful converted by his apostolate than in his bank and amongst those from whom he gathered taxes!

Resolutions and spiritual nosegay as above.

SEPTEMBER 29TH.—ST. MICHAEL AND THE HOLY ANGELS

Summary of the morrow's Meditation.

We will consider tomorrow in our meditation St. Michael: 1st, as our protector; 2nd, as our model, and all the holy angels partaking with him the double title of protector and model. Our resolution shall be: 1st, to renew tomorrow our devotion to St. Michael and to the holy angels; 2nd, often to recall to mind the words with which St Michael overthrew the rebel angels and cast them out of heaven: "*Who is like to God?*" that is to say, who is great, who is amiable, who is terrible, who is just like God? These words will serve as our spiritual nosegay.

Meditation for the morning.

Let us honor St Michael as the chief angel in paradise and the prince of the holy city, always faithful to his God, whose greatness he proclaims by the words which have become his name, "*Mi-ca-el*" that is to say, "*Who is like to God?*" Let us at the same time honor all the holy angels imitating St. Michael, and like him fulfilling towards us the double mission which they have received of being our protectors and our models. Let us thank God for having given them such a mission.

FIRST POINT.

St. Michael and all the Holy Angels are our Protectors.

Two qualities are required for properly fulfilling the mission of protector: power and kindness. Now, St. Michael and all the holy angels possess this double quality in a very high degree, 1st. Who does not admire the power of St. Michael? He casts Lucifer and all the bad angels out of heaven, and when the devil wants to tempt the people of Israel to idolatry under the pretext of honoring the body of Moses, he hinders them by hiding the body in an unknown place. When Pharao pursues the people of God, he drowns the infidel king and all his army in the Red Sea. Lastly, it is to him that is committed the mission of exterminating Antichrist, in the last days that will come upon the earth. For, according to St. Thomas, he is the spirit of Jesus Christ by whom this great enemy of the Saviour of men is to be exterminated (II. Thess. ii. 8 *el seq.).* 2nd. Kindness in St. Michael is equal to his power. First minister of Providence, he is the protector of all the faithful. Under his orders, the angels, sharing his power and kindness, labor for the salvation of men, and together combat the enemy of the human race (Apoc. xii. 7). Under his lofty direction, the angels each fulfil the mission attached to the name given him by the Holy Spirit in the Scriptures; the angels assist each one of us in particular; the archangels lend us a higher kind of assistance, and in extraordinary cases; the virtues perform prodigies by entering into the designs of God in regard to our salvation; the powers sustain us in the strifes and combats of life; the principalities rule kingdoms in the interests of religion; the dominations defend the supreme dominion of God upon earth; the thrones watch over the reign of God in souls; the seraphim and cherubim labor to make lively flames of charity enter into the heart of man. What happiness for us to have such protectors! How do we correspond to their zeal? Have we our salvation at heart even as they have themselves? Are we docile to their inspirations?

SECOND POINT.

St. Michael and all the Holy Angels are our Models.

Models of recollection and of union with God, these celestial intelligences in the midst of the different missions confided to them never lose sight of the presence of God (Matt, xviii. 10). They adore Him unceasingly, they love Him, they pray to Him, they thank Him; they enjoy a holy intercourse with God which nothing can interrupt Models of purity and innocence, they have nothing but holy thoughts and holy desires. Models of humility, they confess that God alone is all, and that every creature ought to tread under foot pride, ambition, vanity. Models of zeal, they aspire after nothing but to make God and Jesus Christ loved. Models of religion, they abase themselves before the greatness of God, and with one voice cry out, *"Who is like to God?"* that is to say, who is just like God, with the justice which does not excuse an act, or a word, or even a thought which is not right? Who is good like God, with the ineffable goodness 'which dispenses all the graces we receive upon earth? Who is excellent like God, with the excellence which includes all perfection, all that can ravish love, admiration, and praise? *"Who is like to God?"* Who could dispute His holding the first place in a heart? Models of charity, they devote themselves, day and night, to what is best for men. Models of gentleness, they perform all their acts with perfect calmness; and, in his disputes with the devil respecting the body of Moses, St. Michael does not allow a word of malediction to escape his lips; he contents himself with saying, *"The Lord command thee"* (Jude i. 9), showing us thereby that modesty, gentleness, patience, are the best kind of weapons to use against our enemies. It is thus that St. Michael and all the angels offer us the model of all virtues.

Resolutions and spiritual nosegay as above.

First Sunday in October.—Our Lady of the Rosary

OCTOBER.

[The Roman liturgy consecrates to the Blessed Virgin the first Sunday in October under the title of Our Lady of the ROSARY; the second under the title of The Divine Maternity of Mary; the third under the title of Her Purity; the fourth under the title of the Patronage of the Blessed Virgin.]

Summary of the Morrow's Meditation.

We will meditate tomorrow upon the chaplet, which is a third part of the Rosary, and we will consider: 1st, the excellence of this prayer; 2nd, the manner in which to say it well. We will then make the resolution: 1st, to say the chaplet every day and to have one constantly about us; 2nd, to say it with great devotion and piety, employing the different means which the saints teach us in order to say it well. Our spiritual nosegay shall be the verse of the angelic salutation: *"Holy Mary, Mother of God, pray for us."*

Meditation for the Morning.

Let us adore the love of the Holy Ghost towards the Blessed Virgin; He has it so much at heart to make her honored that He has inspired the faithful of all times and of all places with the devotion of the chaplet. Let us thank Him for a procedure so glorious to Mary, and one which gives us, at the same time, so easy a means whereby to render her our homage.

FIRST POINT.

The Excellence of the Chaplet.

This excellence consists in: 1st, the prayers of which it is composed, the *"Pater"* and the *"Ave"* which are the most authentic prayers of the Church, the most holy in themselves, the most agreeable to Jesus and to Mary; 2nd, the authority of the Church, which has encouraged this practice by many indulgences, and the authority of God, who has confirmed it by many miracles; 3rd, it consists in the examples afforded us by the saints, of whom several recited it every day, and thereby obtained extraordinary graces; 4th, it consists in the relations which unite us to the Blessed Virgin; for what can be more right or sweeter to the heart of a son than to salute his mother by saying to her, *"Hail, Mary!"* than to praise and exalt her merits and her greatness, as we do when we say: *"Hail, Mary, full of grace, the Lord is with thee, blessed art thou amongst women, and blessed is the fruit of thy womb, Jesus"?* What can be more useful in regard to our salvation than to call to our aid her who, as mother of God, is omnipotent through her prayers, and who, as being the mother of men, is more than maternal in her loving-kindness, always ready to use her omnipotence in protecting us during life, and above all at that decisive moment of death on which eternity depends, as we ask of her when we say, *"Holy Maty, Mother of God, pray for us, now and at the hour of our death"?* Doubtless such a beautiful prayer, when it is recited by routine without any thought of the elevated sense of which it is the expression, becomes insipid and uninteresting, but when it is said intelligently and from the heart, each time it is recited it becomes more interesting, more beautiful, and more touching. Is it thus that we have appreciated the prayer of the chaplet? Have we not felt it to be wearisome, because we said it with a mind given up to distractions and with a careless heart? Have we not spoken of it disrespectfully, looking upon it as a devotion good for the simple and the ignorant? Have we had it at heart to make the advantages of it appreciated and to excite others to say it? Have we carried it about us as a token of our fidelity towards the Blessed Virgin, thereby following the example of St. Francis de Sales and many pious persons? Above all, have we been faithful to the practice of saying it every day, whatever may have been our occupations?

SECOND POINT.

The Manner of Saying the Chaplet Properly.

There are different manners in which to say this prayer well. The first is to attach ourselves to the sense of the words, such as we have explained them; to enjoy them, to penetrate into them; the mind tires and is wearied, the heart never. A second manner is to propose to ourselves, before commencing each decade, a special intention, which, by occupying the mind and the heart whilst reciting it, obviates the weariness of repetition by means of the particular interest attached to each intention. For example: One decade may be said for some fault which requires to be corrected; another for such or such a virtue to be acquired; a third for such or such a grace which we desire; a fourth for the conversion of sinners, or for some sinner in particular; and a fifth for the souls in purgatory. A third manner is to occupy ourselves with the mysteries of the Rosary; one day with the joyful mysteries—the Annunciation, the Visitation, Christmas, the Purification, and the finding of Jesus in the Temple; the second day a meditation may be made on the sorrowful mysteries—Jesus in the Garden of Olives, scourged, crowned with thorns, bearing His cross, crucified; the third day it will be the glorious mysteries—the Resurrection, the Ascension, Pentecost, the Assumption, and the Coronation of the Blessed Virgin in heaven. Is there not abundant and varied matter for our meditations in all these great mysteries, and shall we still dare to speak of monotony? A fourth manner of reciting the chaplet is to consider the Blessed Virgin in the first decade as daughter of the Father; in the second, as mother of the Son; in the third, as spouse of the Holy Ghost; in the fourth, as Queen of the Church triumphant; in the fifth, as Queen of the Church suffering; in the sixth, as Queen of the Church militant These are new points of view eminently suited to sustain piety during the recitation of each decade. Have we recourse to these different means for saying the chaplet well?

Resolutions and spiritual nosegay as above.

Second Sunday in October.—The Divine Maternity of Our Lady.

Summary of the Morrow's Meditation.

We will meditate tomorrow upon the divine maternity of the Blessed Virgin, and we will consider: 1st, what Mary is as mother of God; 2nd, what we owe to her in this quality. We will then make the resolution: 1st, to honor Mary as the mother of God by daily prayers, always accompanied with profound reverence, and to avoid all routine in the different acts of her worship; 2nd, to unite with this reverence unlimited confidence. Our spiritual nosegay shall be the prayer of the Church: *"Holy Mary, pray for us sinners, now and at the hour of our death."*

Meditation for the Morning.

Let us adore the three Persons of the Most Holy Trinity for the share which each one of them had in the great mystery of the divine maternity. God the Father chose a humble virgin of Judea to be the mother of the same Son of whom He is the Father; God the Son accepts as a mother the virgin who until then was unknown; God the Holy Ghost accepts her as His spouse and forms within her the body and the soul of the Incarnate Word. Let us thank the Most Holy

Trinity for this marvel, which is worked solely for our sake, seeing that it has as its object the redemption of the human race and the salvation of the world. Let us congratulate Mary, who therein finds her glory and her happiness, and let us ask her for grace to appreciate as is meet so lofty a mystery.

FIRST POINT.

What Mary is as Mother of God

Mary, inasmuch as she is mother of God, occupies the first rank in the order of created beings, and she even surpasses them by a height which can only be comprehended by an infinite intelligence. When she is called the mother of God, it means that she is a creature essentially elevated not only above all that exists, and consequently that she is queen of the universe, sovereign of earth and of heaven, but also that she is above all which it is possible for God to make or even conceive, on account of this evident reason, that whatever perfections God may give to a being which has issued from His hands or has been conceived in His thoughts, there will be always between such a being and the mother of God the immense disproportion that there is between the servant and the master, between the subject and the sovereign. When she is called the mother of God it means a person associated with the eternal fecundity of the Father, clothed with a legitimate authority over the Master of the world; she commands, and He respects her orders; she speaks, and He obeys (Luke ii. 51). It is a dignity, a grandeur, before which all in heaven are filled with astonishment and overwhelmed with respect and veneration. The loftiest seraphim themselves do not understand aright the greatness of her whom God calls His mother, and who says to God: Thou art my Son (St. Bernard). Therefore Mary, as being mother of God, is all-powerful in heaven and upon earth; not, it is true, on account of her own personal virtue, which is the privilege of God alone, but by the virtue of her prayer, to which nothing can be refused, either by the Father, of whom she is the daughter, or by the Word, of whom she is the mother, or by the Holy Ghost, of whom she is the spouse; and this it is which explains so many miracles worked by her intercession in all places and in all ages, and also in our own day, at Salette, at Lourdes, at Pontmain, at la Delivrande, at Fourviere, at Notre Dame de la Garde, and at a hundred other sanctuaries.

Mary, as being mother of God, is not only all-powerful, she is also supremely kind; that is to say, she is full of the divine benevolence which dwelt in her for so long a time; that is to say, she is clothed by God with the double title of mother of mercy and mother of all mankind, therefore invested with the inexhaustible measure of benevolence necessary under these two titles. She has no other mission except that of being merciful and kind. God is a judge and punishes because He is just; Mary is a mother and asks for grace because she is a mother. To condemn and to punish is not her affair; it is that of God. Oh, how good Mary then is! Do we feel towards her the lofty sentiments of great respect, of profound veneration, of confidence and love, commanded by her position as mother of God?

SECOND POINT.

What we Owe to Mary as Mother of God.

Let us represent to ourselves a great monarch in his palace; he doubtless expects that we should honor the servants who surround his throne, and who have deserved to be treated well by him; but for his mother he asks much more: he expects that honors should be paid her in proportion to her lofty position; and if this should be wanting, if there should be nothing more shown her than the merest shadow of coldness and of carelessness, he would feel himself wounded to the quick in his most tender affections, pierced to the very bottom of his heart, and that to such an extent that all the homage which might be offered to himself would be valueless in his eyes, solely because his mother did not share it. It is a lively picture of what we owe to Mary as mother of God. Jesus Christ accepts the worship offered Him only in proportion to the worship offered to His mother in association with it, by invoking her with confidence, venerating her greatness, lovingly celebrating her festivals, visiting her sanctuaries, praying at her altars, revering her statues or her pictures, and offering her a homage which is above that offered to all the saints, and only below that of which God is the object. Therefore, throughout the whole Church there is unanimous zeal in honoring Mary. The sailor in the midst of the tempest invokes her as star of the sea; he who is unhappy invokes her as being the consolation of the afflicted; the child learns to pronounce her name at the same time as that of Jesus, to recite the Angelic Salutation at the same time as the Lord's Prayer, and the old man sanctifies his dying lips with the blessed name in which he places all his hope. Every portion of public prayers begins and finishes with the name of Mary; all the feasts which celebrate the glory of Jesus repeat the glory of Mary, and it would be impossible to enumerate ail the confraternities, all the pious practices, instituted in her honor. Could the Church better show us how every Christian ought to have at heart the worship of the mother of God? Let us here examine ourselves. Are we not lukewarm in regard to the worship and love of the Blessed Virgin? What is our zeal for her feasts, for prayers offered in her honor, for all that interests her glory and her worship? Do we delight to think of her? Have we her image constantly before our eyes, and, still more, the remembrance of her virtues in our heart?

Resolutions and spiritual nosegay as above.

THIRD SUNDAY IN OCTOBER—THE FEAST OF THE PURITY OF THE BLESSED VIRGIN.

Summary of the Morrow's Meditation.

We will meditate tomorrow upon the purity of the Blessed Virgin, which the Church honors today, and we will consider: 1st, the eminence of this purity; 2nd, the practical consequences to be deduced from it We will then make the resolution: 1st, to have a very special affection for the angelic virtue of purity; 2nd, to be on our guard against everything which may expose it to risk, such as thoughts, imaginations, too free a use of our eyes, speeches and manners which are lacking in modesty, books which are not sufficiently reserved; 3rd, often to ask God for this virtue, as being the most precious thing in the world. We will retain as our spiritual nosegay the invocation of the Litany of Loretto: *"Mother most pure, pray for us."*

Meditation for the morning.

Let us adore the Blessed Trinity laboring together to embellish Mary with all the purity of which a creature is capable. The purity of Mary is the masterpiece of God; it is the subject of His complaisance; let it also be the subject of our praise, of our admiration, and of our love. Let us unite ourselves to the angels in blessing God and in glorifying Mary.

FIRST POINT.

The Eminence of Mary's Purity.

In order to form an idea of the eminence of this purity, we must rise above all human thoughts, and enter into the region of the most lofty mysteries as far as the secret of the councils of God, and meditate in the silence of admiration how God the Father, by associating Mary with the production of His Word, was obliged to communicate to her a measure of purity such as would render her worthy of such ineffable society, and establish her as mother of the Son of whom He is the Father; how God the Son, in taking her as His mother, was obliged to embellish her with innocence in order to fulfil towards her the duty of a good son, who, jealous to do his mother all the good he can, admits her to a participation in his riches and treasures; how God the Holy Ghost, lastly, by elevating her to the dignity of His spouse, was obliged to make holiness overflow upon her. He who gave so much to His apostles, what was it not incumbent upon Him to give to Mary when He communicated to her, not a mere fiery tongue, but, as it were, a torrent of divine flames, an ocean of grace in all its plenitude? (Luke i. 35.) If such were the favors accorded to His servants, what must not have been the presents made to His spouse? O womb of Mary, abyss of purity, infinite treasure! if we had a hundred voices and a hundred tongues we should still be powerless to recount such marvels. God Himself, who after having created the universe contented Himself with saying that *"it was good"* (Gen. i. 12), after having given being to Mary never speaks of His work but in terms of admiration: Thou art beautiful, O My beloved! Thou art all beautiful, and My eyes, which discover spots even in the purest angels, can find no spot in thee (Cant. iv. 7). Angels who surround My throne behold and admire. This chaste dove has no equal and is alone perfect (Cant vi. 8). The angels, in an ecstasy, cry out in their turn, Who is this that has appeared upon the earth? and they compare the splendor with which she shines, now to the sweet and benignant light of the evening star, now to the more brilliant light of the aurora, now to the dazzling splendor of the sun at its zenith (Cant vi. 9). After that, what could we say, mortal men as we are and ignorant? What could we think of the innocence and purity of Mary, a beautiful lily which enchants God and His angels? We can only admire, bless, and love whilst saluting our mother in the plenitude of graces wherein she dwells.

SECOND POINT.

The Practical Consequences with which the Contemplation of the Purity of Mary ought to Inspire us.

The first sentiment with which our meditation on the purity of Mary ought to inspire us is a great love and esteem for purity. Children of so pure a mother, we shall not be worthy of her and we shall not deserve her favors excepting in so far as we strive to be perfectly pure ourselves: pure in our bodies by means of an angelic chastity which will make us lead a heavenly life here below in a body of sin, as though we had no bodies; pure in our minds, never allowing to enter into it any but holy thoughts, never a dangerous thought, a worldly imagination, never reading anything which contains what is too free and is marked by a want of modesty; pure in our hearts, keeping them always free from all affections which are not for God or according to God; lastly, pure in our conscience, avoiding all deliberate sin, and promptly purifying ourselves when human weakness has drawn us into it.

The second consequence which we ought to derive from our meditation on the purity of Mary is to watch continually over our innocence. This innocence is like a beautiful glass which the slightest breath may tarnish; it is a beautiful flower which a nothing can fade; and those alone preserve it who mistrust themselves, who fly from dangerous society and occasions, who nourish piety in themselves by frequenting the sacraments, by good books, by perfect modesty in their manners and conduct.

A third and last consequence is constantly to pray to and greatly to love the Blessed Virgin. Prayer is pointed out to us by the Holy Spirit Himself as a means of preserving ourselves chaste (Wis. viii. 21), and the love of the Blessed Virgin is as an aroma of purity which makes us love virtue and renders its practice full of delight.

Resolutions and spiritual nosegay as above.

Fourth Sunday in October.—Feast of the Patronage of the Blessed Virgin

Summary of the Morrow's Meditation.

We will meditate tomorrow upon the patronage of the Blessed Virgin, which is the object of the feast of tomorrow, and we will consider: 1st, the reasons of the devotion to this patronage; 2nd, the practices of this devotion. We will then make the resolution: 1st, to celebrate with great love the feast of the patronage of Mary; it is the feast of confidence in the Mother of God—what can be sweeter? 2nd, henceforth to honor Mary as our beloved patroness, and often to repeat to her that we place under her maternal patronage the whole of our existence, together with all our spiritual and temporal interests; 3rd, specially to invoke her under this title in all our difficulties, temptations, and dangers, by these words or others like to them: *"O Mary, my patroness, bless me, come to my aid"* Our spiritual nosegay shall be the words of St. Bernard: *"God wills that all graces should be bestowed upon us through Mary."*

Meditation for the Morning.

Let us adore the great design of God in putting the whole universe under the patronage of Mary.

The other saints are patrons of a province or a particular town, but Mary is the universal patroness of Europe, of Africa, of Asia, of America, of the whole of Oceanica. The mother of all men, she is the patroness of them, even as a mother is the patroness of her child; the queen of the universal Church, she is patroness over the whole of it, even as a queen is patroness of her subjects. Let us thank God for having done so much honor to Mary and bestowed such a favor on the world; let us thank Mary for so worthily fulfilling so beautiful a mission, and on our side let us promise to honor her abundantly under her title of Patroness.

FIRST POINT.

Reasons of the Devotion to the Patronage of Mary.

By devotion to the patronage of Mary is meant that unlimited confidence in the Mother of God which leads us to have recourse to her as a protectress, a patroness, a mother, in all the needs of life; and the reason of this confidence is: 1st, that without Mary we can do nothing; 2nd, that with her we can do everything.

1st. We can do nothing without Mary. God is doubtless free in the dispensation of His blessings; He can of Himself and without any intervention grant them to whomsoever He pleases; but the saints and holy doctors teach us that God has established a different order of things. He wills, says St. Bernard, that all graces should pass by the hands of Mary; He wills, says Gerson, that nothing should come to us from heaven except through her. He means that no one should have any portion in His mercies or should obtain salvation except through her, says St. Germain of Constantinople; and the reason of this providential arrangement is that God wishes to bestow on His mother the great honor of being mediatrix between Him and men. To her recourse must necessarily be had, she is the treasurer of heaven, the dispenser of heavenly gifts, and whoever desires to obtain graces must have recourse to her throne, and must offer her his prayers and his homage. It is thus the Eternal Word willed to honor His mother. He obtains everything by His own merits, because He alone is the supreme mediator; but He distributes all through Mary, and without her we can obtain nothing.

2nd. With Mary we can do everything, for she desires all possible good things for us, and the prayer that her heart pours forth in our favor into the heart of God is all-powerful, on the sole condition that we should have full confidence in her. The proof that she desires all good things possible for us is that she is our mother, a very tender and very loving mother, who adopted us as her children at the foot of the cross, who received us as such from the hands of Jesus dying, and who placed us in her heart side by side with Him to love us in Him, love us as she loves Him, and for His sake. On the other hand, we have meditated elsewhere that by the omnipotence of her prayer she can do us all the good she wills, that God the Father can refuse nothing to His beloved daughter, God the Holy Ghost to so good a spouse, and that God the Son could never forget that her entrails bore Him, that He was fed by her milk, that He is bone of her bone and flesh of her flesh. If sometimes the prayers we address to her are without effect, let us lay the blame on ourselves; the reason is that we do not accompany them with sufficient confidence; and not to believe in the omnipotence of the prayer of Mary is to offend the Most Holy Trinity; it is to paralyze our own prayer, which is omnipotent only on condition that we firmly believe in it. Therefore, history in all ages, and contemporary history also, is unanimous in showing us in Mary the channel of all graces. Who has extirpated so many heresies, turned away so many scourges, calmed so many tempests, unless it be Mary called upon with faith? What has cured so many illnesses, consoled so many afflicted persons, converted so many sinners, if it be not recourse to Mary? What is it which still every day works so many miracles of kindness if it be not prayer to Mary and a pilgrimage to one of her sanctuaries? Who does not know that where Mary is loved religion flourishes, and hearts are given to God in proportion as they are given to the Virgin Mother, whilst in places where she is not honored the sacraments are but little frequented and virtue but little practiced—a fact which is so true that devotion to Mary is a sure thermometer of fervor or lukewarmness, whether in parishes or amongst individuals? Who is there, lastly, who has not learnt from saints and doctors that devotion to Mary is the least equivocal sign of predestination, so powerful is the patronage of the Blessed Virgin to obtain everything for those who call upon her? Have we rightly understood it hitherto, and are we faithful in keeping ourselves under the patronage of Mary?

SECOND POINT.

Practices of Devotion to the Patronage of Mary.

1st. Every morning we must salute Mary as our patroness, and offer to her the homage of our whole day; we must pray her to bless every moment of it that they may all be well employed; all our prayers, that they may be well said; all our actions, that they may be holy and according to God; all our words, that they may be without reproach, all within the limits of charity, of meekness, and of truth; lastly, all our intentions, that they may be directed to God alone.

2nd. In the course of the day, we must, every time that the clock strikes, renew the same offering, and call down the blessing of Mary upon the hour, which is about to begin, upon the action which is occupying us or the conversation in which we are engaged.

3rd. In the trials which happen to us we must have recourse to Mary, ask her for an alleviation of these trials, if such alleviation be in the order of Providence; or, if it be not, patience, resignation, perfect conformity to the divine will, and in both the one case and the other the grace to derive from them the greater glory of God and the greater good of our soul.

4th. In the difficulties we may meet with we must beg her to help us to overcome them, to enlighten us respecting what we have to do, and to obtain for us grace to do it well.

5th. Lastly, every day, and above all every evening before we go to sleep, we must place under her patronage the moment of our death, that moment, which is so short, but of which the consequences are eternal. The Church teaches us to honor Mary as the patroness of a good death by means of the last words of the angelic salutation: *"Pray for us sinners, now and it the hour of our death."* Whoever says this prayer piously will die as happily as he will die holily. Whence comes, a dying man was once asked, the joy which beams on your face at the moment when you see you are about to expire? It is, he replied, because having prayed so often during all the days of my life to the Blessed Virgin for the moment of my death, I cannot believe that she will refuse me a favor I have asked for so often. Let us say this prayer with equal attention and fervor, and we shall have the same consolation at our last hour.

Resolutions and spiritual nosegay as above.

October 2nd—The Angel Guardians

Summary of the Morrow's Meditation.

We will consider to-morrow in our meditation: 1st, the goodness of God in instituting angel guardians; 2nd, the duties incumbent on us in consequence. Our resolution shall be: 1st, greatly to respect the presence of our angel guardian, who is with us by night and by day, and not to allow ourselves to do anything in his presence but what is honorable and holy; 2nd, to love him and to thank him often for his benefits; 3rd, to invoke him confidently in our needs and our temptations. Our spiritual nosegay shall be composed of these words of St. Bernard, which will recall to us our resolutions: *"Respect for his presence, gratitude for his good offices, confidence in his protection"* (Serm. xii. *in Rs.* xc. **2,** 6).

Meditation for the Morning.

Let us adore the providence of God, who, in His great love for men, has not only delegated His holy angels to be the protectors of cities, of provinces, and of kingdoms, but has also given to each man in particular a prince of the heavenly court to lead him along the road of life, to help him in his needs, and to defend him against his enemies (Ps. xc. 11). Let us thank Our Lord for such a favor, saying with St. Bernard, "O *admirable goodness! O truly wonderful effect of God's love towards us!"* (Serm. xii. *in Ps.* xc.)

FIRST POINT.

The Goodness of God in the Institution of the Angel Guardians.

How marvelous it is! God lays upon a prince of His court the charge to accompany me always and everywhere, night and day, outside the house as well as in it; to assist me continually, even when I commit the sin which, makes him shudder, even when I resist his inspirations and revolt against him. What goodness on the part of God, what an honor for me, and at the same time what an advantage! This angel has the mission to occupy himself about my interests even as though they were his own, and to render me all kinds of good offices. If I pray, he goes to heaven to carry my prayer thither, and returns to bring me the gifts of God. If I am in trouble, he consoles me by means of the good sentiments with which he inspires me. In whatever state I am he watches over me as a brother; he bears me in his hands, says the Psalmist (Ps. xc. 12), like a tender mother carrying her child; he snatches me away from perils, opens issues for me out of difficult situations; lastly, he is to me what the guide is to the traveler, the doctor to the sick man, the shepherd to his flock, the father to his children, the most faithful of friends to his friend. Hagar in the desert, Lot at Sodom, Isaac upon Mount Moria, Eliezer in Mesopotamia, Jacob pursued by Esau, the people of God at the Red Sea and in the desert, Eliseus, Judith, Jerusalem threatened by Sennacherib, the children of Babylon in the fiery furnace, Daniel in the den of lions, St. Peter in his prison,—did they not all of them experience it and render testimony of it? Do not we also every day have proof of it? Whence come the illuminations which render our faith more lively, those sudden movements impelling us to what is good, those happy moments in which the heart feels itself urged to give itself wholly to God? Ah! it is to the angels we owe all these impulses towards salvation, and when they have succeeded, they make a feast of it in heaven. The misfortune is that so often we will not accept their good offices or listen to their holy inspirations; and when they have forced us to listen, as it were, in spite of ourselves, we still resist them. Let us thank God, let us thank our good angel, and let us be ashamed.

SECOND POINT

Our Duties towards our Angel Guardian.

We owe it to our angel guardian to respect him, to love him, to speak to him, and to imitate him. 1st. We owe him respect. If we ought to respect great and holy personages, how much more ought we to respect the princes of heaven, the officers of the house of God I What a fault it would be not to pay any attention to their presence! What a still more heinous offence if would be to do things in their presence which we would not do in the presence of an honorable man! Since our good angel is with us everywhere, we ought everywhere to recall his presence to mind, and this thought ought to be sufficient to keep us in the path of duty, to make us avoid every word, every action, unworthy of so august a presence. 2nd. We ought to love him. How, indeed, could we help loving such a benefactor, a friend so devoted, so holy, so perfect?

How could we help assuring him a thousand times in the day of our love, thanking him a thousand times for his society, for his good offices, for the good thoughts he gives us, the good sentiments with which he inspires us? 3rd. We ought to speak to him. When we really love anyone, and having the happiness of living with him, we salute him and we speak to him, we tell him our joys and our sorrows, and we pour forth our heart into his. We therefore do not love our good angel if we allow days and nights to pass without speaking to him, without exposing our needs to him, without rendering our homage to him, without saying anything to him; if we do not salute him in the morning at our awaking in order to recommend to him the whole of our day, and in the evening before going to sleep in order to beg him to love and to adore God in our place during the night; if in our affairs and our difficulties, our languors and our disgusts, our combats and our maladies, we do not call on him to assist us; if, lastly, we do not salute on our journeys the angel guardians of the places we pass through, and in our relations with our neighbor the angel guardian of each person with whom we have any intercourse. 4th. We ought to imitate our angel guardian: imitate at church his profound reverence in presence of the tabernacle; in prayer, his recollection and devotion; in business, his union with God; in our temptations, his glorious combats with the devil at the cry of St. Michael: "*Who is like to God?*" in the exercise of charity, his endurance of the faults and defects of our neighbor, his gentleness, his patience, his eagerness to oblige, his devotedness; lastly, in all things, his conformity to the good pleasure of God, the uprightness of his intentions, his pure and innocent life.

Resolutions and spiritual nosegay as above.

OCTOBER 4TH.—ST. FRANCIS OF ASSISI

Summary of the Morrow's Meditation.

We will meditate tomorrow upon the great love of St. Francis of Assisi for Jesus crucified, and we shall see that this love is: 1st, a supreme remedy against sin; 2nd, a means of progressing in all the virtues. Our resolution shall be: 1st, to have henceforth a special devotion to St. Francis of Assisi, as a great model of devotion to the crucifix; 2nd, to maintain this devotion habitually by always wearing a crucifix and often looking at it lovingly; 3rd, to cherish all the sufferings which Heaven may send us as particles of the cross of Jesus Christ Our spiritual nosegay shall be the words of St. Paul: *"I bear the marks of the Lord Jesus in my body "* (Gal. vi. 17).

Meditation for the Morning.

Let us consider St. Francis of Assisi as a perfect image of Jesus Christ crucified. He bears a resemblance to Him: 1st, in his flesh, seeing that he can say, like the Apostle: *"I bear the marks of the Lord Jesus in my body. With Christ I am nailed to the cross"* (Gal. vi. 17; ii. 19); like his Divine Master, his feet and his hands are pierced, his side is open, his whole body shows marks of penance; 2nd, in his heart; like Him he is reduced to a complete detachment from all things, and he burns with an inextinguishable thirst for suffering, contempt, and confusion. Let us honor this living image of Jesus crucified. Let us at the same time adore Jesus so perfectly represented in His servant, and let us thank Him for the special graces He bestowed upon him, above all that of having renewed in the Church devotion to the sacred Passion.

FIRST POINT.

The Love of Jesus Crucified is a Supreme Remedy against Sin.

Who would not conceive a supreme horror of sin when considering the state into which nothing but its mere shadow reduced Jesus Christ? This adorable Saviour was the most beautiful of the children of men in Himself (Ps. xliv. 3), and sin rendered His body hideous with wounds, with blood, with spittle and gashes (Is. liii. 2, 4). Who would not fear to incur the hatred of God for sin on seeing this great God treat with so much severity, and as though He were the greatest of criminals, His own Son, His beloved Son, innocence and holiness itself? (St. Bernard.) Who would allow himself to indulge in sin if he considered deeply that it was sin that scourged, tore, crucified, put to death a God, and made Him suffer more in His soul than even the cross on which He expired, because His death upon the cross was at once voluntary and salutary, whilst the cross, considered in sin, of which it is the penalty, is not desired by Him, nor is it useful to any one; it is the simple evil of him who sins. When we are tempted, let us look lovingly at the cross; let us press our lips to it, let us embrace it, and we shall never sin.

SECOND POINT.

The Love of Jesus Crucified is the Means of Making us Progress in all Virtues.

This mystery, in fact, teaches all the virtues; it gives the example of them, because they show themselves here in a superlative degree; it inspires an attraction to them, because it powerfully inspires us to practice them in the most perfect manner; it merits us the grace of them, since we cannot think of them without being impaled by a desire to lead a better life. Besides, nothing is more suitable than the crucifix to inspire us with that perfect detachment from all things which opens the way to pure love. We may even say that it is impossible to consider Jesus deprived of all things, suffering everything for love of us, without being determined to deprive ourselves of all things for love of Him. This is what was well understood by St. Francis of Assisi when he had a great wooden cross placed in the hall where his religious were wont to pray, and said to them: "Behold, my brethren, the great book on which you ought to meditate every day with faith and love. You do not require any other; this alone is sufficient." Let us be ashamed to have hitherto so little reflected upon, to have so little loved, the crucifix; it is a miserable forgetfulness, and the cause of our small progress in virtue; for that which crucifies sanctifies; Jesus crucified overwhelms with graces those who love Him. The crosses and trials sent by God are the most precious presents that God can make us, even as crosses and trials rightly supported by us are the most precious presents that we can offer to God. Our repugnances do us more harm than our troubles. A Christian soul finds its delight in privation and suffering. Are these out dispositions?

Resolutions and spiritual nosegay as above.

October 10th.—St. Francis Borgia

Summary of the Morrow's Meditation

We will meditate to-morrow upon the admirable life of St. Francis Borgia, and we shall see: 1st, how he loved Our Lord; 2nd, how he strove to imitate Him in all things. Our resolution shall be: 1st, to perform all our actions through love for Our Lord, and with the object of being enabled to love Him always more and more; 2nd, in all things to set before ourselves Jesus Christ as our model, often asking ourselves: What would Jesus Christ have done, what would He have said, what would He have thought in my place? Our spiritual nosegay shall be the words of Our Lord to His apostles: *"Abide in My love"* (John xv. 9).

Meditation for the Morning.

Let us adore Our Lord Jesus Christ taking from out the princes of the world Francis Borgia, Duke of Gandia, Viceroy of Catalonia, to make of him one of the most beautiful models of the perfect life. Let us thank Him for this great example given to the Church and to all ages, and let us ask Him to enable us to love Him and imitate Him, even as St. Francis Borgia loved and imitated Him.

FIRST POINT.

How St. Francis Borgia Loved Jesus Christ.

From his infancy he endeavored to please God by perfect innocence in regard
to morality, by application to all his duties, and by remarkable piety in all his
exercises. He had thus made great progress in virtue when he was given the
mission to take to Granada the corpse of the Empress Isabella, who was to
be interred there, and to assist as a witness at the opening of the coffin and
the translation of the remains into the tomb destined to contain them. At this
spectacle, which revealed, in place of a beauty which had been admired by all,
nothing but hideous putrefaction, he felt more than ever the nothingness of
all human things, and he made a vow to quit the court in order thenceforth to
renounce all things and to devote himself solely to the King of heaven. Realizing
his vow as soon as he could, he entered into the Society of Jesus, and was seen
to lead therein a life full of love for Jesus Christ and full of progress in the
most eminent virtues. Every day he gave to the contemplation of heavenly things
several consecutive hours: often eight hours, sometimes ten. A hundred times
a day he went on his knees to offer God the homage of his adoration and his
love. It was happiness to him to spend as much time as possible in presence of
the tabernacle; he would have liked to remain there always; and when he offered
the holy sacrifice, as well as when he preached, the sacred fire which was in his
heart shone on his face. Hence the eminent purity which inspired him with
indescribable horror of the slightest faults, the smallest imperfections, as being
displeasing to God, and which led him to go to confession every day; hence that
attention to the presence of God from which nothing could distract him, and
which, on the contrary, everything recalled to him. The sight of the heavens and
all the wonders of nature raised him to God. Even when he was in the world and
indulged in the pleasures of the chase, the docility of the falcon, which allows
itself to be tamed by the small amount of food given to it, made him sigh over
the hard-heartedness of men towards God, from whom they receive everything;
and the cunning shown by the animal in seizing its prey recalled to him the
artifices of the devil to ruin souls. The promptitude manifested by the dog in
giving up, at his master's voice, the prey he was carrying, also made him think of
the attachment sinners evince for the vile and dangerous pleasures which God
orders them to quit. Thus, everything served as means to raise his soul to God;
and beneath the eye of the God whom he loved he strove to do everything in
the way which he thought would most please Him. He attached himself above

all to love God, Jesus, and Mary in his neighbor; whence he concluded that he must prefer all others to himself, render them all kinds of attentions and good offices, even to the extent of sacrificing for their sake his repose, his health, even his very life, as he really did during the pestilence which was rife several times in different quarters of Rome. Can love of Our Lord be carried further than this?

SECOND POINT.

How St. Francis Borgia Strove in all Things to Imitate Our Lord.

This great saint, penetrated with the truth that the imitation of Our Lord is the best proof we can give Him of our love, as well as its being the surest guarantee of our salvation, endeavored in all things to conform himself to this divine Model of the elect. Seeing Jesus Christ so humble in His birth, in His life, in His death, in His Eucharistic being, he desired nothing more than to descend from the lofty rank in which his birth had placed him, and to hide himself in the cell of the novitiate of the Society of Jesus, and to perform the most menial offices, such as sweeping the rooms or serving in the kitchen, and to seek everywhere to be abject and despised. Glory seemed to pursue him in proportion as he fled from it; he was offered the Roman purple; he refused it, preferring humility before all else. This humility shone forth in his conduct, in his deportment, in his conversation, in the modesty of his garments, in his deference to the advice of others. Jesus Christ, the King of the humble, was the model which he loved to retrace in all his conduct. Seeing this God-Man poor, in the crib, in the dwelling at Nazareth, in His apostolic life, he conceived a disgust for the riches he enjoyed, he divested himself of them, and he became poor to such an extent that he had to beg his bread, and to wear nothing but mean clothing, and ate no other food than that of the poor. Seeing the Divine Saviour so mortified, so penitent, he renounced all the enjoyments of the senses; he wore a hair-shirt, the coarseness of which was sufficient to cause a shudder; his daily disciplines drew blood, and he seemed to have a body for no other purpose than to make it suffer. He was begged to spare himself: *"I will do so,"* he said, *"when pleasures shall have become torments and torments delights; it is a grace I earnestly pray Our Lord to grant me."* It was a satisfaction to him to be exposed either to the burning heat of the sun in summer or to the piercing cold of winter, to everything disagreeable that frost, wind, and rain can inflict, as well as to the sharp sufferings of illnesses, which God, he said, often gives to those who do not desire them and refuses to those who wish for them. This perfect imitator of Jesus Christ, named, to his great regret, Superior-General of the Society of Jesus, represents to himself Jesus governing His apostles; and, like Him, he gives to his religious the example of devoted attachment to the labors of the apostolate; like Him, he sends them to different points of the globe: to Poland, to the Oceanic Islands, to America, to Peru, and other countries; like Him, lastly, he inspires them with courage to die if necessary for the gospel, and his words kindle in them such a burning thirst for martyrdom, that during the period of his generalship the Society of Jesus had the glory of sending to heaven sixty martyrs. Behold what imitating Jesus Christ did for St. Francis Borgia; what has it done for us up to the present time?

Resolutions and spiritual nosegay as above.

OCTOBER 15TH—ST. TERESA

Summary of the Morrow's Meditation.

As the science and practice of meditation form the most distinctive characteristic of St. Teresa, we will meditate: 1st, upon the great graces she derived from meditation in regard to her own sanctification; 2nd, the great graces which the universal Church has received from it. Our resolution shall be: 1st, to perform our meditation assiduously every morning, preparing it the preceding evening, and preserving the fruits of it during the day; 2nd, to apply ourselves to practice the spirit of sacrifice and renunciation as the sole means of advancing at once in meditation and in Christian perfection. Our spiritual nosegay shall be the words of the Psalmist: *"The meditation of my heart shall be always in Thy sight"* (Ps. xviii. 15).

Meditation for the Morning.

Let us lovingly adore Jesus Christ choosing St. Teresa in order to make of her a model of the most eminent sanctity, a miracle of grace, a masterpiece of His eternal wisdom. Let us praise Him, let us bless Him for this marvel, and let us ask of Him to give us a portion of the spirit of prayer which characterized this great saint.

FIRST POINT.

The Great Graces St. Teresa Obtained from Meditation in Regard to her own Sanctification.

Prayer is an intimate communication of God with the soul, and the soul never enters into this divine intercourse without receiving great graces from it. St. Teresa was only a child when she had already derived from this holy exercise an ardent desire for martyrdom, which led her to take flight from her father's house in order to go amongst the Moors, and there seek the happiness of shedding her blood for Jesus Christ. Frustrated in her design, and not being able to be a martyr, she made herself an anchorite, that she might think solely of God. She made of her garden a desert, of her chamber a chapel, of her heart an altar, of her body and of her soul two victims which she offered every day as a holocaust, the one through penance, the other through the ardor of her love. Every day she strengthened herself by prayer for this double sacrifice, plunging herself in thought into the eternity which follows upon this present life, repeating to herself continually: *"Always, never, eternally"* On a certain occasion vanity attempted to seduce her; she had recourse to prayer, and learnt therein to tread temptation under foot. It was a great happiness for her, for God showed her afterwards the place she would have occupied in the bottom of hell if she had not resisted it. Freed from this peril, she gives herself up with fresh ardor to prayer. In vain aridities, obscurities, desolations, difficulties of all kinds, try her; nothing repels her. She knows that prayer has many steps, that the heavenly Spouse dwells on the summit, which can only be reached by long efforts, and during twenty-two years she perseveres in the strife. It is only then she obtains the end so greatly desired, union with God by the consummation of her soul in holy love; and thanks to this union every kind of virtue is developed in her: love of poverty raises her above all earthly possessions, which are but as dust in her eyes; humility elevates her above all human praise, which is to her but as a cruel torment; confidence in God raises her above all contrarieties and obstacles, patience above all the miseries of life, in which she sees nothing amiable except suffering, so that she exclaims with transport, *"Either suffering or death."* Lastly, divine love raises her to the rank of the apostles, whose immense zeal for the glory of God and the salvation of souls possesses her to such an extent that she cries out: "Heavenly Father, either take me away from the world or cause the great scandal of love which is not loved to cease. I cannot live in a world where

my Jesus is not loved." We might even say that love raised her to the rank of the
seraphim through its ecstasies, which caused her to be known by the name of
the seraphic St. Teresa. Oh, what marvelous things does prayer work in the soul
which gives itself up to it with courage and perseverance!

SECOND POINT.

The Great Graces and Blessings which the Prayers of St. Teresa
Obtained for the Church.

St. Teresa was not the only one to profit by her prayers; the Church gained
thereby the two great blessings which are applicable to all ages as well as to
all countries. The first of these blessings were the immortal writings of this
great saint, in which are contained the marvelous lights she obtained in prayer.
Therein are exposed the highest secrets of her spiritual life, the whole of the
science of the saints, and that with an elevation of language which seizes upon
the soul; with such a certitude that the greatest doctors have not found in
them one single word which is reprehensible; with such lucidity that everyone
is able to understand them; with such unction that it is impossible to read them
without being touched; lastly, with such precision that the original manuscript,
which has for a long time been kept in the palace of the Escorial in Spain,
does not contain a single erasure, and she could dictate her revelations to ten
secretaries at one and the same time. The second blessing with which the prayer
of St. Teresa enriched the Church was the reform of Carmel. The work was one
which was difficult in the extreme, above all for a woman. It pleased God to
choose her, in order to show the world that the work of Carmel was a wholly
divine work and a miracle of grace; that in the hands of Providence the most
simple instruments are the best; that the soul chosen by God for a work ought
never to allow itself to be discouraged either by the difficulties of the enterprise
or by its own weakness; that, lastly, we can do everything by prayer; in fact,
prayer illuminated St. Teresa with such pure light, filled her with so wonderful
a confidence in God, and gave her such celestial eloquence in speaking of divine
things and of the reform, that nothing could resist her. Her words revealed in
her such humility, such patience, such union with God, that, confirmed by her
holy example, they caused her reform to be adopted everywhere, and made of
the Carmelites the most religious, the most edifying, and the most perfect Order

in the whole Church. Oh, what a good and holy thing, therefore, prayer must be! How we ought to love it and be faithful to it every day!

Resolutions and spiritual nosegay as above.

OCTOBER 28TH.—ST. SIMON AND ST. JUDE

Summary of the Morrow's Meditation.

We will meditate tomorrow upon these two apostles, and we shall learn from them: 1st, to be apostles by our zeal in hindering all that is evil and procuring all that is good for religion; 2nd, to be martyrs by means of the spirit of sacrifice and of renunciation of ourselves. We will then make the resolution: 1st, to do all that is possible to lead the hearts of those around us to virtue; 2nd, to renounce an effeminate and sensual life, in order courageously to embrace all that is crucifying in the practice of virtue. We will retain as our spiritual nosegay the words of St Paul to the Hebrews: *"May the God of peace fit you in all goodness that you may do His will"* (Heb. xiii. 20, 21).

Meditation for the Morning.

Let us adore Jesus Christ calling St. Simon and St Jude to follow Him; let us congratulate these two apostles on their vocation. At the first call of Jesus they leave all; Jesus takes the place of all in their hearts. Let us admire their generosity, and let us ask for grace to imitate it.

FIRST POINT.

St. Simon and St. Jude Teach us to be Apostles.

After Pentecost St. Simon goes to evangelize Egypt, St Jude Mesopotamia, and both of them unite together to convert Persia. They attack with intrepidity the idolatry which prevails in those countries; they brave torments and a thousand perils of death; they cast down idols, they chase away devils, and they force the King of Babylon to confess that the apostles of Jesus Christ are more powerful than the gods of paganism (Archiep. Joan., *Serm. de SS. Simone el Juda*). Who is there that would not admire such zeal? But we ought not to confine ourselves to admiring it; we must also imitate it. Zeal is not the duty of apostles only; it is the duty of every Christian; it is the practical consequence of the great precept of charity. If we love God ever so little, we ought to prevent, so far as in us lies, that He should have cause to be offended, that His name should be blasphemed, that His worship should be despised; we ought to use all the means in our power for gaining hearts to Him and making His laws to be respected. In the same way, if we have any love for our neighbor, we shall endeavor to preserve the souls of our brethren from the eternal misfortune of damnation, and obtain for them the happiness of heaven. To see anyone about to be lost, to be able to prevent him from perishing, and not to take the trouble of doing so, is evidently not to love him; and all the more so because such an apostolate as this is easy to everyone. There is the apostolate of prayer; and what soul is there which cannot pray? There is the apostolate of example; and who is there that cannot, by his meekness and his virtues, prove to the world how beautiful religion is, how amiable is true virtue, and thereby open hearts to conversion? There is the apostolate of good advice; and who is there that has not an opportunity of giving it—now to a poor man who is in want of assistance; now to a servant whom we may treat with kindness; now to an equal, or even to a superior, in certain moments of confidence, when friendship is in a frame to be ready to receive advice given delicately? There is the apostolate of good books, which we must contrive prudently to introduce to those we desire to convert. There is the apostolate of the word of God, to the hearing of which we attract sinners by wise procedures. How often have we, until now, fulfilled this duty of the apostolate, above all, in regard to our friends or relatives, to whom we owe it more than to anyone else?

SECOND POINT.

St. Simon and St. Jude Teach us to be Martyrs.

Our two apostles, by dint of moderation and gentleness, gained the good graces of the King of Babylon to the extent of inspiring him with the thought of condemning to death all the pagan priests. He consulted our two apostles with respect to this design, and received from them the truly apostolic reply, that they had not come there to kill the living, but to give life to the dead; and, consequently, they asked that pardon should be granted to the culprits. But they, instead of being grateful for such generosity, only became more furious against the preachers of the gospel: and the king having died, they prejudiced against them his successor, who put them to death. Thus, they were martyrs after having been apostles. It is for us to imitate them also in this respect—not by the martyrdom of blood: God does not ask it of us; what He does ask is the martyrdom of self-love, by the renunciation of all susceptibilities which make us feel wounded and hurt about a mere trifle; it is the martyrdom of our temper, through a perfect serenity which suffers everything from others without allowing any one to suffer, and endeavors to contribute to the happiness of every one; it is the martyrdom of self-will, by condescending to the will of others when charity requires that we should do so; it is the martyrdom of attachments and desires, in order to devote ourselves wholly to duty and to the good pleasure of God, the only desirable thing in this world. Let us heartily embrace this law of sacrifice and of martyrdom. Through it we are at peace with God, at peace with our neighbor, at peace with ourselves; without it, neither God nor our neighbor is satisfied, nor are we satisfied ourselves, for the heart which satisfies itself feels that it is doing wrong.

Resolutions and spiritual nosegay as above.

November 1st.—All Saints

(1st Meditation.)

Summary of the Morrow's Meditation

We will meditate tomorrow upon the great feast of the day, and we shall learn from this solemnity: 1st, what it is to be a saint; 2nd, that we ought to be saints; 3rd, that we can be saints. We will then make the resolution: 1st, to honor the saints by esteem and admiration for their virtues, and to invoke them with confidence; 2nd, to imitate them, saying often to ourselves: "I ought to be a saint, I can be, and I will be; how would a saint perform this action, this prayer; how would he speak, how would he behave in such or such a circumstance?" Our spiritual nosegay shall be the words of St. Augustine: *"What these saints, male and female, have done, why should I not do also?"*

Meditation for the Morning.

Let us raise ourselves in spirit to heaven; let us contemplate the glory and the happiness of the saints, and let us bless the Lord, who so magnificently recompenses His elect *(Invit. Brev. Paris)*. Let us unite our adorations and our praises to those of the blessed, who never cease, day and night, to praise Him, saying: *"Holy, holy, holy, is the Lord God of Hosts"* (Is. vi. 3). *"To Him that sitteth on the throne, and to the Lamb, benediction, and honor, and glory, and power, forever and ever"* (Apoc. v. 13). Let us at the same time render our homage to the saints, in order thereby to repair the faults committed in the celebration of each of their special feasts, and to supply the worship which we have not yet rendered to so many saints whom the world does not yet know, and whom Heaven has crowned.

FIRST POINT.

The Solemnity of Today Teaches us what it is to be a Saint.

Our cowardly spirit, ingenious in deceiving itself, would like to persuade us that there exists an easy road by which to reach heaven, a road in which we need not be under any restraint, but may live at our ease, fly from the cross, and indulge ourselves in everything which is not absolutely mortal sin, wherein we may follow the dictates of self-will and its caprices, self-love and vanity; but let us today question the saints and ask them whether a single one amongst them was saved by walking along this road. They will answer us in the words of the gospel which has been solemnly read today in the assembly of the faithful as a protestation against this system of relaxed morals. What does this gospel say to us, if it be not that the *"blessed,"* or the saints, are the humble who are poor and detached from everything; they are the meek and gentle hearts which suffer everything from every one, without making any one suffer, who render good for evil, praise for blame, love for hatred; they are those who are tried, who spend their days in affliction and tears, far from the joys of the world; they are those who are zealous for their own perfection, who hunger and thirst after an ever increasing righteousness; they are the merciful, who compassionate all human wretchedness; they are the pure of heart, who are horrified at the smallest stains; they are the peacemakers, who do not allow passions to trouble the peace of their soul, and who live in peace with every one; they are the persecuted, who patiently bear insult and calumny? Behold these are saints in the opinion of Christ and of the gospel. Do we find any place in this portrait for cowardice, lukewarmness, and an easy and unrestrained life?

SECOND POINT.

The Solemnity of Today Recalls to us that we also ought to be Saints.

In point of fact, during all eternity there will be no medium between a saint and the damned, in the same manner as there will be none between heaven and hell. It is for us to choose between these two alternatives. Can we hesitate for one moment, and not say to ourselves from the bottom of our hearts: Yes, I will be a saint; I feel I must be, otherwise I shall be one of the damned. I must be, because it is not too great a price to pay for heaven; the ravishing and eternal joys of the saints are worth a million times all earthly privations, all the trials of virtue. I must, because it is not too much to give to escape hell, from which I shall be preserved if I follow in the path of the saints. But if I must, I ought then to be converted, for I am far from being a saint. Where in me is the humility of the saints, their meekness, their patience, their life of faith? Mercy, Lord Jesus, mercy! The feast of today recalls to me that I ought to be a saint, and I will become one.

THIRD POINT.

The Solemnity of Today Shows us that we Can be Saints.

To be a saint! Is it not an enterprise beyond my strength? our weakness will say to us. No, all the saints in heaven reply through their example. We see, in fact, amongst them saints of all ages, of all ranks, and of both sexes. Now, what they have done, why should I not do? Innumerable Christians have preserved themselves pure amidst all the dangers of seduction, recollected amidst dissipation and tumult, poor and detached amidst riches, mortified amidst opportunities for enjoyment. Why cannot I, who am in a better position, do what they did in a more difficult one? There is no room here to say: I have passions which seize upon me, temptations which solicit me. The saints also had them, and of a more violent kind, and they conquered them. Why should I not conquer mine as they did? There is no room here for saying: The seriousness of holiness, the monotony of duty, weary me; I cannot keep to them. Did not the saints also experience this weariness, this disgust? They bore them, and for a longer time than I, and now they are in heaven. How glad they are! How thoroughly they understand that they did well!

But my weakness frightens me; I am afraid of not being able to persevere. Alas! the saints were weak like me; grace sustained them. Why should I not hope that it will sustain me also? It is thus that all pretexts are confounded, all excuses fall down before the words of St. Augustine, few as they are: *"Cannot I do what others have done?"*

Resolutions and spiritual nosegay as above.

November 2nd.—The Souls in Purgatory

(1ST MEDITATION.)

Summary of the Morrow's Meditation.

We will consider tomorrow that we owe it: 1st, to God; 2nd, to our neighbor; 3rd, to ourselves, to help the souls in purgatory. We will then make the resolution: 1st, to say with more devotion our prayers for the souls in purgatory, such as the *"De profundis;"* the verse, *"Fidelium anima per misericordiam Dei requiescant in pace;"* the *"Afemento of the dead"* during the holy sacrifice; 2nd, to offer in their intention a decade of the rosary, and some of our actions or of our good works during the day. Our spiritual nosegay shall be the words of Job, which the Church places today in their mouth: *"Have pity on me, at least you, my friends, because the hand of the Lord hath touched me"* (Job xix 21).

Meditation for the Morning.

Let us descend in spirit into the dark prison where the souls in purgatory are detained until the entire and perfect expiation of their sins has been accomplished. Let us adore the infinite justice of God, who never passes over any fault, even the slightest; His ineffable purity, which cannot endure in His court anything which is not perfectly pure; His ineffable holiness, which cannot ally itself with the shadow of a stain; and at the sight of purgatory, as well as at the sight of heaven, let us repeat the eternal canticle: *"Holy, holy, holy, is the Lord."*

FIRST POINT.

We Owe it to God to Help the Souls in Purgatory.

What, in fact, in relation to God, are the souls in purgatory? They are His elect, His beloved children, the heirs of His glory, called to bless Him eternally in heaven, His spouses whom He tenderly loves. His heart will delight to introduce them into His paradise, to inundate them with a torrent of delights; but His justice and His holiness require that all the satisfaction due from these souls should be paid down to the last farthing. If some Christian or other upon earth paid the debt of one of these souls, God would receive it with joy into His bosom, and a saint would sing His praises in heaven. Now, things being thus, should we love God if, having at our disposition several means for reuniting to Him the souls He desires and loves, we should leave them separated from Him, without trying to put Him in possession of them? Should we love His honor and His glory if, being able to make new worshippers enter into heaven, and enable another mouth to sing His praises, another heart to love Him, we took no trouble about it?

SECOND POINT.

We Owe it through Charity towards our Neighbor to Help the Souls in Purgatory.

For, 1st, they are persons who are in great suffering; they suffer above all from the privation of God. Sighing with indescribable ardor for their reunion to the Supreme Good, they dart towards Him as the arrow shoots towards the target, and are always repelled. They endure in addition sufferings which are unknown to nature, the least of which, the saints tell us, incomparably surpass the greatest torments it is possible to suffer here below. Now, would there be charity in our hearts if, being able to obtain for these souls the great blessing for which they sigh, we were not to procure it for them; if, being able to withdraw them from the extreme sufferings they endure, we were not to withdraw them? 2nd. They are unfortunate beings who, sighing beneath the weight of misery, could not make their voices heard if they were to cry for help; and to whom could they cry?—to God? But justice, which is there, replies: The debt must be paid, the soul must be purified. If they were to cry to us, alas! we should not hear tthem;their only resource is to borrow the voice in which the Church speaks today, exclaiming; *"Have pity on me, you at least, my friends, because the hand of the Lord hath touched me!"* Evidently, we have no charity in our heart if this voice does not touch us. 3rd. They are persons worthy of all our interest, called to reign with us in glory. Would it not be unworthy of us to allow such excellent persons to perish without putting ourselves to any trouble to help them? 4th. They are perhaps a father or a mother, a brother or a sister, a person dear to us for more than one reason, but in any case they are Christians, that is to say, brethren in Jesus Christ, members of the same body, heirs of the same kingdom, companions of eternity, souls that we are commanded to love as we love ourselves, or rather to love as Jesus Christ has loved us. Let us judge, after having made these considerations, where our charity is if we do not help them.

THIRD POINT.

We Owe it to our own Interests to Help the Souls in Purgatory

For, 1st, these good souls, which we have withdrawn from their prison and introduced into heaven, will be our protectors in the presence of God, and will there pray continually for us. 2nd. Jesus Christ Himself will be our advocate, as being also indebted to us, seeing that He was in prison in the person of one of His members, and we withdrew Him from it; He was thirsty, and we made Him drink from the fountain of life; He was naked, and we clothed Him with eternal glory. Oh, if the works of mercy here below, if the glass of cold water given to a poor man, touch His heart and obtain for us an eternal recompense, what will He not do in return for the still more excellent mercy which is exercised on behalf of the suffering souls in purgatory? 3rd. If it be written that we shall be treated as we treat others, God will not permit us to be forgotten when we in our turn shall be in the place of expiation, or He Himself will apply to us the merits which have no other destination, such as there are when those for whom they are offered have been damned or have already entered into heaven; whilst He will allow those who have not been helpful to their deceased brethren to languish without any succor being given them. 4th. At the same time that we procure for ourselves such great advantages, we shall lose nothing of the merits which we offer for the solace of these souls; for there will always remain to us the merit of charity, which abundantly compensates all that we give up for their deliverance. Would it not then be to understand our own interests very badly if we had no zeal for the solace of the souls in purgatory? Let us examine whether we have nothing to reproach ourselves with on this head.

Resolutions and spiritual nosegay as above.

NOVEMBER 3RD.—ALL SAINTS

(SECOND MEDITATION.)

Summary of the Morrow's Meditation.

We will consider tomorrow that the feast of All Saints is eminently calculated to perfect in us: 1st, faith; 2nd, hope; 3rd, charity. Our resolution shall be: 1st, to pass the whole day tomorrow in spirit in heaven, that we may there share in the feast of the holy city; 2nd, to reanimate, by means of this spectacle, our faith, hope, and charity. We will retain as our spiritual nosegay the words of the Psalmist: "*Woe is me that my sojourning is prolonged: my soul hath been long a sojourner*" (Ps. cxix. 5).

Meditation for the Morning.

Let us adore God, who is admirable in His saints (Ps. lxvii. 36). He is admirable in the virtues His grace causes to be practiced, admirable in the glory with which He crowns them in paradise, admirable in the power He gives them to protect us and help us. Let us render to Him all our homage of admiration, of praise, and of thanks.

FIRST POINT.

The Feast of All Saints is Calculated to Perfect us in Faith.

As long as our mind is circumscribed within the narrow circle of earthly things, it is difficult to believe certain hard truths of the gospel; for example, that we

must renounce everything and ourselves also, do violence to ourselves, bear
our cross, bring our vanity and self-love under subjection, prefer a hidden life
to the splendor of glory and of reputation, obedience to our own will. When
these doctrines are only enunciated, nature shudders. But if we raise ourselves
in thought into the midst of all the saints, whose octave we are celebrating; if we
but contemplate them resting from their trials, in the midst of immortal glory;
if we consider that those who have suffered the most here below are now the
happiest in heaven, that those who have been the most forgotten are now the
highest in glory; and if we recall to mind that what lasted so short a time has given
place to eternal happiness, then faith accepts with transports the evangelical
maxims which it costs the most to believe, and utters the cry of faith: "What a
nothing the earth and its false goods are to him who looks up to heaven! Happy
the poor, happy the afflicted, happy those who suffer or those who are a prey to
calumny! There is no proportion between the crosses of the present life and the
glory of the future life; for a moment of light tribulation an immense weight
of glory (Matt v. 12). What an excellent bargain!" It is then we enjoy and enter
with delight into the words of the Imitation: "Oh, if you had seen the eternal
crowns of the saints in heaven, the transports of joy of those who formerly on
earth were counted as nothing, and who were even deemed unworthy to live,
you would humble yourselves in the dust, and prefer to be subject to all rather
than to command even one single person. Far from desiring pleasure in this life,
you would rejoice to suffer for God, and you would esteem it a great grace to
be looked upon as nothing amongst men" (III. Imit. xlvii. 3). It is thus that, by
raising our eyes to heaven, the soul is elevated and its faith perfected.

SECOND POINT.

The Feast of All Saints Perfects Hope in us.

Let us look up to heaven where the saints await us (Ps. cxl. 8). They call to us
and invite us to rejoin them; they encourage us, and show us the throne which
awaits us, the crown which will encircle our brow, the recompense which God
reserves for every good work, for each prayer, for each sacrifice, for each sigh
that is uttered for Him. Oh, how well suited is such a spectacle to inflame hope,
how it urges us to depart for the eternal country! Not only do the saints await
us, but they pray for us, they give us the benefit of their merits: the martyrs of

their broken limbs, the confessors of their tortured bodies, the anchorites of their penances; and at the thought of such fervent prayers our courage rises, our confidence is reanimated. And why then should I not do what the saints have done? They are so happy, why should I not share their happiness? They see God no longer far off, in enigmas and imperfect images, but close by, revealed, face to face, such as He is in Himself. And I am called to enjoy the same felicity; the thing depends only on me; it suffices for me to will it. Yes, Lord, I will it; I desire to go and lose myself in Thy infinite essence; I am impatient for this happiness. When will it be, Lord? O life too long! O death too much delayed! I desire with a great desire to associate myself with the angels, with the patriarchs, with the prophets, with the company of the apostles, with the army of martyrs, to see them, to speak to them, to embrace them (Ps. cxix. 5; Philipp, i. 23; Ps. lxxxiii. 3). O Christian hope, thou dost ravish my heart, thou dost detach it from earth, and thou dost raise it to heaven!

THIRD POINT.

The Feast of All Saints Perfects us in Charity.

Religion, in fact, teaches us that the means for attaining the felicity of the saints is greatly to love them (Rom. xiii. 10). To love God upon earth is the means for loving Him in heaven: to love is the only way to happiness. If, then, we desire to go to heaven, we must live by love alone; we must increase every day in love, and in doing so we are sure of paradise (Ibid. 8). And who would not love a God who is so magnificent towards those who serve Him? Who would not love a God whom the angels always think so amiable that they are never weary of loving Him; the God whom the seraphim celebrate by means of the eternal canticle: *"Holy, holy, holy, is the Lord God of hosts"* (Is. vi. 3); the God to whom the virgins sing the song which they alone can sing; and at whose feet the elders lay their crowns, exclaiming that to Him alone belong honor, praise, and benediction? Oh, how well calculated are all these lofty thoughts, which recall to memory the festival of today, to make our hearts kindle with love!

Resolutions and spiritual nosegay as above.

November 4th.—St. Charles

Summary of the Morrow's Meditation.

We will meditate tomorrow upon St Charles, and we will consider: 1st, the elevation of his soul above all that passes away; 2nd, his union with God. We will then make the resolution: 1st, to consecrate ourselves to God without reserve, without allowing ourselves to indulge in any attachment; 2nd, to give ourselves up more and more to a life of recollection and of union with God. Our spiritual nosegay shall be the words of God to Abraham: *"Walk before Me and be perfect"* (Gen. xvii. 1).

Meditation for the Morning.

Let us adore God, whose powerful grace formed in St. Charles an admirable type of the purest and loftiest virtues. This great man was like a luminous lighthouse, placed by God in the midst of the sixteenth century to enlighten it amidst the darkness which covered the earth, and to show to the world that at all epochs, even amidst scandals and disorders, it is still possible to be a saint.

Let us thank God for so great an example offered to all the children of the Church, and let us ask Him to enable us to profit by it.

FIRST POINT.

How the Great Soul of St. Charles was Raised above all that Passes Away.

This elevation of soul appeared from his childhood. When he was still only a boy his pleasure already consisted in decorating chapels, ornamenting altars, imitating the ceremonies and the songs of the Church. At college all his tastes were serious, and he divided his time between prayer and study. Provided at an early period with a rich benefice, he took from it only what was strictly necessary; all the rest was for the poor. Raised to honors, he saw in them only matter for a more terrible account to be rendered, but one more reason for being more humble and more holy. For, he said to himself, being in a position in which I am more exposed to be looked at, I ought to give a better example; being drawn nearer to Jesus Christ, I ought to live more by His life and to be filled with His spirit. Superior to the outward things by which he was surrounded, he is still more raised above himself; he controls his own will, which he keeps bent beneath a severe rule, which assures the wise distribution of his time, the economy of every moment, without caprice or dislike ever being able to derange the beautiful ordering of it all; he rules his temper, and masters it to such an extent as to maintain it in a state of constant serenity, which neither prosperity inebriates or dissipates, nor adverse circumstances render melancholy or less agreeable; never a word of ill-humor, never a sharp remark, escapes him; he conquers the curiosity which is always in search of news, and he fears all such things as are calculated to dissipate the recollection of the soul; he overcomes the delicacies of sensuality to the point of fighting against them by means of hair-shirts, which tear his innocent flesh; by disciplines, which make his noble blood to flow; by watchings, which only leave him a few moments for sleep taken upon the bare ground, in order that he may give more time to prayer and study; lastly, by fastings on bread and water, his only nourishment, and which he allows himself to take only once a day. How, above all, shall we give expression to the elevation of his soul above all self-love? He esteems himself so little that he calls himself a worm which ought to be trodden under foot; a useless servant, sinful and idle, the least of men and the most ungrateful of creatures. He blushes and is confounded when he is honored, he rejoices when he is humbled and when evil is spoken of him, and, in so far as he can, he hides everything that might make him to be esteemed.

SECOND POINT.

How the Great Soul of St. Charles was United to God.

Three links concurred together in forming this union: faith, hope, charity. Faith showed to him God present everywhere, and everywhere he respected Him by a holy recollection and a religious attitude. It showed him God present in the bottom of his heart (II. Cor. vi. 16), and in this interior sanctuary he remained with Him in so intimate and assiduous a manner that it was easy to recognize it by the calmness of his conversation and a certain tranquil joy which was spread over his face. It showed him still more clearly God present in our churches; this fervent prelate was often to be seen there, prostrate, motionless, during long hours, and when necessity tore him away, he left his heart behind him, for there, he said, is the center of all my joys. If he fulfilled some function or other, it was with a modesty, a piety, a religious attitude, which seized hold upon the spectators and reanimated even the most lukewarm. His faith occupied him with God even in his journeys, and he always carried about with him several subjects of meditation with which to feed his heart. To this vigilance to keep himself united with God during the day he added the night, and he then retired into a little cell under the roof of his palace. There, alone with God, prostrate before the Supreme Majesty, he gave himself up to all the fervor of prayer. Being thus united to God by faith, St. Charles also united himself to God by hope. Confiding in God alone, he kept close to Him, in the same way as a child who, not being able to walk alone, clings to its mother's hand; and, tranquil in this confidence, he preserved his soul in peace in the midst of all events, without anything being able to trouble or distract him. Lastly, more powerful still than hope and faith, charity united the heart of St. Charles to God. Possessed by holy love, he had a horror of the slightest faults, for the sole reason that they displeased God, whom alone he loved; of even the smallest imperfections, because they diminished, he said, the beauty of virtue; and, jealous to preserve himself from them, he watched over his senses to keep them at a distance from evil; over his exterior, to avoid too great freedom in his gestures and not sufficient restraint over his eyes; over his thoughts, to have none but such as were holy; over his words, to utter none but such as were edifying. Moreover, he confessed every day, often even with great abundance of tears, and he was always accompanied by two priests, to whom was confided the duty of warning him of his smallest imperfections. It was thus that charity kept him always pure, always united to God, who is infinite purity.

Resolutions and spiritual nosegay as above.

November 5th – The poor Souls in Purgatory

(SECOND MEDITATION.)

Summary of the Morrow's Meditation.

We will consider tomorrow: 1st, the means of solacing the souls in purgatory; 2nd, the lessons we ought to derive from meditating on their sufferings. Our resolution shall be: 1st, to gain as many indulgences as we can, and to offer each one of our actions for the solace of these poor souls; 2nd, carefully to avoid the slightest faults, since they are so severely punished in purgatory; 3rd, to accept and to offer to God all the trials of life in penance for our faults. Our spiritual nosegay shall be the words of the Maccabees: *"It is a holy and wholesome thought to pray for the dead"* (II. Mach. xii. 46).

Meditation for the Morning.

Let us take back our thoughts to purgatory, let us consider with a fraternal compassion the poor souls who there endure so much suffering, and let us listen to the cry that they utter: *"Have pity on me, at least you, my friends!"* Let us prostrate ourselves in presence of the mercy of God, and let us implore it in favor of these dear souls.

FIRST POINT.

The Means whereby we Solace the Souls in Purgatory.

We should be all the more inexcusable if we did not solace the souls in purgatory when the means of doing it are so easy and abundant We can do it, 1st, by indulgences, a precious treasure composed of the superabundant merits of Jesus Christ and of the saints, of which the Supreme Pontiff has the principal dispensation. It costs us so little to draw from this treasure, and thereby to abridge the duration of the suffering of these poor souls, or else to diminish ours by gaining for ourselves the indulgences which will hasten our entrance into paradise. What does it cost us to say at every communion which we make: *"O good and most sweet Jesus!" to* which is attached a plenary indulgence? What does it cost us to make from time to time the "Stations *of the Cross,"* to which are attached several plenary indulgences? Is it not the same thing with other indulgences, some of which are plenary, some partial, and all of which it is easy to gain?—indulgences for the *"Angelus,"* mental prayer, the rosary, and different prayers or good works, the details of which are given in prayer-books. We can, 2nd, solace the souls in purgatory by means of our prayers said attentively and piously, as we would that, if we were in their place, they should be said for us; never letting a single day pass without remembering them, if it be only by uttering the pious aspiration: *"Good Jesus, give them eternal rest,"* or by a decade of the rosary said for their intention. We can, 3rd, solace them by alms or different good works of which we may apply the merit to them; by the Holy Sacrifice or by Communion; by various mortifications of the taste, of the will, of curiosity, and of other inclinations; lastly, by means of even the most common actions, by offering them to God for their intention. Where is our charity if with so many and easy means for solacing these poor souls, we do not do it?

SECOND POINT.

Instructions to be Gathered for our Personal Conduct.

We ought to deduce from it, 1st, a great horror of the smallest sins. We take great care not to commit any action for which human justice would inflict upon us even a single year's imprisonment. With still more reason we ought to abstain from all the venial faults which divine justice punishes with sufferings infinitely more terrible than all earthly dungeons and prisons. What strange forgetfulness of our faith! We know that the penalties of purgatory will be the chastisement of every word we have spoken which is untrue, which is contrary to charity or humility; of all acts of sensuality and of selfishness, of all fits of bad temper, of all the complaisance we derive from vanity, of all the time we have lost or have employed badly; and spite of that we allow ourselves to commit all these faults. What folly to expose ourselves for so little to such great punishments, and to permit ourselves so easily to do things which will bring down such terrible chastisements upon us! We ought, 2nd, to deduce by meditating on purgatory a spirit of penance. We have great debts to pay to divine justice, whether it be for the temporal punishment due to sins which are already pardoned, whether for venial sins which we so often commit. Now, in order to acquit ourselves of these great debts, we have only two means to choose from: either penance in this world, or purgatory in the next. Purgatory is terrible, penance here below is easy; for in proportion as God is severe after death, He is good and indulgent during life. With this alternative, does not prudence tell us to make our payments here below, where they are easy, rather than to put them off to a future life, when they will be very terrible? It was this consideration which inspired the saints with so great a spirit of penance. They mortified themselves as much as they could; for they said, What is this compared with purgatory, which I am thus sparing myself? If we do not imitate the austerity of the saints, why, at least, do we not accept in a spirit of penance all the "troubles of life, the sicknesses which come upon us, the disagreeable events which take place? Why have we not courage to impose upon ourselves some little privation, a slight mortification of self-will, of sensuality, of curiosity, of the taste, of the imagination, of our own comfort? Why do we not often utter aspirations of penitence, *"Spare, O Lord, spare Thy people"* (Joel ii. 17), acts of contrition, and other acts, which would diminish the season of purgatory for us?

Resolutions and spiritual nosegay as above.

November 6th.—All Saints.

(THIRD MEDITATION.)

Summary of the Morrow's Meditation.

We will profit by this holy octave for meditating upon an article in the Creed, the dogma of the Communion of Saints; and we shall see: 1st, what the Communion of Saints is; 2nd, what are the advantages it obtains for us; 3rd, what are the duties it imposes upon us. Our resolution shall be: 1st, to have recourse to the saints with confidence in all our troubles, and to excite ourselves to imitate them in our manner of acting, of speaking, and of thinking; 2nd, to exercise a tender charity towards each other. Our spiritual nosegay shall be the prayer Our Lord addressed to His Father: Grant that Christians "may be but one as Thou, Father, art in Me, and I in Thee" (John xvii. 21).

Meditation for the Morning.

Let us adore Jesus Christ founding the dogma of the Communion of Saints, to unite together in one single family, of which He is head, the Church triumphant, the Church suffering, and the Church militant. Let us thank Him for this magnificent institution, of which St. Bernard said: "There are saints in heaven and there are saints on earth; this feast is the festival of them all taken together."

FIRST POINT.

What is the Communion of Saints?

It is a divine institution whereby all the saints who are in heaven, all the just who are in purgatory, all the children of the Church who are upon earth, form but one sole and same thing, even as the Father and the Son are but one. After the divine nature, where even the number terminates in a perfect unity, nothing is more beautiful than this Communion of Saints, wherein the divine unity is represented. We are one with the Father, who calls us His children; one with the Son by resemblance to His divine life; one with the Holy Spirit, who gives Himself to us to sanctify us; one with all the saints: with all the martyrs, the confessors, and the virgins; one with all the great heroes of Christianity: the Pauls, the Xaviers, the Francis de Sales; one with Jesus Christ, and by Jesus Christ one with God. O holy and beautiful unity! At the beginning God was alone with His Word and His Holy Spirit; He created the world, and He wills that unity should result from it: unity of all men, unity of all the saints, unity of all the angels, and unity in Him, not out of Him; otherwise there would be no longer unity (John xvii. 11).

SECOND POINT.

What are the Advantages the Communion of Saints Obtains for us?

1st. It ennobles us; because it is great, the nobility of the Christian, whose family raises itself up to the skies, where it reigns upon immortal thrones, and extends to the very extremities of the earth, everywhere where the Church, its mother, has children; and where has she not? How noble is the Christian, who, on entering into heaven, does not find himself among strangers, but in his own family and amongst brethren; and what brethren they are!—the Pauls, the Chrysostoms, the Augustines, and innumerable others (Tob. ii. 18; Eph. ii. 19). O Communion of Saints, how deaf you are to me! Living here below in your unity and your faith, I will never leave you; on departing this life I shall find you again above in the most beautiful portion of yourself, in my co-citizens and my brethren of heaven. Here below I salute you in faith, O holy city of my God! Soon, soon, in a moment, I shall be united to you. I shall be inebriated by your beauty and your delights. Oh, how I long for that moment! O Jerusalem, I am at your door, I am standing there, my feet move, my whole body presses itself forward, that it may enter into your glorious unity. 2nd. The Communion of Saints enriches us. Of ourselves alone we are miserably poor; but when I recite the Creed: "I believe in the Communion of Saints," I feel myself to be rich, like the indigent man who finds a treasure. This treasure is the merits of Jesus Christ and of all the saints, family possessions which are not divided amongst the members, because charity does not know anything about mine and thine, but which are as a common heritage of which I may avail myself in the presence of God to such an extent as to be able to say to Him: Lord, I offer Thee, in order to cover my poverty and strengthen my prayer, the torments of the martyrs, the labors of the apostles and of apostolic men, the austerities of the anchorites, the merits of all the saints an inexhaustible fund of which the Church continually dispenses to me the product by indulgences. 3rd. The Communion of Saints assures us of powerful protectors in heaven and of brethren upon earth. In heaven a portion of the happiness of the saints consists in interesting themselves in us, in praying for us; tranquil in regard to their own lot, they occupy themselves with ours and only await our petitions before presenting them to God and supporting them by their merits. What an advantage and a consolation for us who are on earth! In virtue of the same principle, I am nowhere either a foreigner or unknown; I am in my own family; I am a brother. O consoling dogma!

THIRD POINT.

What are the Duties which the Dogma of the Communion of Saints Imposes on us?

1st. It obliges us to show, by a holy life, that we are worthy of the great family of which we are members. Remember, we say to the children of a family, the blood that flows in your veins; it is the blood of heroes. Be worthy of them, and do not be the scandal of a degenerate race. The saints from out of heaven use the like language to us: Members of our family, members of our body, be worthy of us; live as we lived. What we did, why should not you also do? 2nd. The Communion of Saints imposes on us the duty of invoking the saints with confidence, of honoring them above all on the days of their feasts, of loving them as our benefactors, of thinking often of them as our models, of looking upon this earth as an exile, and of sighing after our reunion with them. 3rd. It imposes on us the duty of praying often for the souls in purgatory, and gaining as many indulgences as possible for them. 4th, and lastly. It prescribes us tenderly to love each other as members of one same body. The word communion excludes division and coldness. It was thus that it was understood by the primitive Christians, who formed but one heart and one soul; it was thus that St. Paul understood it when he said to the faithful: Have all of you but one same spirit, one same soul, one same understanding, one same heart (Philipp, i. 27 ; ii. 2).

Resolutions and spiritual nosegay as above.

Feast of the Dedication of a Church

(FIRST MEDITATION.)

Summary of the Sorrow's Meditation.

We will meditate tomorrow: 1st, upon the respect, 2nd, upon the love, that we owe to churches. We will then make the resolution: 1st, to maintain a profoundly religious demeanor, joined to an interior full of faith, when we are in church; 2nd, to hold in great esteem our visits to the Holy Sacrament, and to look upon the time which we consecrate to them as most precious. Our spiritual nosegay shall be the words of Jacob: "*How terrible is this place! This is no other but the house of God and the gate of heaven*" (Gen. xxviii. 17).

Meditation for the Morning.

Let us humbly adore the immense majesty of God, who, although filling the whole universe with His presence, and consequently having in all places a right to our respect and love, wills nevertheless to be honored and loved in a special manner in our churches, where He has for that purpose established His dwelling. "*Behold,*" says the apostle St. John, "*the tabernacle of God with men, and He will dwell with them*" (Apoc. xxi. 3). It is there that He wills to see all His children gathered together before His eyes, offering to Him the solemn and public homage of their religion. Let us enter into His views, and let us renew the great sentiments of respect and love in this holy place with which we ought to be inspired (Ps. xciv. 6). Let us delight to go there and adore God, and prostrate ourselves in His presence.

FIRST POINT.

The Respect Due to our Churches.

We cannot read in the Old Testament without being deeply impressed by it, of all the respect which God demanded, whether for the tabernacle or for the different places where He manifested His presence. *"Reverence My sanctuary"* (Lev. xxvi. 2), He said. *"Put off the shoes from thy feet,"* He said to Moses, *"for the place whereon thou standest is holy ground" (Ex.* iii. 5). How shall I dare speak to my Lord, cries out Abraham with his face bowed to the ground, *"I who am but dust and ashes"* (Gen. xviii. 27.) *"How terrible is this place, indeed the Lord is in this place"* (Gen. xxviii. 17, 16), cries out Jacob. Lord, says David in his turn, I will enter into Thy house, but it will be with reverential fear. For Thou art He who has His throne in the heavens (Ps. v. 8; x. 5). Let us recall to mind the dedication of the temple of Solomon ; the fire descends from heaven, the majesty of the Lord fills the holy place; all the children of Israel fall down prostrate with their faces to the ground; they adore and praise the Lord, who is so good and merciful as to lower Himself to His creatures (II. Paral. vii. 3). Now if such respect was felt for the ancient temple, how much greater is the respect due to our churches; for here there are no longer signs and types, a rude ark and the images of seraphim which are honored, but God Himself as substantially present by His Word in the tabernacle as He is in paradise; God surrounded by millions of angels, who form by day and by night an invisible guard around His throne. Oh, how right and seemly it is to maintain a profoundly reverential demeanor, to keep a restraint over our eyes, our words, and our smiles, to avoid the slightest appearance of freedom and familiarity, hastiness of manner, quick genuflexions, all lazy and disrespectful postures! How above all ought we to keep our interior pure and without spot, recollected and occupied with the great Majesty in whose presence we are! How we ought, lastly, to have at heart the decoration of churches, the decency and majesty of divine worship!

SECOND POINT.

The Love Due to our Churches.

What could we love here below if we did not love a place where are gathered together all the memorials of the love of God for men, a place which God inhabits in person, where He invites us to come and present to Him our prayers, which He promises to grant? Now this is what our churches are: 1st. There are assembled all the memorials of divine love: the sacred baptismal font, which, by regenerating us, has made us children of God, brethren of Jesus Christ, heirs of heaven; the pulpit, whence descends into our souls the holy word, to make us bring forth all virtues; the tribunal of mercy, which restores to us, together with our innocence, our rights to heaven when we have lost them; the holy table, where we are fed with the bread of angels; the image of Jesus crucified, the memorial of so much love; the holy altar, on which the God-Man immolates Himself every day for us; and the portraits or statues of the Blessed Virgin and the saints, the remembrance of whom recalls so many wonders of grace and preaches all the virtues so eloquently to us. 2nd. It is there that God dwells. Solomon formerly exclaimed: *"Is it credible that God should dwell with men on the earths"* (II. Paral. vi. 18.) That which Solomon found it so difficult to believe we see realized in our churches. There God holds His court within our reach; the entrance is always open for us. We can, when we will, draw near to Him, speak to Him, and listen to Him, let our hearts flow forth into His, and gather therefrom consolation in our troubles, strength in our weaknesses, find there a paradise upon earth whilst awaiting paradise in heaven. Let us judge from this how much we ought to love our churches. It is there, 3rd, that God invites us to come and present to Him our petitions, promising that He will grant them. Moses said of the ancient tabernacle: *"Neither is there any other nation that hath gods so nigh them, as our God is present to all our petitions"* (Deut. iv. 7). David sang, when alluding to the old temple: *"How lovely are Thy tabernacles, O Lord of hosts. For better is one day in Thy courts above thousands. I have chosen to be an abject in the house of God rather than to dwell in the tabernacles of sinners"* (Ps. lxxxiii. 2, 11). Thou Thyself, Lord, didst say of that temple: *"My eyes shall be open and My ears attentive to the prayer of him that shall pray in this place"* (II. Paral. vii. 15). *"I have chosen this place that My eyes and My heart may remain there perpetually"* (Ibid. 16). There *"I will hear from heaven, and will forgive their sins, and will heal their land"* (Ibid. 14). Now, if such magnificent promises were made to the ancient temple, what ought we not to hope from prayers offered in our churches before the throne of grace which is raised therein in order that all may find there help and mercy? Jesus Christ awaits us there, calls us there, invites us to come to Him and ask for anything confidently, and He promises to hear us (Matt. xi. 28). Let us reply to His appeal and let us come with confidence and open to Him our heart and tell Him our needs (Heb. iv. 16). Let us hence conclude how much we ought to love our churches, these Vestibules of heaven, these meeting-places given by God to His creatures, the true paradise of earth.

Resolutions and spiritual nosegay as above.

— • —

FEAST OF THE DEDICATION OF A CHURCH

(SECOND MEDITATION.)

Summary of the Morrow's Meditation.

We will meditate tomorrow upon the temple of God which is in us, according to the doctrine of the Apostle (II. Cor. vi. 16). We will first penetrate ourselves with the truth that we are really the temple of God, and in a second reflection we will study the duties which are to be deduced from it. Our resolution shall be: 1st, to respect our body and our soul as the sanctuary of God; 2nd, to delight to live in a state of recollection in this sanctuary alone with God only. Our spiritual nosegay shall be the words of the Apostle: *"You are the temple of the living God"* (Ibid.).

Habitation for the Morning.

Let us adore God dwelling in our breasts as in His sanctuary; that is the church of which He is the most jealous and where He best loves to be honored; the church the dedication of which has no octave, because it is a festival belonging to every day, a festival of time and of eternity. Let us thank God for having willed of His goodness to establish His temple in the bottom of our soul; let us beg Him. to penetrate us with this great truth and with its beautiful consequences.

FIRST POINT.

We are the Temple of God.

It is the teaching of St. Paul, who tells us so in formal terms. It is the doctrine of the prophets, according to the remark of the Apostle (II. Cor. vi. 16). And it is not only in our souls, it is in our bodies that God thus dwells; He dwells therein by communion, which makes us the living tabernacle of the Eucharist; He dwells there by the grace of baptism, of which St Paul says: "*Do you not that your members are the temple of the Holy Ghost, who is in you?*" (I. Cor. vi. 19.) O greatness of the Christian! how august is his soul, how venerable is his body! And how remarkable it is that this privilege does not belong only to this present life: it applies to the whole of eternity. We are, says the Apostle, living stones destined for the construction of this immortal temple which God has prepared here below for His glory throughout eternity; an august temple of which each holy soul will form a portion, counting from the prophets and the apostles, who are the foundation of it, the martyrs, who are its victims, the virgins, who are its flowers, down to the most unknown amongst the saints, who will each shine in his place by the variety of their merits; a temple always progressing and rising every day until it attains the plenitude of its perfection, and the dedication of which will take place in heaven on the day when Jesus shall present it to His Father, His church pure and without spot, to be forever united with Him (Eph. ii. 21, 22).

SECOND POINT.

What are the Duties Incumbent on us through the Honor of being Temples of God?

The first thing to be done in building an edifice is to cut and polish all the stones. In the same way, in order that a soul may be worthy to enter into the construction of the temple of God, it is necessary that the chisel and the hammer of mortification should have removed all the asperities of the temper and all the inequalities of the will. He who will not endure this hammer and this chisel will be cast away as refuse by the divine Architect. If, on the contrary, we allow ourselves to be hewn and carved and polished without murmuring, we shall have a place of honor in the temple of God (Hymn of the Dedication). This is the meaning which is conveyed to us in what is recounted of the temple of Solomon, in the construction of which not a single stroke of a hammer or of a chisel was heard, because the stones, before having been brought to the place where the edifice was being raised, had been so perfectly carved that nothing remained to be done but to put them in their place. 2nd. The stones once cut and well-polished, it is necessary to join them and place them in position in the exact proportion of each part to the whole. It is charity which operates this perfect joining and this beautiful harmony in the temple of God of which the Apostle speaks (Eph. iv. 15, 16). 3rd. In a temple all ought to be pure and holy (Ps. xcii. 5). It is thus that in our soul, the true temple of God, all which is not pure, and holy is a profanation (I. Cor. iii. 17). Even our bodies ought to be pure like heaven, and to have in a body of sin something which is not of the flesh, says St. Augustine. 4th. A temple is a place of prayer. We ought not to allow ourselves to indulge when we are in it in any dissipation or anything that is profane, in useless thoughts or wandering imaginations, but we ought to occupy ourselves with God, with His perfections, with His praises, with His love. It ought to be the same with our soul. Since it is a temple, we must be recollected in it, we must pray, we must adore and love, we must give thanks, we must ask and we must listen to God, who speaks to us there when we listen to Him. St. Teresa teaches us that she owes to the understanding of this truth her progress in perfection and the facility which she experienced in leading a life of recollection in God.

Resolutions and spiritual nosegay as above.

November 11th.—St. Martin

Summary of the Morrow's Meditation.

We will meditate tomorrow upon St. Martin, and we shall see: 1st, that this great saint carried evangelical renunciation to the very highest degree; 2nd, that raised thereby above all that passes away, he lived entirely for God alone. Our resolution shall be: 1st, to imitate St. Martin in his love of prayer, which was the soul of all his virtues; 2nd, to renounce all attachments which we may remark in ourselves. As our spiritual nosegay we will retain what Sulpicius Severus said of St. Martin: "*He, always kept himself in the presence of God.*"

Meditation for the Morning.

Let us render glory to God for all the graces which He heaped upon St. Martin, for all the miracles which He worked through him, for the conversion of so many sinners whom He converted by his ministry. Let us at the same time congratulate this great saint on his perfect correspondence with grace, on his virtues and his merits; and let us conceive lofty sentiments of veneration and of confidence for this illustrious miracle-worker of the Gauls, the light of his age, the glory of France, the model of the perfect life.

FIRST POINT.

Martin Carried to the Highest Degree Evangelical Renunciation.

In him there was no love of his own ease; he seemed to have a body for no other purpose than to martyrize it; he lived upon roots only, and even with that he fasted almost continually; he took the smallest possible amount of repose, and even then it was upon a haircloth laid upon the ground. The heretics whom he strove to convert scourged him cruelly, to punish him for his zeal; he rejoiced at it as for a special favor. Julian the Apostate put him in prison, in order to deliver him up the next day to the fury of the barbarians; he blessed God. Twice the iron of the assassin threatened his life; he escaped only as by a miracle. In him there was no attachment to the world. Whilst still a child of twelve years old he was about to leave everything, country and parents, friends and possessions, that he might retreat into a solitude, when the obligation of following his father to the wars made him give up the carrying out of his project. He resumes it as soon as he can, and goes and places himself under the direction of St. Hilary of Poitiers. In him there was no attachment to self-love. Whilst he was still only a catechumen he exposed himself to the ridicule of the whole army, by appearing before it with the half of a mantle, because he had given the other half to a poor man. The military career offered him a brilliant future; he made the sacrifice of it that he might give himself wholly to God alone. Called to the diaconate, he esteemed himself to be so unworthy of it, that he meets all solicitations to his acceptance of it with nothing but cries and tears. Obliged later on to become a bishop, he only shows himself all the more humble. In the midst of honors he preserves a simple and common aspect. For raiment he has nothing but the poorest of garments, for a palace nothing but a little wooden cell near the church. Honored by the respect of emperors, who receive him as an angel from heaven; by the veneration of the empress, who deems herself happy to be permitted to serve him at table; by the confidence of the whole world, which canonizes him, he only looks upon himself as a sinner worthy of the greatest contempt, and he desires to die as such upon a hair-cloth and ashes. In him there were no fits of bad temper, nor any variations in his character. No one, says his historian, ever saw him angry or giving way to emotion, never either melancholy or jovial; he always preserved an unchangeable sweetness, always a serene brow, an affable manner, a kind way of speaking. Brice, one of his disciples, mocks at and insults him; he replies with the calmness of patience and amenity of manner: *"If Jesus Christ"* he said, *"suffered Judas, why should I not endure Brice?"* Therefore, when he was at the point of death, our saint was able to say to the devil, who presented himself to him in order to tempt him: *"What dost thou do here, cruel beast! Thou wilt find nothing in me which belongs to thee."* Such is the peace which evangelical renunciation gives at death.

SECOND POINT.

St. Martin Lived Wholly for God Alone.

At the epoch when St. Martin lived idolatry or heresy still reigned in portions of Gaul. St. Martin, burning with the desire to make God loved, attacked at one and the same time idolaters and heretics with a zeal which made him brave all fatigues, all the perils of death, and which enabled him to say: *"Without having any other weapon or defensive armor than the name of Jesus and the sign of the cross, I would throw myself willingly into the midst of the squadrons of a whole army,"* and at the same time having so wonderful a gift of working miracles that he chases away devils, cures the sick, raises the dead, and performs nearly as many miracles as others perform actions. Therefore, it would be impossible to say either the number of idolaters whom he converted, or the heretics he brought back to the fold, or the heathen temples which he cast down, or the churches which he raised on their ruins. Living thus for God exteriorly, he lived still more for God interiorly. There was in the bottom of his heart such love for Jesus Christ that his historian said of him that he loved Him with all his bowels, and that, "if he had lived in the time of Nero or of Decius, he would have joyfully ascended the scaffold, he would have thrown himself into the fire, and would have sung the praises of the Lord amidst the flames, even as the children of Babylon did in the furnace. I attest," says his historian, "in the presence of the God of heaven and of earth that it is so." Heaven, indeed, proved it by causing to appear upon his head, whilst he was at the altar, a globe of fire in sign of the love with which his whole heart burned, and this great love had this special characteristic, that he saw Jesus Christ in all with whom he had to do. He saw Jesus Christ in the poor and the sick, and was thereby inspired with a more than maternal tenderness towards them; he saw Him in servants, and on that account he delighted to serve them himself; he saw Him in sinners, and looking upon them as members of Jesus Christ covered with wounds, he shed over them torrents of tears; he saw Him in his enemies, and in consequence he revenged himself on them only by fasting and praying for them. Seeing things in this light during his life, he saw them still better at his death. Those by whom he was surrounded wished, in order to alleviate his suffering, to turn him towards the wall. *"Let me"* he said, *"look up to the sky, that my soul may see the road by which it is going to unite itself to Jesus Christ."* When he was conjured to ask Jesus Christ to cure him: *"Lord,"* he replied, *"if I am still necessary to Thy people, I do not refuse labor; I would willingly postpone my entrance into paradise as long as the interests of Thy glory may demand it."* O heroism of charity! O perfection of holiness! exclaims St Bernard.

Resolutions and spiritual nosegay as above.

November 13th.—St. Stanislaus Kostka

Summary of the Morrow's Meditation.

We will meditate tomorrow upon this angelic young man, who died at the age of eighteen, and who in such a short space of time won so beautiful a place in heaven. We will consider that he was: 1st, an angel through his love; 2nd, a martyr by his abnegation. We will thence deduce the resolution: 1st, to strive every day to increase holy love within us by frequent aspirations of love and by ardent desires to love God more and more; 2nd, to prove our love to Jesus Christ by making in a cheerful spirit all the sacrifices or acts of abnegation for which opportunities may occur. Our spiritual nosegay shall be the words which the Holy Scriptures apply to the just man: *"Being made perfect in a short space, he fulfilled a long time"* (Wis. iv. 13).

Meditation for the Morning.

Let us adore the Holy Spirit taking possession of the heart of Stanislaus Kostka whilst he was still a child, and from that time embellishing him with angelic purity, turning his affections from earth and raising them all towards heaven, filling him with divine strength to conquer himself, and setting him on fire with love for God alone. Let us praise and glorify the Holy Spirit for this marvel of grace and let us beg Him to have pity on our miseries and to convert us.

FIRST POINT.

St. Stanislaus Kostka was an Angel through his Love for God.

Such was the love with which St. Stanislaus burned for God that it raised him above all visible things, which were as nothing to him, and made him concentrate all his affections in God alone. As soon as he began his mental prayer his mind and his heart were absorbed in God, and he did not know what it was to have distractions. His face became inflamed, tears of love flowed from his eyes; such an ardor of charity burned in his breast that he could not bear its flumes, and he was obliged to temper them by means of cold water. When not engaged in prayer, in the whole course of his actions, his heart was never separated from God; he did everything in union with God and through love for God. *"I was not born for the things of this present world"* he said, *"but for those which are for the future and eternal."* Therefore, his life was that of a wholly heavenly soul. In church and when he was praying he manifested a recollection which deeply impressed all who were witnesses of it; outside the church he showed a modesty which revealed how entirely united was his interior with God; in conversation he spoke the language of heaven, and people thought that they were listening to a seraphim. The spectacle of the sins committed upon earth filled his heart with grief, and he was often seen spending as much as five or six hours on his knees, with his arms stretched out, his eyes bathed in tears, to ask God to pardon the offences committed against His adorable majesty, and to make Him honorable amends by offering himself as an expiatory victim for all the iniquities of the world. He even felt a great disgust for life, and sighed with inexpressible ardor for heaven, where God is no longer offended, where He is always loved, and where He is seen to be always loved. O God, inspire our hearts with the same sentiments 1 When will the beautiful day which knows no night dawn for me, because Thou art therein no longer offended? When shall I enter into the country where charity unites all hearts? *(Brev. Paris,* Hymn *Complet.)* Thou delayest too long, O day so greatly desired! Oh, how gladly would I leave the prison of my body in order to enter the beautiful heaven where I shall not cease to contemplate Thee, O my God, and to sing Thy praises 1 *(Brev. Paris,* Hymn *Vesp. Domin.)*

SECOND POINT.

St. Stanislaus Kostka Was a Martyr by his Abnegation.

As this holy young man was very agreeable to God, it was necessary he should pass through the crucible of tribulation (Tob. xii. 13). From his earliest infancy he subjected himself to privations and to a life of austerity in the midst of all the comforts of which his paternal home was full. Sent to Vienna for his studies in the company of his brother, he found a persecutor in his very brother, who could not bear his recollected life, separated from the pleasures and amusements of the world, his long hours of prayer, the whole of his angelic life, which was such a notable condemnation of the dissipated worldly life he himself led. Not content with persecuting this earthly angel, he stirred up his companions against him and made him odious to them. They all vied with each other in persecuting him with bitter satire and with insulting speeches; they even went so far as to strike him and heap upon him the worst kind of treatment. During the space of two years the holy young man bore this martyrdom without complaint or murmur, without meeting it with anything but patience, gentleness, and amiability. Called to the Society of Jesus by the Blessed Virgin, who appeared to him, but wanting resources to pay the expenses of the journey because of the opposition his father made to his vocation, he did not hesitate to go five hundred leagues on foot, wearing a poor garment and asking alms; and having reached Rome and arrived at the Novitiate of the Society, he submitted himself joyfully to all the austerities of his new life. He followed the rule with a strictness which admitted of neither exception nor dispensation; he was content to live in a continual immolation of his own will, founded upon the principle that it is better to do little things through obedience than great ones in following our own will. He saw in his rule or in his superiors the will of God, and lovingly following this holy will, he rose from virtue to virtue, and was the admiration of his masters as well as of his companions. Soon he was ripe for heaven, and death came to add another angel and another martyr to the heavenly court. May I profit by this beautiful example and comprehend that we cannot go to heaven without passing through suffering and tribulation.

Resolutions and spiritual nosegay as above.

November 21st—The Presentation of the Blessed Virgin.

(First Meditation.)

Summary of the Morrow's inebriation.

We will meditate tomorrow upon the mystery of the day, and we shall learn from the Blessed Virgin to give ourselves to God: 1st, without delay; 2nd, without reserve; 3rd, without return. We will then make the resolution; 1st, to make tomorrow the consecration of our whole being to God, that we may love and serve Him better than we have hitherto done; 2nd, to sacrifice to Him the attachments to which we cling the most. Our spiritual nosegay shall be the words of the Psalmist: "O *Lord, I am Thine*" (Ps. cxviii. 94).

Meditation for the Morning.

Let us adore the Holy Spirit inspiring Mary, whilst she was still a child, with the resolution to leave her family and all the pleasures of the domestic hearth, in order to shut herself up in the solitude of the temple, and there lead a life of entire devotion to God and in God. Let us congratulate the Blessed Virgin on her perfect correspondence to grace, and let us rejoice at seeing her, whilst she was so young, already so great a saint.

FIRST POINT.

Mary Teaches us to Give ourselves to God without Delay.

There were in the appurtenances of the temple at Jerusalem two kinds of monasteries, where were received children of both sexes who were dedicated to God by their parents, as is proved by the example of the youthful Samuel, and of Anne, the daughter of Phanuel. They were occupied there, according to their sex, either in the functions of the holy place or in its decoration, and in keeping in good condition the sacred vestments. Venerable priests were appointed for the education of the boys, and the girls were under the supervision of holy women filled with the spirit of wisdom—a true picture of our religious communities, shining with innocence and virtue. Mary was only at the entrance of life—she was hardly three years old—when she asked her parents to permit her to go and shut herself up in this holy asylum; they, knowing that children belong to God before belonging to their father and mother, consent to her wishes; and immediately the tender infant, docile to the voice of the heavenly Spouse who calls her (Ps. xliv. 11), betakes herself to Jerusalem. Her feet can hardly carry her before she ascends the steps of the temple, and the angels cry out in ecstasy: *"How beautiful are Thy steps, O prince's daughter!"* (Cant. vii. 1.) Her tongue is scarcely loosed before she confidently pronounces the holy engagement of belonging to God alone. It is a beautiful lesson for parents, teaching them to form their children for piety from their very earliest years, and to give them to God when He asks them, whether it be that He calls them to the religious state, or that He withdraws them from this world to place them in His paradise. It is a beautiful lesson for childhood and youth, which teaches them to consecrate to God the first-fruits of their life. A beautiful lesson also for Christians, which tells them not to put off to a later period their leading a better life. It sometimes seems to us that at a future period we shall be better disposed, that courage will come to us, that circumstances will be more favorable. Meanwhile we should not like to die such as we are; we know very well that God has no reason to be pleased with us, that He has many reproaches to address to us, that we are deficient in many virtues, that many faults remain to be corrected, that it is not by living in this way that the saints reached heaven. We feel all this, and we say to ourselves: I must certainly become better someday. But when will that be? We answer: Later on. Alas! has death promised to wait till later on? Is it possible that one will, by dint of making evil into a habit, become more inclined to what is good? Will the grace of God become more abundant in proportion as we abuse it more here below? What a deception! Let us then not put off from one day to another (Ecclus. v. 8). Let us begin this very day to lead the life in which we should like to die (Ps. lxxvi. 11). We have already delayed too long to love Thee, O beauty always ancient and ever new! (St. Augustine.)

SECOND POINT.

Mary in her Presentation Teaches us to Give ourselves to God without Reserve.

Behold this holy child; she renounces the world and its hopes, her family and all the joys of the domestic hearth, all the comforts of life, in order to embrace the austerity of community life; her self-will, in order henceforth to live by obedience; her senses and her body, by the vow of virginity; all that is not God, in order to belong only to God; lastly, she sacrifices all that she has, all that she is, all that she can do (St. Bernard). Let us hence learn to give ourselves to God without reserve or division. We belong wholly to the Lord : wholly because He has created us, wholly because He has redeemed us at the cost of His blood. Body and soul, all belongs to Him, and we can dispose of nothing except in accordance with His good pleasure. With Him, it is all or nothing. He hates rapine in a holocaust (Is. lxi. 8), and to give Him only almost all is not a religious act; to retain the least portion is injustice and fraud. Oh, how little understood is this doctrine! We give the whole of ourselves to God in general and we take it back in detail. We give to God a portion of ourselves, but on condition of keeping another portion. We give ourselves to God by a good work, but on condition of keeping our avarice, self-love, self-will, and temper.

THIRD POINT.

Mary in her Presentation Teaches us to Give Ourselves to God without Return.

The Blessed Virgin, having once given herself to God, never took herself back; she always persevered in the immolation of the whole of her being to the Lord, and lived only for Him. How far we are from this beautiful model! In a moment of fervor, we give ourselves wholly to God. But let disgust or weariness come, and we belong once more wholly to ourselves. If we have to fear *"what people will say,"* we leave off the good we had begun, dissipation succeeds to recollection, lukewarmness to fervor, love of self to the love of God; whence it results that our life is a continual alternative of good and evil, of virtue and vice, of returns and backslidings. We promise without keeping our promises, we make projects without executing them. It is not thus that we save ourselves. We attain salvation only by means of a firm and constant determination to walk always in the line of duty, even when it is displeasing to us. There is salvation and nowhere else. Let us examine ourselves as to whether these are our dispositions.

Resolutions and spiritual nosegay as above.

November 22nd.—The Presentation of the Blessed Virgin.

(SECOND MEDITATION.)

Summary of the Morrow's Meditation.

We will meditate tomorrow on the life of Mary in the temple, and we shall see: 1st, what it was in relation to God; 2nd, what it was in relation to her neighbor; 3rd, what it was in relation to herself. Our resolution shall be: 1st, to infuse more fervor into our exercises of piety, more recollection into the whole of our life, and, 2nd, to treat our neighbor with more charity. Our spiritual nosegay shall be the words of St. Ambrose: *"The life of Mary was such as to serve as a model for all."*

Meditation for the Morning.

Let us transport ourselves in spirit to the temple at Jerusalem, where Mary after her consecration wished to dwell, entirely shut up, in order there to lead a wholly celestial life. No created intelligence will ever be able to conceive all that the Spirit of God did that was holy and perfect in a soul that was so well disposed, so jealous of its perfection, so pure, and so loving. Let us glorify the Holy Spirit for it; let us beg of Him to enable us to perceive something of this magnificent picture, and to grant us the grace to reproduce some features of it in ourselves.

FIRST POINT.

What the Life of Mary in the Temple was in Regard to God.

We commit two great offences against God; they consist in forgetfulness and want of respect. We only think of God at rare intervals; with that exception God is to us as though He did not exist; and when we do think of Him we treat Him without reverence, at prayer, in church, everywhere, since He is everywhere. It was otherwise with Mary in the temple. There God occupied all her thoughts, filled all her affections, so that the whole world was as nothing to her, or rather only served her as steps by which to raise herself to God. She honored God in her superiors, she loved Him in her companions, she admired Him in the splendor of the skies, in the verdure of plants, in the beauty of flowers. If she spoke, it was of God and for God; if she worked or read, if she took a walk, if she granted her body food and repose, it was in order to please God, who willed that it should be thus. And who could give expression to the profound reverence with which this habitual remembrance of God was accompanied? What recollection in all her senses, what modesty in the whole of her deportment! When she prayed, with what humility did she not abase her nothingness in presence of the divine greatness, like a poor servant before the most august of masters! (Luke i. 38.) With what confidence and abandonment she poured forth her soul into the heart of God! When she assisted at the sacrifices which were offered in the temple, very different from the carnal Jew, who thought only of the blood which he saw flowing, she meditated on the significance of the sacrifice, through which we tell God that we recognize His supreme dominion over our life and death, His infinite excellence, in presence of which not a single being deserves to exist, and such a plenitude of good in Himself that He has no need of bur gifts. Filled with these lofty thoughts, she was inspired with the most profound reverence and a devotion in proportion to the more perfect knowledge she had of the divine greatness. Under the figure of these rude victims, incapable of honoring God as He deserves to be honored, she saw the future Messias, the great Victim of Calvary, alone capable of rendering to the Supreme Being a homage worthy of Him; and in advance she offered Him to the heavenly Father with ineffable sentiments of adoration, of praise, and of love. This, in relation to God, was the life Mary led in the temple. Let us be edified by it, and let us encourage ourselves to imitate it.

SECOND POINT.

What the Life of Mary was in Regard to her Neighbor.

How beautiful was it to see Mary in the temple in her relations with her superiors and her companions! With regard to the first, what respect, what docility, what obedience, did she not show, not only to their commands, but to their slightest wishes! With the second, what charity, what gentleness, what forethought, what delicate attentions, did she not manifest! Bearing everything from everyone without making anyone suffer, she excused all their faults, concealed all their imperfections, pardoned all the wrongs done to her. Never did she show any rudeness of manner; never did she indulge in a sharp word or a critical remark; never did she allow herself to enter into any disputes or permit herself to contradict others, because she loved better to yield through condescension than to gain a victory at the expense of meekness; never was her behavior cold and careless; she always had an amiable welcome for every one; she was gentle and gracious, always ready to render a service and to oblige others, not through natural kindness and sympathy or through human love, but from a sentiment of faith, from love to God, whom she loved and served in the person of her neighbor. Such a beautiful example embellished and sanctified the community, leading all hearts to God, and the edification was universal. It if thus that Mary teaches us charity towards our neighbor.

THIRD POINT.

What the Life of Mary in the Temple was Considered in Herself

It was a life of abnegation and humility; of *abnegation,* in order to combat all self-seeking and all desire of ministering to her own comforts, to self-will, and to all defects of character; of humility, to prevent all vain complaisance in self, all susceptibility, and all pretensions. Never did the holy child seek herself in anything; forgetting self, she desired only to please God and to make herself all in all to her neighbor. Placing herself in her own esteem below all her companions, she venerated in them the children of God, of whom she herself was only the humble servant. She placed herself consequently in the lowest rank, yielding whatever was best in everything to them, and taking for herself what was least. She did not even esteem herself to be worthy of this least part, for she always kept herself abased in the sentiment of her indignity in everything and for everything. Oh, how far she was from the little tricks of vanity, from the manners that are assumed and the words that are said in order to attract the good opinion of others. She possessed what would have caused her to be admired, and she only aspired after being forgotten. Let us beg for a portion of her abnegation and humility.

Resolutions and spiritual nosegay as above.

NOVEMBER 30TH.—ST. ANDREW

Summary of the Morrow's Meditation.

We will consider St Andrew: 1st, as a fervent disciple of the cross; 2nd, as an eloquent preacher of the cross; 3rd, as a martyr of the cross. Our resolution shall be: 1st, cheerfully to accept all the crosses which Providence offers us; 2nd, to crucify ourselves by mortifying our own will through obedience, our temper by the practice of gentleness, our curiosity and our sensuality by privation. Our spiritual nosegay shall be the words of St. Andrew: *"O good cross! may He who has redeemed me through thee receive me through thee."*

Meditation for the Morning.

Let us adore Our Lord calling St. Andrew to the apostolate before all the other apostles, before St Peter himself, whom this apostle had the happiness to bring to Jesus (John i. 42). Let us thank the Saviour for this predilection, and let us congratulate St. Andrew for having so promptly and generously replied to the divine appeal, so that he was at once the disciple, the preacher, and the martyr of the cross.

FIRST POINT.

St. Andrew, a Disciple of the Cross.

Hardly had this humble fisherman of Galilee heard Jesus Christ proclaim that whoever does not bear His cross and renounce himself cannot be His disciple, that happy are those who suffer, miserable those who enjoy, than he instantly frees himself from the false ideas of the world in regard to happiness and misery; henceforth he loves nothing but the cross; he thirsts and languishes with love for it. Jesus Christ announces to him the difficulties and labors of the apostolate prisons, persecutions, and death. What would have alarmed numerous others becomes for him an attraction and a charm. Later on, when the apostles share the world between them, he desires to have as his portion the two most barbarous nations, Scythia and Thrace, where he hoped to meet with martyrdom; and finding there nothing but recognition of his virtues, he passes over into Achaia and thence to Patras, where at last he meets with what he longs for. He is condemned to be crucified, and he is led without delay to the place of execution. When he perceives from afar the cross which is destined for him, joyous as a warrior who, after long combats, perceives the triumphal chariot— "Good cross," he exclaims, "cross the source of all good, cross. so long desired, so passionately loved, so continually sought after, thou art at last granted to my longing desires! Holy cross, I salute thee! I come to thee full of confidence and hope! August cross, triumphant cross, empurpled with the blood of my Master! Receive me within thine arms, in order to remit me into the hands of my Jesus, who has redeemed me through thee" (St. Andrew). How well such words as these reveal a fervent disciple of the cross, a disciple who has studied its lessons and enjoyed its doctrines! At what point have we arrived in regard to such sentiments? Do we, at any rate, love those little crosses of Providence of which life is full, and do we salute them as did St Andrew, when he exclaimed: *"O good cross!"*

SECOND POINT.

St. Andrew, a Preacher of the Cross.

St. Andrew raised upon the cross, and from there overlooking the multitude which had gathered together to see him crucified, considers himself as occupying the most beautiful pulpit in the world whence to evangelize the people. He believes that it is not possible to preach the cross better than from the cross itself, and Jesus crucified than by being crucified one's self. He therefore raises his voice and speaks with force and dignity during two whole days; and the pulpit whence he speaks gives so much efficacy to his words, that many of his auditors who had come thither as infidels go away as Christians. Made fruitful by the blood of the apostle, the Church of Achaia becomes one of the most fervent and the most numerous of the infant Churches. It was because preaching always bears fruit when it has as its minister a man who is truly crucified, who places his happiness in suffering, his treasure in poverty, his repose in labor. The contrary will happen if the priest be one of those men who are lovers of themselves, who do not know how to bear restraint, and to suffer, to mortify, and renounce themselves.

THIRD POINT.

St. Andrew, a Martyr of the Cross.

From the midst of the assembly, touched and converted, a cry goes forth to demand the deliverance of the holy apostle. A revolt is about to snatch him away from the fury of the proconsul who has condemned him. "O God!" exclaims St. Andrew, "do not Thou permit me to be separated from my beloved cross." He is heard and his prayer is granted; the people yield with tears to the power of the Roman spears, and Andrew dies, according to his desire, upon his bed of honor, like a worthy lieutenant of the armies of Jesus Christ, like a perfect martyr, happy to render witness, by his death, to the cross of the Saviour, and thus teach men to love suffering and privation. What a lesson for us! How far we are from fearing that our cross will be taken away from us, we who so greatly love situations in which we have nothing to suffer; who are always endeavoring to put away anything that is disagreeable, to obtain that which flatters, pleases, and amuses us ; we whose whole life is nothing, so to say, but an habitual protest against the cross of the Saviour!

Resolutions and spiritual nosegay as above.